NOW THE VOLCANO

Painting by Darcy Penteado (Brazil)

NOW THE VOLCANO

An Anthology of
Latin American Gay Literature

Edited by Winston Leyland

Translated by
Erskine Lane
Franklin D. Blanton
Simon Karlinsky

Gay Sunshine Press
San Francisco

Spanish texts of the poems by Salvador Novo, Xavier Villaurrutia, and Luis Cernuda are published with permission of Fondo de Cultura Economica, Mexico City.

The Brazilian contemporary short fiction and poetry in the present anthology is from the following sources: Gasparino Damata: *Os Solteirões,* Pallas, S.A., Rio de Janeiro, 1976. Aguinaldo Silva: *Vida Cachorra,* Editora Civilização Brasileira, S.A., Rio de Janeiro, 1977 (for "Greek Love"); *A Republica dos Assassinos,* Editora Civilização Brasileira, S.A., Rio de Janeiro, 1976 (for "Eloina's Letter and Testimony"); *Extra* (magazine), no. 4, March 1977 (for "Cinema Iris"). Darcy Penteado: *A Meta,* Edições Simbolo, São Paulo, 1976 (for "Snow White Revisited"); *Crescilda e os Espartanos,* Edições Simbolo, São Paulo, 1977 (for "Jarbas the Imaginative"). Edilberto Coutinho: *Um Negro Vai à Forra,* Editora Moderna, São Paulo, 1977 (for "Lost in Recife"). *Ficção* (magazine) (for "One Foot over the Abyss" in an earlier version). Caio Fernando Abreu: *O Ovo Apunhalado,* Editora Globo, Porto Alegre, 1976 (for "Visit," "Requiem for a Fugitive," and "Portraits"); *Pedras de Calcutá,* Editora Alfa-Omega, São Paulo, 1977 (for "A Story about Butterflies"). João Silverio Trevisan: *Testamento de Jônatas Deixado a David,* Editora Brasiliense, São Paulo, 1976 (for "Testimony of Jonathan to David"). Cassiano Nunes: *Madrugada,* Pool Editorial Ltda., Recife, 1975. Franklin Jorge: *Improprio para Menores de 18 Amores,* Coleção Limiar, Natal, 1976. Valery Pereleshin: *Ariel,* Rio de Janeiro, 1976 (for "A Declaration of Love").

Colombia: X-504 (pen name of Jaime Jaramillo Escobar): *Los Poemas de la Ofensa,* Tercer Mundo, Bogotá, 1967.

Publication of this book was made possible in part by a grant from the National Endowment for the Arts in Washington, D.C.

Library of Congress Cataloging in Publication Data:
Main entry under title:
Now the volcano.

English, Portuguese, or Spanish.
1. Homosexuality - Literary collections. 2. Brazilian fiction - 20th century - Translations into English. 3. Latin American poetry - 20th century. 4. Latin American poetry - 20th century - Translations into English. 5. English literature - Translations from Portuguese. 6. English poetry - Translations from Spanish. I. Leyland, Winston, 1940-
PQ9637.E5N68   869   79-15055
ISBN 0-917342-66-6 hardbound   ISBN 0-917342-67-4 paperback

First edition 1979
Gay Sunshine Press, P.O. Box 40397, San Francisco, CA 94140

Contents

Introduction

FIVE YEARS AGO I decided to compile and publish an anthology of Latin American literature, concentrating on twentieth-century writers who were using (or had used) gay themes in an innovative, liberated way. In the past few years many Latin American writers have been translated into English (Borges, Neruda, García Márquez, Octavio Paz, Vargas Llosa, Amado, to name a few), but large numbers of first-rate writers, especially Brazilian, still remain untranslated, their work mainly unknown in the United States. It became necessary for me to research the literary material I needed by travel and personal contact with Latin American writers.

In the course of four years (1974–1978) I made visits to Mexico, Brazil, and Colombia in order to meet with gay writers and evaluate their work. Some of the material I gathered was published in the two Latin American issues of *Gay Sunshine* Journal which I edit: Issue 26/27, 1976, and Issue 38/39, 1979. The rest of the material, with only a few duplications from the journal, is presented in *Now the Volcano.* (Readers are also referred to E. A. Lacey's in-depth essay on homosexuality in Latin America and on the present anthology in *Gay Sunshine* No. 40, Summer/Fall 1979).

The title of the anthology, *Now the Volcano,* so similar to that of Malcolm Lowry's famous novel *Under the Volcano,* expresses the book's intention of documenting the emerging gay consciousness in Latin American literature. Recent biographies have made known Lowry's own bisexuality, the full implications of which he seems to have evaded. So it is perhaps fitting that this anthology should bear a title reminiscent of his masterpiece but with the signification of real sexual liberation. The title, *Now the Volcano,* also reflects my belief that the Gay Cultural Renaissance is a world-wide phenomenon. Just as the United States has experienced a flourishing of gay liberated literature by major and new writers in the past decade (Ginsberg, Norse, Wieners, Rechy, etc.), so has Brazil experienced a similar renaissance (Aguinaldo Silva, Gasparino Damata, etc.) and, to a much lesser extent, Spanish Latin America. Just as we have our precursor gay liberation writers (Walt Whitman, Hart Crane, Charles Warren Stoddard), so does Latin America have *its* precursors (Salvador Novo and Xavier Villaurrutia for Mexico; Adolfo Caminha for Brazil; Porfirio Barba-Jacob for Colombia/ Central America).

This anthology is not intended to be a definitive collection of contemporary Latin American gay literature. Most of the material is from two countries: Brazil and Mexico. It is important for the reader to be aware of the great cultural differences between Brazil and Spanish Latin America, a difference reflected in the literatures of the two linguistically different areas.

Undoubtedly Brazil offers the richest lode of gay literature in all Latin America. Two-thirds of the material in the present anthology is from that country. The first openly gay novel published anywhere in the world appeared there in 1895: Adolfo Caminha's *Bom-Crioulo*. It detailed the love affair between a black sailor and an adolescent cabin boy and caused a sensation at the time of its publication, resulting in the author being threatened with arrest. Selections from this novel appear in *Now the Volcano*.

Short stories on homosexual themes appeared in Brazil in the nineteen-forties, fifties, and sixties. Many of these were collected and published in Gasparino Damata's pioneering anthology *Historias do Amor Maldito* (1970). This was followed very soon after by Damata's anthology of gay Brazilian poetry, *Poemas do Amor Maldito*. In the present decade there has been a real flourishing of gay short fiction in Brazil, very open and frank: some of it in gay collections by one author (for example, Damata's *Os Solteirões*), and other material in collections of stories on diverse themes by writers such as Penteado, Abreu, Silva, Coutinho, and Trevisan—all represented in the present anthology. Yet in this same period there has strangely been a dearth of poetry on homosexual themes—at least poetry of a high literary level (with occasional exceptions like the poems of Cassiano Nunes).

In summer 1977 I visited Brazil and met with many writers and artists in Bahia, Rio de Janeiro and São Paulo, including most of those mentioned above. All the writers I met were most hospitable and open, and I obtained a wealth of literary material, especially short fiction. There does not appear to be an equal wealth of contemporary gay short fiction in Spanish Latin America. During my visit I was interviewed on the projected anthology by several magazines, including *Véja* and *Istoé*, the Brazilian equivalents of *Time* and *Newsweek*, as well as by alternative journals such as *Pasquim*. I was able to speak on gay liberation, on its connections with feminism, and on gay literature. Two special gatherings of gay writers and intellectuals were held in São Paulo and Rio de Janeiro to welcome me and to exchange information. One positive result was the formation of a group which has started the first gay cultural Brazilian journal, *Lampião,* in Rio de Janeiro.

Now the Volcano comprises thirteen short stories (two of them long enough to be almost considered novellas), two excerpts from novels, twenty-nine poems, one long memoir, and seven reproductions of paintings/drawings by artists from four countries. All the material is by men, since the publisher, Gay Sunshine, is an avowedly gay male press. Poetry is presented bilingually, with the exception of the work of the Russian/Brazilian poet Valery Pereleshin. Due to space limitations it was not possible to do the same for the prose selections. Translator for more than ninety per cent of the present volume, including all the prose, is Erskine Lane, author of the recent *Game-Texts: A Guatemalan Journal.* Other translators are Simon Karlinsky (for Pereleshin) and Franklin D. Blanton (for all the Cernuda poems.).

My special thanks to those Brazilians who were my hosts during my trip to their country, especially to João Antonio de Souza Mascarenhas (Rio de Janeiro) who was indefatigable in contacting writers and arranging introductions to them. My thanks also to Royal Murdoch in Mexico City. And, of course, I offer gratitude to all the writers and artists in this anthology who so graciously consented to have their work published.

WINSTON LEYLAND
San Francisco

Salvador Novo

SALVADOR NOVO was born on July 30, 1904, in Mexico City. In 1910 his parents moved to the north Mexican city of Torreón— "the barbarous North," as Novo often referred to it later—and did not return to the capital until 1916.

With his entrance into preparatory school in 1917, Novo's prolific literary career began. If his place in Mexican letters is not monumental, it is at least enduring and unavoidable. No unbiased history of twentieth-century Mexican intellectual life could be written without frequent reference to him. He held numerous official posts and appointments: director of the editorial department of the Ministry of Education from 1924 until 1932; professor of theatrical history at the National Conservatory from 1930 to 1933; official Mexican representative to the First Pan-Pacific Conference on Education, held in Hawaii in 1928; delegate to the Seventh Pan-American conference, Buenos Aires, 1933; member of the Mexican Academy of the Language; and "Official Chronicler of Mexico City," a title bestowed on him, with great honors, in 1965.

Salvador Novo's output as a writer is enormous and enormously varied: he published numerous translations, mostly from English and French; edited and/or collaborated with some of the most important Mexican literary journals of his time (*Vida Mexicana, México Moderno,* and *Ulises*); did extensive work as a journalist for leading Mexican newspapers; produced a series of travel books (including *Return Ticket,* 1928; *Jalisco–Michoacán,* 1933; and *Empty Continent: A Trip to South America,* 1935); was prolific as a critic and essayist (*In Defense of the Used,* 1938, and *Expired Letters,* 1962); wrote scripts for innumerable films; and was a central figure in mid-century Mexican theatrical life as playwright, actor, director, critic, and theorist (*Ten Lessons on the Technique of Acting,* 1951). In addition to all this, he earned a reputation as a historian through his *Brief History of Coyoacán,* 1962, which won him the title of "Official Chronicler" mentioned above, and through his two-volume study of life in Mexico during the terms of presidents Cárdenas and Camacho.

His reputation, nevertheless, rests most squarely on his poetry. As preparatory students, he and his life-long friend Xavier Villaurrutia began to publish their verse in local newspapers and small literary journals. Soon Novo's countless volumes of poetry began to appear. Most notable among these are *XX Poems* in 1925; *Mirror* and *New Love* in 1933; *Proletarian Poems* and *Seamen Rhymes* in 1934 (the latter with illustrations by his friend Federico García Lorca); *Selected Poems* in 1938; *Master of Mine* in 1944; and *XVIII Sonnets* in 1955. In 1961 his collected *Poetry* was published by the Editorial del Fondo de Cultura Económica.

Novo has been referred to as "one of the most elegant writers of the Spanish language." On numerous occasions he referred to his early exposure to Cervantes' *Don Quijote* as having a crucial influence on his style. His prose was often intricate and ornate, playfully euphuistic, and his poetry, when cast in traditional forms, tended to be impeccably correct—though in both poetry and prose he enjoyed jolting his reader by mixing levels of diction, combining elegantly polished phrases with language that was likely to register as vulgar or obscene.

His *Memoir* provides ample evidence of that tendency. Privately circulated in manuscript form among his friends, and still considered unpublishable in Mexico, it here receives its first printing in English translation. It deals with his life in Mexico City in the second and third decades of this century.

Salvador Novo died in Mexico City in 1974.

MEMOIR

I WATCHED THE LANDSCAPE slip rapidly by beyond the windows of the train taking us back to Mexico City, and in one unbroken feat of introspection my mind retraced the five long, gravid years that began when I was seven and now were ending with a journey that severed me forever from all the things that had endowed those years with their intimate charms and anguishes, their revelations and their awakenings. My health had never been perfect. Subjected to quinine at one time, to cod liver oil at another, on two occasions I was on the verge of death. Those illnesses left me skinny and weak, coinciding as they had with the usual growth pains of youth. I was much in need of a healthy, sunny way of life—a need which my mother mistakenly tried to satisfy with tonics and indoor seclusion.

In my sickly condition I resembled my father more than my mother. She scarcely recalled having once been at the edge of the grave with acute peritonitis, from which, without surgery, Dr. Parra saved her. After that time she never suffered any further illness of any sort whatever. Until this day she still has all of her teeth, enviably white, even and strong, as well as a full head of black hair which with defiant relish she brushes vigorously in the presence of my baldness.

My father, on the other hand, was always pale and frail. For hours at a time he used to sit in silence with a long black cigarette smoldering between fingers that, like his blond mustache, had long since been conquered by nicotine. His light-green eyes, gazing emptily, had already turned yellowish like his thin wavy hair. Only now can I understand and admire the strength of his will and the bitterness of his struggle, poorly gifted as he was to maintain it against the dominance of a household meekly resigned to the rule of my mother, all in an environment which, in addition to being foreign to him, reserved its triumphs for the daring and action-minded men of the North. A flagrant inferiority complex, rooted in his impotence or perhaps its most direct cause, had stabilized within my father a mechanism of abdication before my mother's will—a mechanism whereby he buried his protests in silence, in apparent conformity, or in the mute elaboration of fresh scenes for attaining an economic well-being that would eventually entail the restitution of his strength and authority. My mother allowed him his plans, as convinced beforehand of their failure as she was desirous of it, thus nudging him each time further away from any possible intervention in a world where I was already beginning to take his place. When his habitual cough grew dried and more frequent, when it began to be accompanied by daily fevers and a glossy sheen in his eyes—all of which, he said, was due to a cold he caught in a Turkish bath—my mother coldly pronounced him consumptive, stopped sleeping in the same bed with him, and firmly warned him that he was not to kiss me or even to touch, as he so enjoyed doing, the books and toys that he bought for me whenever he could afford to do so.

I sided with my mother. Soon I felt sickened by the mere nearness of my father, by his weary breathing, by the odor of his clothing and his black cigarettes. In the delightful daydreams that the idea of returning to the capital stirred up in me, in the images of well-dressed relatives, perfumed and smiling, who would shower me with affectionate caresses and gifts, the figure of my father, stooped, beaten, weak and sad, simply did not fit. He hindered; he was out of place; he was not needed. Old Laïus was blocking Oedipus' path.

If today I consider what other shape my life might have taken had my father won out in the struggle for my favor and had I, since childhood, helped him in any of his undertakings, could such conjectures serve as anything more than a futile and belated apology to his memory?

It takes little effort to imagine what might have happened if, instead of placing my hopes and aspirations in the return to Mexico City and the completion of a university degree, I had managed to become adept at business, sharing my father's burdens and labors, immersing myself in the activities to which my classmates at the Escuela del Centenario were going to dedicate themselves. In time the small sign that hung on the door of the office he set up for his timid commercial adventures could have been broadened from ANDRES NOVO, MERCHANT AND COMMISSION AGENT to ANDRES NOVO AND SON, and, still later, when its founder had already lavished caresses upon his grandchildren and then serenely closed his large green eyes, the enterprise would have passed wholly into the keeping of Salvador Novo.

Or I could have accepted the offer of a scholarship to study for a career in teaching at the Ateneo Fuente in Saltillo. In spite of all the ill will my sixth-grade teacher bore me, he failed to prevent my final exams from providing me with the choice of one of the scholarships awarded by the government to the most outstanding students. But that possibility, in my mother's eyes, was so ridiculous that she did not even condescend to acknowledge it. Her sentence of exile had expired, its length being determined by my elementary education. Preparatory school awaited me now, just as the bosom of her family awaited her. She had ventured forth from Mexico City without full awareness of what she was doing, and now, a prodigal daughter, she was returning home with a son belonging to her alone, a son for whose fate she alone would have to answer.

My first days in Mexico City were filled with innumerable pleasant surprises. Large, clean, with fresh clear air, the city in those days allowed one to admire its venerable old buildings and Porfirian edifices still unprofaned by the pickaxe and not yet overwhelmed by skyscrapers. The traffic was moderate, like the number of inhabitants who, as pedestrians, could leisurely stroll the streets and cross them safely with no fear of being run down.

On Avenida Madero, in stores called Regal and High Life, I was taken to buy the white-soled shoes I had long dreamed of. There one could observe the city's distinguished, decadent, indolent elite —the dandies, or *fifís,* as they were called, who multiplied like store-window mannequins in obedience to the daring trends set by Bucher Brothers, the haberdashery that dictated the modes of masculine elegance along Madero and Bolívar, publishing its dictates through the hackneyed drawings of Carlos Neve: tight-fitting trousers with high cuffs that revealed light-colored socks or elegant leggings, laced half-boots with rubber soles, and short belted jackets, vented in the back, with extremely broad lapels and a single button. The hat was an indispensable accessory. A widely circulated advertisement of the time, done by a store called La Vencedora, caught the public's attention with a sketch of the smiling wrinkled face of an old man, who, pointing to his battered hat, proclaimed IF I HAD GONE TO LA VENCEDORA TO BUY MY HAT, IT WOULDN'T LOOK LIKE THAT. Another ad, also done by Carlos Neve, challenged La Vencedora's claim to primacy by declaring that FROM SONORA TO YUCATAN, IT'S HATS BY TARDAN. Much attention was necessary if one were to keep abreast of the latest fashion, which varied unpredictably in the width of the brim or in the boldness of the band, or perhaps in the shape of the crown, changing constantly until it attained its final degree of wantonness and daring in a type of straw known as the "basket." At that point it immediately became stable and uniform. It was precisely on the tenth day of February that this new triumphant model appeared in the store-windows and hastily took its place on the heads of all the well-dressed gentlemen. And so, prescribed by the dictatorial statutes of Carlos Neve and purveyed by Bucher Brothers, La Vencedora, Tardán, and Sanjenis, this paragon of masculine elegance moved from the realm of art into the realm of life, from the stereotyped sketches of the ads into the graceful bearing of the *fifis* who, standing firm on their left foot or perhaps leaning on a cane, allowed their right foot to trail languorously behind them, giving the impression that they had just deployed it in tossing back the imaginary train of an evening gown such as primadonnas wear, displaying all the while the powdered faces and plucked eyebrows which the hat, jauntily tilted back according to the demands of fashion, left boldly uncovered.

Our life soon settled into a normal routine. The furniture arrived from Torreón and we moved into a house around the corner from where my mother's family lived. They suggested that my father remain in the city, and they arranged a night job for him with the railroads. But the many circumstances and contingencies, clear and inexorable, that would send him back to Torreón were already at work; rather than inspire him to flee of his own accord, they would soon expel him from our midst against his own will. My mother, sure of her family's support, treated him harshly and coldly, with open hostility. His health deteriorated rapidly, and far from being a reason for consoling him with tenderness, it was the justification for imposing upon him an ever stricter quarantine that severed him from the dining table, restricted him to his bedroom, and repeatedly forbade him to touch the new textbooks that my relatives now hurried to buy for me. So it was that he returned to the North, alone, as when he first made the trip six years earlier, though this time he was stripped of any illusion that he was leaving behind a son who, though never very loving, would soon follow him. His departure eliminated for my mother and me the need to maintain a house of our own. In my grandmother's household there opened up a space for just the two of us, fusing us forever with that family, offering me the status of a younger brother to my uncles, and imposing my grandmother's supreme authority over that of my mother.

Once the daily routine of cohabitation had been established, the gifts and outings with which my relatives had tumultuously assaulted me at the beginning came to a halt, quickly giving way to a matter-of-fact indifference which, by way of positive compensation, left them largely oblivious to my incipient forays into territory they would have regarded as negative and disturbing.

The first-year preparatory students were housed in what was called the San Pedro and San Pablo Annex, prudently segregated from the upperclassmen. At the time I was totally unaware of what was going on inside an educational system still reverberating with the changes, disorders, and retrogressions that came in the wake of the Revolution. The University, rendered ineffectual since the demise of Don Justo Sierra, was the feudal domain of the Directory of Public Education. The Directory in turn was controlled by a gang of *normalistas* who merrily distributed among themselves the preparatory classes which, before the Revolution, had been taught by professors with respectable academic backgrounds.* A picturesque *normalista* named Enrique Olivares—he heightened his forehead by shaving back his hair, and he dressed according to the latest Bucher Brothers styles—was, so to speak, the autonomous director of the glorified elementary school which the first year of the Preparatoria turned out to be. Geography, arithmetic, grammar, history—all of these were taught by *normalistas*. The survival of Porfirianism was observable in the voluminous presence of Dr. Jesús Díaz de León, who taught Greek and Latin roots from his own text, written, in actual fact, by Bouret. He was the author of *The Immortality of the Soul,* one of the books I had read back in Torreón. Though I read it with no great interest I was now awestruck by meeting its author in the flesh, and so one day before classes I decided to let him know that I had read his book before meeting him. I approached him and to broach the subject asked him if the soul was really immortal. His curt reply—"That, young man, is something one doesn't ask in the corridor of a school!"—instantly cancelled any liking I might have had for him.

My schooldays were converted into interminable and highly discomforting jail sentences by our hourly shift from one classroom to another, each with its own teacher, forcing me to plow my way through the hurried bustle of so many students eager to conserve

---

*Graduates of a professional teaching program as opposed to an academic curriculum.

their precious time, as well as by the fact that the door to the street was kept closed and carefully guarded by an ill-tempered custodian. Between the school and my home stretched the great city, seductive and unknown, constantly beckoning me to explore it, to exercise my unedited freedom in the pleasures it could afford. I was scarcely enthralled even by my drawing classes, of which there were two. One was called Constructive Drawing, taught by a Mr. Centeno who at the time was about to complete his degree in engineering, and the other, as I recall, was called Decorative Drawing. It was taught by Don Fidencio Nava, who made us draw vases of flowers with colored crayons on gray paper. Whenever I possibly could I fled the physical and military exercises that were commanded in a stentorian manner by a comically corpulent, mustached officer who reminded me of the ringmaster of a circus. Three afternoons each week he marched us around the courtyard of the school.

With no real surprise I soon learned that Jorge González had also moved to Mexico City from Torreón and that he too had entered the Preparatoria, though in another first-year class. He seemed unmoved by the fact that his change of habitats had brought him into an environment brimming over with captivating attractions and mysteries. We talked, naturally, but not often, and then about things of no particular interest or importance. He was already aware of my "flaw," and he even hinted that he had some stubborn but weak right to use any means necessary in opening for himself a path into my affections. He was like an old suitor who, years later, visits the girl he once could have married, only to find that she has become a prostitute. Perhaps, as a tribute to memory—a memory so quickly grown stale and inert—perhaps I would have consented to his demand that I comply with the terms of what he saw as an old tacit agreement. But, aside from my sincere lack of interest in him and my feeling that the whole question was closed, two circumstances eliminated the possibility of such compliance. First, if Jorge back in Torreón had never had at his disposal a hideaway to which he could take me, much less could he find a propitious place in a city that was unfamiliar to him, and it hardly occurred to him that we could have done the deed in the Woods of Chapultepec, so remote and unfrequented in those days. Second, he soon dropped out of school. An orphan, he lived with his grandmother in Tacubaya, and one day on his way back to her house he was involved in a streetcar accident that left him crippled for life.

THE THIRD YEAR of the Preparatoria opened for us the doors to the big courtyard of the school and admitted us to classes with very appealing names: psychology, ethics, logic, literature, physics, chemistry, trigonometry. For political reasons which I didn't understand then, we had a broad assortment of teachers as far as training and competence were concerned. There were some survivors from Porfirian days, such as Don Samuel García, furiously positivistic, always immaculately groomed, gray-haired, and Don Ezequiel A. Chávez, who taught psychology with a text by Titchener that he himself had translated. His intellectual agility was such that he could teach a history course from time to time with equal ease. But the majority of the teachers were *normalistas* like the director, Moses Sáenz, who, according to a nasty rumor, served as the pastor of a Protestant church every Sunday. He was from the North, supposedly, and his brother Aaron—also biblically named—had been an important revolutionary.

Aside from his activities as director of the school, Moses Sáenz taught ethics and chemistry. He was tall, dark, strong, with a stern countenance, thick lips, sparkling white teeth, and a penetrating gaze. He had something to do with the YMCA and he placed great emphasis on sports and physical education. "Red" Ochoa and "Cat" Velásquez, the gymnastics teachers, invited us to take part in early-morning training for some kind of athletic competition I never heard mentioned again. On two or three occasions I got up early and went to run before having breakfast in the YMCA; there I had my first experience with a breakfast of fruit, cereal, eggs, and coffee, so different from the cocoa and sweet biscuits we had at home.

Several doctors have told me that my bone structure was ideal for an athlete, unusually solid and sturdy in relation to my height. But an invincible laziness and a neurotic shyness about showing my body conspired to arrest my muscular development and set me on the path toward the slouching posture and languid, graceless bearing that would identify me for life. A resolution of Moses Sáenz further contributed to my emancipation from gymnastics: he decided to confer the attributes of leadership upon those students whose grades were consistently the highest, and we, the leaders, would simply supervise, felicitously exempt from any obligation to participate in sweaty physical exercises.

A third group of young teachers, few but brilliant, taught their classes with a fresh approach that contrasted strongly with the tedious pedantry of old Don Ezequiel and Don Samuel, with the clumsiness of Nica Rangel and the neuroses of Don Erasmo Castellanos Quinto, and with the blabbering witlessness of the *normalistas*.

Don Erasmo was a case apart. Afflicted with paranoia, fatherly in the extreme, he scattered greetings left and right by lifting his hat as if it were the lid of a sugar bowl and then sticking his head forward, away from the space the hat covered. His head, kept in custody by a beard just beginning to turn gray, looked vaguely like that of a turtle. After poking it forward he would then draw it back, like a turtle retreating into its shell, and, last of all, his hat, never brushed or cleaned, would make a vertical descent back into place. Don Erasmo took a particular liking to me. He read my poems and recited his own to me. After a short while I stopped attending his classes—Spanish literature and literature in general—because in my solitary readings back in Torreón, I had already covered the material that he was presenting in class. So he exempted me from attendance; I would simply take the exams and he would give me a perfect score.

Still, we remained friends, seeing each other frequently. He trusted me, confided in me, and secretly, because of laziness or lack of time, he passed his students' examinations papers on to me to be corrected. Or perhaps he acted through paternal generosity, using the papers as a decorous pretext for allowing me to pick up a few extra pesos each month.

Don Erasmo lived in San Pedro de los Pinos, still a village then, far off at the edge of the city, and it was there that I had to go by slow streetcar to pick up and return the exam papers. His house was small, with books stashed away in piles under furniture of the most unpretentious sort. After he had been made a widower by the death of his beloved Bella, whom I had met, he filled his house with errant cats. At night, looking like some poor scavenger, he roamed the streets picking them up and stuffing them into a sack, bringing them back to his private asylum for homeless animals where he could feed and care for them.

Without my being clearly aware of it, off beyond the cloistered corridors of the Preparatoria, which the chance changes of the Revolution had let fall into the clutch of the *normalistas,* a movement to rescue and redeem the system was brewing. The younger teachers, recently graduated, were the vanguard or spearhead of the protest. One afternoon, thronged together in the courtyard, the students rioted. On such occasions I always tried to get away before-hand but this time they closed the doors. There were speeches and lots of shouting; a certain Heriberto Barrón, notoriously older than the rest of us, led the kindled multitude to the room where Moses Sáenz was holding his chemistry class. There they demanded his resignation. Pale, his face the color of ashes, he came to the door. I never saw him again. The following day we learned that a mys-terious someone had conceded to the students the right to appoint their new director.

We all liked Don Ezequiel—so fine in character, always carrying a stack of books under his arm with the hand in the right pocket of his loose coat, his big white thumb sticking out. I remember his immaculately childlike skin and his long yellowish eyeteeth, his unctuous manner, and his repetitive way of expressing himself, of which the affectionate dedication he wrote for me in my Titchener is a good sample: "Your name is Salvador, Savior. Always live up to that name; always entertain thoughts that save, never thoughts that harm or hurt, never thoughts that kill. Affectionately and cordially, with sincere wishes for your success and good, your teacher, Eze-quiel A. Chávez."

Don Ezequiel, with the good will and applause of all, was ap-pointed our new director. In his small sunny office opening onto one of the smaller courtyards there soon appeared a young secre-tary. A fair-skinned young man, trim and spruce, with beautiful wavy hair, the secretary was named Jaime Torres Bodet.*

Months earlier I had embarked upon a casual friendship with a boy a year ahead of me. He was in his fourth year, the last, and his class shared with my third-year class the rooms bordering the large courtyard. I don't recall how the friendship began, but, given his inquisitive nature, it must have been he who approached me, at-tracted, perhaps, by the discovery that, like him, I wrote poetry and that both of us had had some of our work printed in *Policromías,* our school magazine. We had no classes together but always met and chatted before or after class. When I learned that he lived at No. 95 Mina, not far from my home on Guerrero, little by little I fell into the habit of passing by his house on the way to school so that we could walk together through the streets, so little transited at the time.

---

*Jaime Torres Bodet (1902–1974). Important figure in the literary and intellec-tual life of twentieth-century Mexico and director-general of UNESCO from 1948 to 1951.

Xavier's family was quite large and he was one of many children.* They lived on the ground floor of a large stone house that had a patio surrounded by an open hallway with an iron railing. The hallway ran from a living room with two balconies facing the street to the numerous bedrooms and back around to the dining room. Once Xavier invited me to eat with them and so I met his mother and several of his brothers and sisters. His older brothers had some kind of bank or loan agency on Avenida Cinco de Mayo. Once I went with him there to check on the monthly allowance they gave him. Little by little I learned that in his family there had been literati, artists, people of wealth. They owned originals by Ruelas, which Xavier pointed out to me with obvious pride. I learned, too, through things he told me in the strictest of confidence, that his family's history also included conjugal tragedies and nervous disorders of pitiable types.

The special liking that Don Ezequiel showed for me must have induced him to introduce his "distinguished student" to his young secretary, who, according to Xavier, was a poet and at the same time was giving brilliant lectures on literature in a school near ours. Between classes, then, I began to visit Jaime Torres Bodet. In his office he introduced me to another poet and constant companion of his, Bernardo Ortiz de Montellano. Somewhat before that time my family had moved to San Rafael where we occupied a large house on the corner of Icazbalceta and Altamirano. Jaime lived at No. 116 Altamirano. In the afternoon, when he had finished his work at the Preparatoria, we often took the same bus back to San Rafael, where, he said, he was going to prepare a lecture on Greek literature for the following day. On afternoons when he had no lecture to prepare, Bernardo usually stopped by for him and once they invited me to have tea and English muffins with orange marmalade at "Selecty," a small café across from the Hotel Iturbide.

One morning I took Xavier to Jaime's office to introduce them. The passion they both had for French literature led to a quick rapport between them. Jaime and Bernardo had already had books of their poems published—Jaime's *Fervor* in 1918, and Bernardo's *Avidez* a short time afterwards. But the first book Jaime presented to me as a gift was an edition of Gide which he had adorned with comments, erudite quotes, and a scintillating prologue for the "Cultura" series of publications.

---

*The poet Xavier Villaurrutia. See page 65.

Gide and Huysmans were the two authors that Xavier revealed to me. *A Rebours* and *L'Immoraliste,* which seem so harmless and naïve to us today, shook us then with their revelations. We had also read, certainly, and with guilty admiration, *The Portrait of Dorian Gray.* It was through discussions of Wilde that we slowly began to confide in each other. I made no attempt to conceal my inclinations, but Xavier seemed not to have discovered his, or, at least, he was not eager to acknowledge them. His surrender or self-definition finally occurred in the letters we exchanged during the last trip my mother and I undertook to Torreón. It was entirely fitting that it should be so within the context of a life such as his, always girded in the most rigid literary restraints. In my letters to him I wrote about the shock of finding myself face to face with the vestiges and scraps of my childhood, about the boys that I now saw with different eyes, and about a certain Angel Gallardo whom I looked up and hauled off to bed as if, in an act of neurotic revenge, I were trying to usurp the role of seducer and switch my own image for his.

In his letters Xavier at last confided to me the joy arising from his own discovery of himself, and he wrote about his love, apparently hopeless, for Paco Argüelles, the son of our history teacher. His letters were exquisitely wrought and I will never forgive myself for having lost them.

About that same time I felt flowering within me an amorous desire toward one of my classmates, Fernando Robert. Lighthearted, athletic, free of prepossessions, he was an excellent dancer; always surrounded by admiring girls and involved in gallant adventures, he avoided me and by so doing only fanned the flames of my desire all the more.

My life was split into three parts—home and family, where I felt increasingly foreign, constrained, and ill at ease; the school; and the long walks and adventures into which my friend Ricardo dragged me. He liked to introduce me to people of the most offbeat sorts— and then gleefully watch as they possessed me almost in his presence. Following that pattern he dumped me into the hot arms of a young military man one New Year's Day, and later, when I confessed to him that I was attracted to Pichón Vallejo, a beautiful boy who recklessly played the piano in our "cultural assemblies" at school, Ricardo schemed and maneuvered so that I could persuade Pichón to accompany me on a visit to Ricardo's room, whereupon Ricardo soon left us alone. That was the first time that my mouth, acting with some sudden but glad expertise, went all the way in the execution of a loving act that left me overcome with pleasure.

Ricardo left for Europe. President de la Huerta, a close friend of his revolutionary family, gave him a pension so he could perfect his artistry at the piano. But I was no longer wholly dependent upon his complicity. Once I had discovered the oblique world of those who understand each other with sidewise glances, I encountered those glances simply by going out into the streets. They were especially bountiful on Avenida Madero where, at a leisurely pace, so many people strolled away their afternoons. There, as if guarding the door to "El Globo," gazing vaguely but alertly through his pince-nez glasses, Mr. Aristi could invariably be seen with his cane and his fashionable leggings, his silk vest, and his stiff gray mustache. His nickname was *la Nalga que Aprieta*—Tight Ass or Clutching Buttock. It was through the door beside "El Globo" that you climbed up to the office of Mr. Solórzano, a lawyer who, according to Ricardo, sang operatic arias at home—"Ninon, Ninon, qu'as-tu fait de la vie?"—and was dubbed Miss Tamales because he always made his conquests by inviting the prospective young man to "a few tamales and some beer." There one could always find Mother Meza too, out on the prowl for clientele or fresh stock. He never sampled the merchandise he procured for his clients, mostly refined survivors of Porfirian days. He made his approach by convincing boys that they should learn to play the guitar and then offering to teach them free of charge. Once in his room, he assessed their pricks with a tape measure and then proceeded to put them into peremptory but immediately lucrative circulation among his many distinguished and well-heeled customers.

In that same building Mother Meza rented one of the many large rooms that were occupied by his congeners—Father Tortolero, for example, whose room was replete with chasubles and ecclesiastical ornaments, or Salvador Acosta, who left his bare except for one wide bed that was always in use. There were others I didn't know. When I visited those I did know, it was not to go to bed with them but rather to use their quarters for sex with my own tricks—an arrangement which they consented to on the understanding that I would later do it with them. In those rooms I met most of the fauna of that epoch—Father Vallejo Macouzet, affectionately known as Sister Demonio, who sported a scar from a knife wound on his lip and was famous for the throngs of young cadets that called upon him in his Church of Santo Domingo; Father Garbuno from Guadalajara, always in the company of Sister Demonio; the Devil on the Corner, in reality a Mr. Martell, well known because it was rumored that he had once paid a bullfighter one thousand gold pesos for a very personal sort of sword thrust; a lawyer named Marmolejo, ugly as a graven image, who pulled from a drawer in his desk the pillow that he burpingly placed beneath him and his tricks, and the Goddess of Water, an antiquarian, married with grown children and numerous grandchildren, who nevertheless was convinced that all of tricks fell madly in love with him.

Aside from Mother Meza there was another procuress known as la Golondrina. His most devoted client, whom la Golondrina served as a highly efficient and industrious purveyor of boys, was Richard Lancaster Jones. So pale that he almost looked transparent, Jones owned but never occupied a sumptuous house on Puente de Alvarado; he preferred instead to live in a hotel on Avenida Madero where he kept all of his clothes and a wide variety of medicines. Every afternoon he crammed a good fistful of pesos into his pocket and went to station himself in a shabby room that la Golondrina reserved for him on the way to the Lagunilla Market. La Golondrina would then deliver the wares—unknown boys at two pesos a head—until Mr. Lancaster Jones' endurance and that day's provision of pesos had been simultaneously exhausted. Being accustomed to the luxury of the mansion he scorned and to the clean comfort of his downtown hotel, only some rampant species of masochism could have compelled him to enjoy, in the sordidness of la Golondrina's room, the invigorating youthfulness of his victims.

The communicating arteries of that anonymous solidarity led to another memorable building, now demolished, which we referred to as the Vatican. Many other members lived there but I visited only two—Chucha Cojines, and, with greater assiduity, Dr. Enrique Mendoza Albarrán, known to his friends as Suzuki because of his nearsighted, Japanese-like countenance. Gustavo Villa—the Virgin of Istanbul—took both Xavier and me to visit Dr. Mendoza Albarrán on the same occasion. At the age of twenty-four, which I then considered scandalously advanced, Villa was still a student. In the Preparatoria he readily worked his way into our friendship, and, once we had reached a stage of mutual trust, once the ice had been broken and complicity had been established, he invited us to accompany him on the aforementioned visit. Actually, like a new

Mother Meza or la Golondrina, he was taking me to meet Dr. Mendoza who had heard about the Little Fawn and wanted to go to bed with him. In the process he took possession of Xavier too, liked him, and later fell in love with him.

Suzuki had discovered his sexual calling rather belatedly, when he was already fully mature, bald, shortsighted, and on the verge of marrying some old sweetheart from the provinces. Once awakened, he hurriedly made up for lost time. His practice as a specialist in problems of the urinary tract supplied him with a broad choice of cocks; they came to him in a sickly state and he took it upon himself to restore them to a use in which he then gladly engaged them, moaning ecstatically on his wide bed of carved wood.

He enjoyed company and was fond of small, quiet gatherings. He would sit us down at his table to drink hot chocolate or milk with candies or sweet rolls divided in halves, and then he would pump the pedals of his pianola for our enjoyment, pausing to tell us, with great displays of emotion, about his latest adventure with someone who had "a prick like the neck of a swan."

Beside the Olimpia Theatre there was another ancient, lugubrious house, and, inside it, an apartment where I was taken on a visit one night. The usual musty smell of closed places, of perfumes turned rancid; thick heavy drapes, low lights. The apartment was shared by Carlos Meneses, whose ridiculously small stature had caused him to be cruelly nicknamed Miss Bottled Fart, and by Antonio Adalid. I was surprised to recognize the latter as one of the English teachers from the Preparatoria.

The Virgin of Istanbul lavished her fine blond beauty upon a circle of people quite different from that which Clara [i.e., Ricardo] had revealed to me. Clara's scandalous, shameless friends were for the most part poor and homely. In her circle were characters such as la Semillona, who always pulled away just at the last moment so that his hustler-friends would not ejaculate inside him, because, he said, "it was unhealthy." The Virgin's friends, by contrast, were of a higher class, less obvious. She had been the lover of the owner of the most fashionable haberdashery of that epoch, Bucher Brothers, and she knew many rich gentlemen with handsome young lovers—acquaintances which she made the most of, either for her personal use or for broadening her business contacts. One of these gentlemen was Ignacio Moctezuma, the congressman. He lived in the

Hotel Iturbide and had as a lover a young athlete of German descent, Agustín Fink, whose mammoth cock only Nacho Moctezuma himself could boast of being able to accommodate.*

In his room at the Iturbide, though grossly ill-equipped to compete with the magnitude to which his steady lover had accustomed him, I did my best to comply with Nacho's expressed desire to sleep with the Little Fawn—all of which, for him, was merely a passing whim. Our bedspread conversation, as such conversations usually do, took an autobiographical turn. I told him the story of my hopeless passion for Fernando Robert, and he solicitously offered to help me appease my longing. Somehow I managed to inveigle Fernando into going with me to pay a call on Nacho. Once we were inside his room, Nacho vigorously propounded the legitimacy of my sexual claims and Fernando dutifully complied.

It was in the same Hotel Iturbide that I paid a visit one morning to a representative or impresario of Anna Pavlova's ballet troupe, which, at the time, was touring Mexico. He had seen me in the theatre, had approached me and suggested that I could become a dancer and leave Mexico with the troupe. I was, of course, immediately enthusiastic about the prospect. I was fifteen then, a good age, he said, to begin training. We made an appointment at his hotel to discuss the matter. When I arrived he was still in bed in blue pajamas left open over a chest lightly covered with fuzz. Little by little he seduced me into an act that seemed to me as ridiculous as it was harmless: he wanted me to bite him briskly on his right nipple. That was the extent of it. I never heard from him again.

For a quick orgasm the shabby rooms rented by la Golondrina or Salvador Acosta were a handy solution; for visitations of a more purely social nature we preferred Suzuki's house or apartments such as those of Antonio Adalid and Miss Bottled Fart. They all served as a home, so to speak, places where we could freely let down our hair and openly indulge in chatter meant only for our ears. Still they did not fulfill all of our needs, and so Xavier, the Virgin of Istanbul, and I—the three most dedicated partners in crime—decided, at the Virgin's suggestion, to set up a household of our own. Xavier and the Virgin were lovers at the time; I was still free and uncommitted. Between the three of us we would pay the rent—thirty pesos a month, electricity included—on a large

*See Xavier Villaurrutia's poem "Nocturno de Los Angeles," dedicated to Agustín Fink and printed on pages 66-69.

room in the office building on the corner of Donceles and Argentina streets, very near the Preparatoria where we were in our final year of study.

That year—1921—was the consummation of independence and the centennial was being celebrated with a clamorous resurrection of decorative nationalism—local volcanic stone in all the new buildings, and the publication of Dr. Atl's *Popular Arts of Mexico* in two giant volumes that sought to exalt the potsherd, edited by the powerful Minister of Industry, Miguel Alessio Robles, who also happened to be Clara's brother. In a near rapture we all went to see the exhibit of folk art mounted in the Regis Hotel. A painter named Montenegro, fresh back from Europe, had decorated the pavilion with frieze-like cutouts of cactuses and prickly pears done in green and red flannel. Gourds had been made into hanging lamps, rudely usurping the place of Porfirian chandeliers, and *sarapes* from Oaxaca, Saltillo, and Tlaxcala were on display where Gobelin tapestries and Persian carpets had been.

With scissors, a needle, a hammer, and boundless enthusiasm I consecrated my energies to the task of redecorating our room in that style. A little Aztec idol with a fat butt hung above the couch—our sacrificial stone, as it were—where it could dutifully preside over our ceremonies, and an exaggerated spirit of patriotism led me to choose a small typical gourd as the most fitting receptacle for the vaseline we used in our rites. We bought a typical pottery tea set and each afternoon had tea and heavy pastries that I bought at one of the neighborhood bakeries. Happy to have a place of our own, we gave a housewarming for our friends, and it was not long until we were known, in our own milieu, as "the Girls of Donceles Street."

We were not always able to pay our rent on time. Of the three roommates, Xavier was the only one with a monthly income adequate to his needs. But the Virgin skillfully made the most of her wealthy contacts. Once she brought home an enamored suitor of hers, Don Tito Gasca Rojo, a short, dark-complexioned old man who owned several pharmacies and a record shop on Madero. We left them alone. That month the Virgin paid the rent. The next month it was my turn to submit to a bulky and burping visit from Mr. Marmolejo, Attorney at Law.

The balcony of our fourth-floor room overlooked Donceles Street, just across from the main offices of the Secretariat of Industry. On a certain afternoon I sat down and gazed toward the street.

It must have been around five. Several weeks earlier, at the exit of the Preparatoria, Jaime Torres Bodet had introduced me to a Central American poet of the type that won Vasconcelos' approval.* With a sweep of his pale manicured hand he had said, "Rafael Heliodoro Valle, the poet," and then, with a gently mocking smile, "Salvador Novo, the poet."

Heliodoro's interest in my writing grew by leaps and bounds. I introduced him to Xavier; he read Xavier's poems and then published work by both of us in the newspapers he worked for. With him we talked about Ricardo Arenales, another poet about whose behavior horrifying rumors had been known to circulate. In one description we had heard of him he was "the man who looked like a horse." At first sight I found his ugliness as repulsive as his uncalled-for brashness. I asked him if he liked some poet or other, and, flapping his purplish blubbery lips, he answered, "What I like, honey, is to have it shoved into me h-a-r-d!" Then he took out some cigarettes and passed them around. We lit them and took deep draws three times each, holding it in as he told us to do. He began to recite his poems. I continued to gaze at the street. Time had come to a complete halt; the light was white, blindingly white; the silence was absolute, as if I had suddenly grown deaf.

When I came to I was stretched out on the couch. The worried faces of Xavier, the Virgin, and Dr. Mendoza hovered above me. They had revived me with injections. It was already ten o'clock at night. Frightened by their own doings, Heliodoro and the pot-smoking poet had long since taken their leave.

The marijuana, strangely enough, had had no effect at all on the Virgin and Xavier. Perhaps they had not inhaled it with the same relish as I, considered my tendency to surrender myself completely to any kind of unfamiliar and alluring excess. The Virgin told us that in other flats, as in a scene from the novels of Jean Lorrain, she had sniffed ether. It was marvelous, she said, how one attained a nirvanic state enveloped in the lulling, soothing sound of bells.

On another night—one which, in retrospect, we would refer to as Walpurgis Night—we all got together in couples to get drunk on

*José Vasconcelos (1882–1959). Author of *The Cosmic Race* and *Indology*. Widely known for his theories of supranational Latin-American cultural identity and his speculations on the destiny of Latin-American society. Among other important posts, he served as rector of the National University and director of the National Library.

anisette. The Virgin had introduced me to a very appetizing boy named Gaitán; she, as usual, would sleep with Xavier. For the first time that night we had invited Delfino Ramírez Tovar, a classmate from the Preparatoria whom we suspected of being a latent and undecided accomplice. Skinny as a skeleton, timid and withdrawn, dressed in provincial white, he sat in a corner and simply observed the drinking, the endless smooching, and the numerous nude dances which I, still charmed by the possibility of becoming a dancer, performed to brighten the gathering. When we were all very drunk we turned out the lights and panted in the sweaty darkness. "I was blind and deaf during it all," Delfino said afterwards from his corner. "But there was nothing wrong with your hands," we replied.

Engraving by José Clemente Orozco (1883–1949, Mexico)

That confirmatory initiation, nevertheless, was enough to launch our timid provincial young man toward the full recognition of his true calling. Some days later he told us the story of his first adventure with a Fernando whose memory he would cling to for years to come. With the discovery of himself a luminous change of character came over him. His intelligence and his natural talents awoke inside him; soon he joined me in my nude dance numbers, joking, reciting poetry, singing—all with a humorous but healthy awareness of his own lack of physical charms. Soon he even bleached his hair with peroxide. We christened him Porfiria and, with his entry into the household, the popular trio known as "the Girls of Donceles Street" became a gay quartet.

The Virgin insisted that it was to my best advantage to find a steady friend to provide me with decent companionship, just as he and Xavier had each other. A good candidate, he decided, was Enoch Paniagua, a nice boy, handsome for someone of his pale gynecomastic type, always attractively dressed with an operatic felt hat tilted over a fresh and somewhat freckled face that blushed with the slightest provocation. Enoch contributed several baubles and knickknacks to our interior decor. He usually came calling with his friend Rafael Pérez Gavilán, who resembled Torres Bodet in ugliness. Both were opera buffs and Pérez Gavilán played the piano. They peered into our way of life, as scandalous to them as it was seductive, and when I later moved into a furnished room of my own, which I occupied only long enough to enjoy a fleeting idyll with a massive, blond railroad employee, they lingered on as friends of Xavier and the Virgin. Then one day they moved to Los Angeles, where several years later I ran into them again. Pérez Gavilán was the cousin of Ramón Novarro, the famous film star of the time, and he hoped to follow in the footsteps of his kinsman.

La Golondrina located another lodging for me, one nearer his own. It was a huge empty room with two balconies opening onto the quiet Street of the Mexican Thinker. He bought me two wooden crates from a store, I covered them with cretonne, and every afternoon after classes Delfino and I went there together. La Golondrina would stick his head in to check if we were home—"Have the princesses arrived yet?"—and then with a "back in a moment" he would be off. From the balconies we could watch him head down the street, proudly erect, noteworthy and dominating in spite of his shabby suit, his frayed hat, and the blackish scab on his right cheek. A short while later his deliveries would begin. "Let yourselves sink into languor," he would purr as he ushered the next unknown pick-up into the room.

At other times he preferred to take me to his own room, better appointed than mine in spite of its shabbiness. There one afternoon he shut me up with a guy who had just set off a bomb in the American Embassy—ugly, but the bearer of a piece of hardware of such colossal proportions that only with considerable difficulty could one find a ready use for it. La Golondrina questioned my abilities and I accepted the challenge. Accompanied by other curiosity seekers, she locked me up with the anarchist, went away, and then shortly returned to stick her aquiline face in the door and ask, "Did you? Did you?" I did, I said. "All of it?" she asked incredulously. All of it, I said. And then, turning to the witnesses that crowded around her, with the solemn intonation of a Papam Habemus, she proclaimed, "He did it—the *whole* thing!"

ANTONIO ADALID'S apartment, after he moved away from the one he had shared with the Bottled Fart, was at No. 123 Hidalgo Avenue, not far from the gardens of San Fernando. It was actually a sealed-off half of a spacious flat on the second floor of a building that at the time was comfortable and modern. A discreet door at the top of a flight of service stairs opened onto a small hallway; to the left were two rooms with windows, to the right a bedroom, and, at the end of the hallway, a tiny kitchen. Once he had it decorated and furnished according to his liking hs invited me over and introduced me to Antonio Jr.

Antonio Jr. was twenty-eight at the time, Antonio Sr. fifty-three. The latter spent two days each week teaching English in the Preparatoria and three days in the School of Agriculture far out in Chapingo. He usually got back home around seven. By that time Antonio Jr. had awakened from his siesta and donned his kimono; then, with a cigarette in a long holder held between nicotine-stained fingers, he would light the little stove to brew coffee and proceed to set the round table in the second of the living rooms. The table, sporting a service of fine blue English porcelain, was between the corner sofa and the round-backed armchairs which the guests—never more than four—could pull into place at the appropriate moment.

A tapestrylike wallpaper covered the walls of these two rooms, somber but inviting with fine antique armchairs and curtains in the best of taste. In a corner of the first room, just beside the window, stood a pianola over which, smiling down peacefully, hung a life-size oil painting of Antonio Jr. in a red velvet cape. The cameo of his ring glimmered on a handsome hand held dramatically against his chest. Some stray bit of chinoiserie on a wall, a blue and gold mandarin skirt, a piece of lacquered furniture—these relics sub-stantiated or commemorated the fact that the two Antonios had resided for some time in San Francisco, California. A Guatemalan saint here or there, carved from wood or ivory, marked the onset of the collector's fever that would later gain control of Antonio Adalid.

Home from his classes, Antonio Sr. would take a good-sized bowl from his kitchenette and leave the apartment again. Sometimes I went with him to the Chinese restaurant down on the corner where he would have the bowl filled with some dish or other to take back to the apartment for dinner. Stripped of his coat, his diamond-studded tie clasp glittering on a tie knotted around an impeccably stiff collar, he stationed himself in the middle of the sofa, as if seated on a throne, while Antonio Jr. served the meal and the two ritual cups of American coffee, pushing a little ornate metal box of violet-scented cigarettes into our reach.

Between the two of them, I learned, the flesh had long since ceased its clamoring. Theirs was a friendship that one could have called fraternal if it had not been for the great disparity in their ages and if their relationship had not been ultimately rooted in an inci-dent that altered forever Antonio Adalid's image of himself and marked the end of the golden age in which he had spent the years of his youth.

The Adalids were one of the older and wealthier families of Mexico. The Marquesa Calderón de la Barca constantly mentions Señora Adalid—Antonio's grandmother—and the family's hacienda of Goicochea in San Angel, only one of their many ranches dedi-cated to the production of *pulque.* The Emperor Maximilan had con-ferred the rank of gentleman upon Antonio's father, Don José Adalid, whom I met before his death. The old man balked at the idea of riding in a car or touching a telephone, and so, until carriages were banned from the city, his coach drawn by gray horses transported him to and from his enormous house at No. 13 Cosme Street. Antonio himself and all of his brothers and sisters had been chris-tened by the Emperor and Empress. Don José's legitimate family—legitimate, because, in keeping with the most venerable traditions of manliness among the Mexican elite, it was suspected that he had others—consisted of five children: three females—la Pita, la Tarra, and la Toto—and two males—Pepe and Antonio. Antonio had been sent to school in England while Pepe stayed home and learned to manage the family's estates. Antonio returned from England in the full bloom of his youth and in the middle of the most opulent period of Porfirianism. That was the time when exquisite aristocrats threw lavish parties which, though private, no doubt made them wary of the small, placid city's thirst for gossip and scandal. In short, that was the time of the famous Dance of the 41 Faggots. Antonio was the life of those parties—Toña the Fellatrix, as he was nicknamed because of his fondness for a form of lovemaking which must have been not at all current at that time, or which, perhaps, he performed according to the highest European standards of proficiency and dedication.

Perked up by his second cup of coffee, Antonio would blow out a big mouthful of smoke from a cigarette he didn't know how to handle, holding it awkwardly in chubby hands that reminded me of those of a cardinal, and then he would laughingly summon up memories of early-morning outings to Xochimilco with all the participants dressed in immaculate blue jackets and straw hats.

There were pimps—Mother Meza among them—who procured boys for the entertainment of the aristocrats. At a certain party one night Toña made a dramatic appearance, slowly descending the great stairway in splendid attire worthy of a ballerina. The guests applauded his grand entrance, but at the foot of the stairs the mute reproach of one pair of glaring eyes froze him in his tracks. "Ridiculous old man!" those eyes seemed to say. More than slightly taken aback, Toña scurried back up the stairs, took off his sumptuous drag, and then rushed back down to find the beautiful boy who had chided him with such sternly disapproving silence. Just at that moment the young man in question was being auctioned off to the highest bidder. Antonio bought him. His name was Antonio too.

Whether it was at the Dance of the 41 Faggots or some similar gathering, Antonio's life was soon touched by scandal. Don José Adalid disinherited and disowned the degenerate son who had so besmirched the family's honored name. Stunned and helpless, not knowing where to turn, Antonio fled. After a while he reached San Francisco, California, with a few dollars in his pocket and no idea of what to do with himself. There he went into a church, entered the confessional, and disemburdened himself of his sins.

"God Himself must have sent you," the priest told him. "We need a Spanish teacher at Saint Mary's College. There's a nice salary with room and board and free laundry if you want the job."

It was as if heaven itself had smiled upon poor Antonio. He began to teach at Saint Mary's, putting his fine British English to good use, and in the solitude of his little apartment he mulled over the memories of things past. He had no contact at all with Mexico and wanted nothing more to do with it. It was as if he had died to that world, as if he were now living in some new, strange dream.

One afternoon he heard a light knock at his door. He opened. "Here I am," the younger Antonio told him. "You understand," he murmured, "you understand that . . . that from this moment on I will never leave you."

Antonio Jr. learned English. Together they led a simple but free and comfortable life in San Francisco. When the elder Antonio's mother died and left him a sizable inheritance and a full pardon, Don José, in turn, saw fit to forgive his errant son. Both of the Antonios then returned to Mexico. Wealthy once more, Antonio did not have to work but by that time he had acquired the habit. Besides, he enjoyed teaching—enjoyed screaming in class and dealing sonorous slaps and affectionate blows to his boys. He soon took a job teaching English at the Preparatoria. There I met him and there we formed the basis for a long friendship in which he never in any way sought to impose his physical contact upon me.

Fully convinced that his pattern of life with Antonio was an ideal for all, he insisted that it would be to my best advantage to enter into a similar relationship with a well-to-do, mature man who would appreciate my beauty and nourish my talents, who would support me and eventually bequeath to me his fortune. He made two brave attempts to marry me off. The first prospect was Don Luís Amieva, a bald-headed old man who had been Inspector General of the Police Department. Don Luís at the time was shopping around for someone to replace the boy who had lived with him. He was a great fan of the bullfight, and the night Antonio introduced us in his apartment, Don Luís, just before leaving, wrapped himself in his Spanish cape and pressed a hundred-peso gold piece into my palm. I could use part of it to buy myself a ticket to the coming fight, he said, and we could see each other there.

His illusion that we might become lovers was short-lived; not even greed for his wealth could move me to share it. The first time we met in his house, full of valuable antique porcelain and such, we lay across a bed with a richly brocaded cover. No act of imagination on my part and no display of skill on his part could suffice; his leechlike mouth—opportunely but inconspicuously toothless—failed to get me erect.

The second attempt at matrimony failed for reasons of a different sort. Don Carlos Gutiérrez Palacios lived in an apartment in a building on Balderas Street. The building, I think, was his. He had surrounded himself with austere antique furniture, real museum pieces soberly positioned on the cushiony green carpet that covered all of his rooms. His hobby was Death. From Ruelas on, artists, painters, poets, and writers had fulfilled his request that they execute and dedicate to him some work with a funereal theme. Don Carlos himself was skinny and frail, dark-complexioned, with a slight voice. Dressed always in black, with carefully groomed white hair and a thin cane that his nervous hands waved about like a magic wand, he looked like a Hamlet precipitously grown old in the middle of the scene with Yorick's skull. When Antonio invited him over to meet me, he picked me over with his sly but searching gaze. We talked about art. He had just bought "some ruins" in San Angel and he intended to transform them into a home for himself and his collection of antiques. He had no heirs. He subtly hinted that he would like to find a young friend to whom he might bequeath his earthly goods, and, he said, one of his fondest wishes was to take a trip to Mallorca before dying—accompanied of course by his new-found friend.

He showed no particular haste in courting my affections. That night he walked me to my house and said good night to me at the door. The following day a package arrived from a bookstore containing his first gift: Elie Fauré's *History of Art,* which we had talked about the night before. I went to his apartment to thank him and then returned on several other occasions without his ever daring to touch me. He listened attentively to what I said, gazed at me dreamily, and smiled. Sometimes he bought tickets for the theatre, but he always gave me mine in advance so that we could meet there as if by chance, and after the performance he would always take me out for a snack in some nearly deserted café. I was puzzled by his reluctance to visit the two Antonios since their apartment was always so pleasant for me. Soon he confessed that, supposing me to have been a lover of Antonio's, he felt jealous.

His hesitancy and his low-keyed companionship bored me beyond words. I avoided him, bowing gracefully out of several dates and then stopping by to visit Antonio. He laughed heartily at the ridiculous jealousy and absurd behavior of poor Don Carlos, who should have been grateful to him for having introduced us in the first place. All the while, alone, I continued in the pursuit of autonomous adventures. My most fervent predilection was for truck drivers and taxi drivers. I climbed into their trucks and struck up a conversation that usually ended with our making a date for the night, or I took the taxis and simply had the drivers seek out some propitious shaded spot. One of the taxi drivers stationed on San Juan de Letrán, famous among the queens for his sexaggeration, took me to a house at No. 4 Pescaditos Street where someone named Fidencio rented out his bedroom with a wide brass bed for a mere two pesos.

Unknown to me at the time, Don Carlos Gutiérrez Palacios kept a close check on my movements. One afternoon I went to his apartment and was received with cold hostility. He knew everything. The whole scene was grotesque: he wanted me with all his strength but had never had the nerve to touch me. He looked upon me as a god of sorts; he respected me. Without my ever conceding him the least caress, he smoldered with a repressed desire to kiss me each time I came calling. At last, in desperation, he had tried to pacify his passion with a sordid nocturnal advanture, such as those I so enjoyed, and, in so doing, he had learned from the truck driver before whom he had degraded himself in his need for consolation that I—I, his child, his brilliant young poet—habitually indulged in identical acts with members of that unsavory guild.

Months later, through Antonio, I learned that Don Carlos had at long last found the guiltless angel to whom he would leave his priceless antiques and his ruins in San Angel, and that he had finally sailed for Mallorca in the company of his blond German boy.

Antonio had little taste for an active social life. His apartment was his refuge, so to speak—an eagerly awaited home which he now enjoyed, just as, back in San Francisco, he had enjoyed the home that he and his Antonio had made for themselves. My own cheerful, simple company answered their social needs. Still he could not entirely seal himself off against old friends who had the habit of dropping in unexpectedly, though his displeasure at their arrival was sometimes apparent. Sometimes it was the antique dealers with whom he was negotiating for some coveted piece, such as the elaborately gilded Guatemalan saints he loved to collect. Sometimes it was the Goddess of Water, that utterly loathsome being, or old decrepit Mr. Valdés of La Lagunilla, who had a house crammed with furniture, or Antonio Peña, a lighthearted old bachelor from Jalisco, recently fired from his job in the Ministry of Finance, and who, in partnership with his young friend Pepe Lascuraín, opened up on Gante Street the first antique shop that specifically catered to the needs of interior decorators. Or sometimes it was Pepe Alcalde with his face like a Chinese mask. He had just set up another antique business almost in the shadow of Antonio Peña's. Tall, bald, and fair-skinned, he made the usual rounds of Madero Avenue in the company of the dark and voluminous Don Rafael Manzo, brother of a battle-scarred general of the Revolution and owner of a small palace on the Paseo de la Reforma. The pair were known as "Nelly Fernández and her Low-down Mama"—the name of a comedy team much in vogue at the time. With more dedication than success, Manzo haunted the pissoirs in the movie theatres.

From time to time too the chubby figure of Genaro Estrada made an appearance in Antonio's hideaway. Then he was a high-ranking official in the Department of Foreign Relations; later he became a government minister and ambassador, for which post he was obliged to find himself a wife. From his position in Foreign Relations he discreetly paved the way for the infiltration of the honorable diplomatic and consular corps by the many young, well-bred queens who sought his favor. In that way he served the cause well by placing a handsome member of the fellowship in each of Mexico's delegations abroad, while fulfilling at the same time his appointees' dreams of living beyond the reach of local criticism and censure, far away in romantic capitals more amply stocked with beautiful sailors, soldiers, and Buckingham guards. Those whom he protected and promoted were not necessarily those who plumbed his heart's affections. At night one could see him pacing "the Slide," a cryptic name for the corner of Avenida 16 de Septiembre and San Juan de Letrán. Having sent his official limousine on its way, he lingered there under the pretext that he was waiting for the streetcar to take him to his book-lined home.

Another fortuitous caller at the abode of the two Antonios was Chavitos. Like Mr. Amieva, he had been Inspector General of the Police. Small, dark and plump, he amused us with his incredible tales of Porfirian Mexico, such as one about a very rich and elderly gentleman with a great many grown children. It seems that one day the gentleman in question suddenly decided to station himself in Alameda Park, from which, by scattering a trail of pesos in his wake, he managed to coax a horde of ragged, barefoot boys into following him home. When one of his sons chanced to catch him in the act, down on all fours with his snow-white beard sweeping the floor, the poor man promptly committed suicide.

One final caller was Dr. Land, an enormous bald-headed Swede with the voice of a soprano. He was a masseur and the owner of a house across from the Alameda where he brewed his own sweet but terribly potent liqueurs. Once I prevailed upon his hospitality by asking if I could use his quarters to fuck with a bus-ticket collector I had just met. Dr. Land opened the door and disappeared while I ushered the poor fellow in. Just as I finished stripping him of all his clothes the good doctor graciously returned with a tray of his liqueurs. He screamed with alarm and let the tray fall to the floor, convinced that my big raunchy pickup could easily have killed me.

WHEN THE CLASSES at the Preparatoria were over I had the option of studying law at the University. Torres Bodet by that time was already working as a secretary to Vasconcelos, the rector, and I rarely saw him. He was too involved in the university scene, where, at the expense of his person, he was busily inventing and developing his persona. Xavier enrolled in the law school with me, but we saw each other less at school than at night in other more palatable places.

I suffered through the boring morning classes only by anticipating the diversions of the afternoon and evening. To pass the time I set out to compose a romantic novelized autobiography, full of details, entitled simply *I*. In spite of the constant and copious evidence to the contrary, I was still persuaded that my proclivities made me somehow exceptional and unique. I quickly dashed off a great many pages which, for lack of a safe place at home, I kept in a locker in the gymnasium at the law school. Each morning I took out the notebook and, seated on a bench in the courtyard, cutting classes, I proceeded with the composition of my great and sorrowful novel. Xavier knew about it and was alarmed by its crudeness and directness, by my use of actual names instead of pseudonyms. He was so alarmed, in fact, that one day he forced the lock on the locker and carried off my manuscript—an act he would repeat later with a sketch in which Diego Rivera had caught me in the full beauteous bloom of adolescence, as well as with the original copies of my sonnets, which he filched from a chest in my house. After a discussion of the matter he returned the manuscript of the novel, but, as if by profaning it he had stripped it of all the virginity and worth it had held for me, I soon destroyed that first confession written in my sixteenth year.

One day I was standing in the door of the law school when a dark, negroid man appeared. He was dressed all in black, and he was obviously not a student. We exchanged a quick glance; intrigued, I followed him in. He went into a classroom that soon filled with gringo students. They took their seats and the stranger began a lecture on Mexican literature. He talked about the poetry of Sor Juana Inés de la Cruz,* and while he rambled on in his slow mellow voice his eyes remained fixed on me where I sat in the last row. "What is a gloss?" he asked the class. No one offered to answer. "Doesn't anyone know?" he said—"anyone, even though he isn't a member of the class. You back there . . ."

I answered, he smiled, and then he dismissed the class. Still intrigued, I waited for him at the door. We walked together, talking. He was Pedro Henríquez Ureña, of whose existence, erudition, and stature I knew nothing.† Without my noticing it, I was little by little drawn into the nets wherein he socratized a small group of reverent disciples. An old friend of Vasconcelos, and now his protégé, Pedro Henríquez Ureña had been the heart of the famous Ateneo de la Juventud and the contented mentor of a certain Alfonso Reyes whom Xavier greatly admired and whose books he owned. In the University, revived by Vasconcelos, he had founded an exchange program and set up a summer school for foreigners. The classes of the summer school were held wherever space was available—in the Preparatoria, in the law school, or in the building where Pedro had an office dominated by a huge desk stuffed with papers and notes written in his elegant calligraphy. He lived at No. 27 Rosas Moreno, just a block from my house. Once he was perfectly confident in my English he appointed me to teach a class in Mexican literature at the summer school. He had something to do with the "Modern Mexico" series of publications and with the magazine of the same name. He put me in charge of a section of the magazine and urged me to edit an anthology of Spanish-American

---

*Juana Inés de la Cruz (1651-95), a nun, considered the greatest lyric poet of the colonial period in Mexico.

†Pedro Henríquez Ureña (1884-1946). A key figure in Spanish-American criticism and interpretative writing. Best known for his *Literary Currents in Hispanic America* and *A Cultural History of Hispanic America.*

short stories, which he had published. In lengthy monologues, while we walked home from the University, he explored, instructed, and calibrated me. He skewered me with unexpected questions—"Why don't you become a philologist?"—and often he suggested that I have dinner at his house. Over the meals of rice with plantains I received the curious, questioning stares of his other disciples, who accepted me with silent reserve.

From all the group there was only one—Salomón—who immediately treated me in familiar terms, and it was he who was designated to put me to the test. The plan was naïve and transparent: one night he would take me to visit some Czechoslovakian whores who plied their trade in front of the Venecia Moviehouse. Salomón shut himself up in a room with one of them, leaving me alone with another. As had been the case with Mr. Amieva, her bold and determined oral techniques were powerless to arouse me from my frigidity. But on our way out of the shabby hotel Salomón seemed convinced of my orthodoxy, and the other disciples from that day on benevolently accepted me as one of the circle.

Pedro went off to South American in the intellectual and artistic Noah's Ark with which Vasconcelos objectified his ardent Ibero-Americanism. They took a statue of Cuauhtémoc, other Mexican curios, and local editions of the Classics. (Such marvelous moral support we found in the *Symposium,* where all the Grecian queens engage in lofty discussions under the wise baton of Socrates the Philosophess, the greatest faggot of all and a madame of sorts). The sculptor Centurión and the painters Fernández Ledesma and Montenegro had already been shipped off to Rio de Janeiro to decorate the Mexican pavilion at the exposition there.* A short time before that I had gone to the Hotel Iturbide to see the exhibit with which Roberto Montenegro had reintegrated himself into the Mexican cultural scene. His talkativeness was coupled with the mute dialogue of his penetrating gaze. He invited me to his studio on Balderas Street where a group of his artsy-litsy friends were going to meet. They paid scant notice to me at the beginning, and what attention they did give me was no doubt due more to my plucked eyebrows than to my poetry, which they consented to hear read in that studio with its gilded walls, black floors, Chinese red-lacquer furniture, and dim hanging lamps faintly scented with amber.

---

*These writers and artists were visiting Rio de Janeiro to participate in the celebration of the centenary of Brazilian independence, 1922.

The jobs that Pedro had conferred upon me before his departure for South America gave me a nice income, and so, financed by that money and unrestrained by his vigilant tutelage, my adventures multiplied. Confidence in my own beauty and in my ability to buy caresses gave me a boldness that served my insatiable thirst for flesh, throwing me into a mad chase after the type of boys I most loved to hunt out, entice, and embrace. They, of course, were those who drove trucks, buses, and taxis—the new generation to which, in the small Mexico City of the time, had fallen the task of handling the machines and living dangerously.

One day a newspaper called *El Chafirete* appeared, designed for that guild and written in the slang the drivers used. To amuse myself I submitted an article and they published it immediately. Soon I paid a visit to the editorial staff in what was then the Callejón de la Palma. Downstairs there was an eating-house run by the same chubby, dark-skinned man who directed the newspaper from the offices above. He himself wrote almost all of the eight pages of the paper, but he signed the different sections of his weekly with a variety of pseudonyms. The other accomplice was a goggle-eyed individual who collected news from the terminals and reported it under the name of Don Derrapadas.

Within a few short weeks I was running the paper. A sure instinct had led me to associate myself with the founders of a weekly that provided me easy and abundant access to its specialized readers. Some of the best bodies of the time were lured into my arms by *El Chafirete*. The director preferred the ticket collectors or the news-boys who hawked the paper; I preferred the more solidly built drivers who read it. At times I overtaxed my own resistance and abused my competitive capacity for handling pieces of unwonted proportions. As if I had vowed to win some kind of championship, I dared to take on Agustín Fink, to whose phenomenal prick, according to the legends of the time, only Nacho Moctezuma, his lover, had been able to adapt. In thickness it was like a can of salmon. Well aware of its outlandish size, I cautiously took it in while it was still dozing, having first thoroughly anointed it with vaseline, the preferred lubricant in those days prior to the meritorious advent of KY. But once inside me it flared out like an umbrella, bursting the narrow straits that confined it. I was left with a fissure that did not respond even to the healing applications of a black zinc oxide pomade which Suzuki resorted to on such occasions, and so I became the daily patient of a certain Dr. Voiers, whose waiting room was filled with plaintive sufferers from hemorrhoids and other posterior ailments. He hoisted me onto his operating table, spread wide my cheeks, and inserted a roll of cotton saturated with burning salves. I was to leave it in place all day, he said.

I was still undergoing that treatment when Pedro returned from South America. His disciples had nasty stories to tell him about my person. I sensed it in the suspicious seriousness with which he summoned me to his office. With much beating around the bush he slowly lured me to the brink of a confession in which I was more than eager to oblige him. I had never seen him so nervous before. His small jet-black eyes blinked compulsively; he cleared his throat again and again; he wiggled his toes inside his shoes. Finally the question came out—"Would you do it with me?" As he formed the question he drew closer to me, as if waiting for a kiss.

The whole thing struck me as ridiculous, grotesque, but I sensed that it was to my advantage to go along with his wishes, considering the jobs he had arranged for me, the easy money they brought in, the agreeableness of the work, and so on. And, after all, the big black fellow was no more ugly or repugnant than Heliodoro, who had received me in his pajamas one Sunday when he induced me to visit him.

"Yes," I said, "if you would like to . . ."

"Well, that's not the way I would want it," he blurted as he suddenly moved away, gathered himself together, and sat back down at his desk. "It's a filthy and untoward act. Certainly cases of attraction between men can occur—the urge to kiss each other, for example. At the university where I taught in the United States there was a very beautiful boy who was quite taken with me. We talked a lot, like you and I talk. Then one day he told me he felt like kissing me. I told him to go ahead and he kissed me here, on the cheek. But even that is too much. Such things should not be allowed to happen."

Fortunately someone came in at that point and interrupted the scene. But, to my disgrace, I failed to notice as I left that the roll of cotton which Dr. Voiers had deposited in my ass a few hours before had slipped out and worked its way down my pants leg to the floor. There I unknowingly left it as concrete evidence of my wrongdoing. It must have infuriated poor Pedro, for the favors he once showered upon me gave way to a furiously belligerent enmity.

Meanwhile, politics had been at work on the court of the omnipotent Vasconcelos. From the University, to which he had summoned Pedro, he moved to the Ministry of Education which he himself had founded. As head of the library department he appointed Jaime Torres Bodet, who thus embarked upon the long, steady, sure, and aseptic career that years later would twice make him minister of education. Jaime surrounded himself with a select cortège of poets and journalists, both Mexican and Central American, who visited him every morning to bestow their praises upon him.

The complacent rector of the University was the philosopher Antonio Caso, who liked to shave back his forehead, climb into his Ford, and drive to the Café Lady Baltimore for snacks. Pedro Henríquez Ureña's addict-followers were in constant rivalry with those of Bodet and Vasconcelos. Vicente Lombardo Toledano, director of the Preparatoria, and Daniel Cosío Villegas, director of the University Extension Service, were members of the former faction. (Cosío Villegas, at Pedro's suggestion, had once appointed me "lecturer." Two afternoons each week I had to take a streetcar to the outlying towns of San Gregorio Atlapulco and Tulyehualco to lecture the Indians on matters they could not understand. To keep the thing from being a complete loss I took on the streetcar conductor there on the spot, though somewhat hurriedly.) As if in reply to *La Falange,* the magazine published by the Education clique, in which a sizable hunk of my story "The Young Man" first.appeared, the University clique came out with *Mexican Life,* which survived for one issue only.

The pointless feuding between Vasconcelos' group and Henríquez Ureña's ended with the defeat of the latter. Both Antonio Caso and Pedro resigned their positions. But long before he bowed out of the picture Pedro had violently divested me of my professorial charges. My divestiture took place after a torrid scene in which he proclaimed that my eventual salvation would come only after I had undergone severe trials and tribulations. I would have "to shovel snow in New York," he said, in order to inure myself to hardship. Soon after he announced his forthcoming marriage to Isabel Lombardo, the youngest and prettiest sister of Vicente. With perverse and ill-advised pleasure I attended the wedding ceremony in the Church of San Cosme. Later a scandalous rumor would circulate about how I, in the middle of the solemn proceedings, had kneeled, opened my arms, and prayed aloud: "Lord, take care of him for me; protect him, Lord, for what on earth is he going to do with a woman?"

Still, all things considered, I was not faring poorly. With the enthusiastic approbation of the gringas who found me "oh so young, so cute, and yet so learned," I had acquired a certain right to hold on to the Mexican literature class I taught in the summer school. Its new director, now that Pedro had gone off to Argentina on a honeymoon from which he would never return, was old familiar Moses Sáenz, dark and sullen, just back from Europe—the same Moses Sáenz whom I had seen kicked out of the Preparatoria one tumultuous afternoon. He left the class in my hands but he treated me with notorious reserve. It was much later, after we had come to more friendly terms, that he confided to me that Pedro, before leaving for Argentina, had expressly recommended that I be banned from teaching.

Clarita—née Ricardo—returned from Europe. His natural ebullience was now accentuated by a refinement he had contracted there: cocaine. He kept his crystalline powder in a little metallic box encrusted with fake jewels, and he taught me to savor the delight it brought—that sudden, accelerated, pervasive, and total quickening of the intelligence as it prowled about the world, grasping details and nuances that go unnoticed in the torpor of our normal state.

I could hardly wait to share my new pleasure with Xavier and Delfino. It was easy for me to filch a sheet from my Uncle Manuel's prescription pad, which I could then fill out according to my needs and sign with an illegible scrawl. Any drugstore would fill the prescription: pure, high-grade cocaine at two and a half pesos per gram. Though our sampling of the substance began behind closed doors, a restless hyperkinesia soon drove us into the streets where we rambled about beyond the reach of fatigue, talking endlessly, drained of the lowly need for nourishment and sleep. Sex receded into the background. Our only real joy was that state of nervous exaltation, that purified synesthesia, so lofty and marvelous, which heightened perceptions to a paroxysmal degree and gave rise to the most astonishing and lucid metaphors when, under the influence of the drug, I tried to work out the poems that a sleeplessness marked by clamorous coronary palpitations had spawned in my mind.

Satisfied that he had made new converts to his "snow," Clara took us to visit his new acquaintances. One night we happened to call on Violeta, an aged whore who had erased all traces of her gringo parentage. In her small house she played hostess to the lovers of her daughter Irene and a niece named Milagros. At times Violeta relied too heavily on her cognac, which she mixed with cocaine, and then she would sink into a melancholy silence. With her owllike gaze fixed on the floor, she would occasionally moan, "God, how awful it is to be in love with a faggot." In that state, it seems, she always thought she was in love with Clara.

As he gave himself more and more to his love of cocaine, poor Clara began to lose control of his life. One of his crankier whims was that of falling in love with a queen—he who had so often flaunted his superstitious belief that one queen could only soil and cheapen herself by sleeping with another. Carlos Luquín—Elena Luca, as Clara himself had baptized him—was suddenly the object of his attentions. He was the type of authority-figure he longed for. Though he was well aware that Luquín frequented the baths, freely rubbing his physique against those of the other habitués, Clara faithfully waited for him night after night, poised tremulously on the balcony of his gloomy apartment overlooking Plaza Rio de Janeiro. Sometimes he waited all night, frantically tapping his little box until its stock of "snow" was exhausted, and then, at dawn, he would shoot Sedol and collapse his bed—the same bed from which his powerful family one day removed his squalid corpse, pitifully consumed by life, and hurried it off to a surreptitious burial.

While I was under his Socratic tutelage, Pedro Henríquez Ureña forced upon me editorial exercises which, he hoped, would degrade my prose into a state of intelligibility. "You must learn to write like Carlos González Peña," he said with ill-concealed malice for the editor of *El Universal*. Under his guidance I earned extra money by submitting articles and editorials to *El Mundo,* a paper edited by Martín Luís Guzmán. In that way he opened for me the facile doors of journalism. *El Universal Ilustrado* accepted my submissions with excessively enthusiastic praise, and so, though the pay was slight in those days—ten pesos for an article that filled three-quarters of a copy sheet—I was not left completely without an income when the swift and deadly animosity of my disillusioned mentor took from me the teaching posts he had bestowed upon me.

By that time I was almost twenty. When I abandoned my law studies my family were not overly disappointed. They knew that

I was working, as all of my uncles had done since their childhood, and that knowledge calmed them, or, at least, explained their indifference toward my decision. From time to time I could even contribute a little toward the expenses of the household. I provided my own clothing, and insofar as possible, my own food, thereby sparing myself the torture of sitting at the family table. There I would have had to mull over my sins, confronted by the bourgeois normality of my Uncle Felipe, the haughty indifference of Manuel, the sorrowful tenuity of Aunt Julia, and the hoary matriarchy of my grandmother. So I gulped down my breakfast and lunch and managed to condition my relatives not to expect me for the evening meal.

I met Enrique Jiménez in the apartment of the two Antonios. He was teaching an English literature course at the time and was a friend and peer of important people such as Antonio Caso and Genaro Fernández MacGregor, but he pursued a more intimate friendship with Honorato Bolaños, known familiarly as Totó. As faculty secretary or director, Totó ranked second to Antonio Caso himself.

Enrique regarded Totó with an admiration in which he shielded his own sexual timidity, his disinclination to take the risks that Totó took in procuring for himself an enormous clientele of cadets, firemen, and gendarmes with whom he staged private orgies. If Enrique had asked Totó to loan him one of another of his surplus tricks, the old man, in all probability, would have gladly ceded him those who had begun to bore him. But, knowing well that he could only end up with the rejects, Enrique somehow preferred to pass by Totó's house and catch them on their way in or out. In his car, driving in endless circles through the dark streets of the city, he would pass again and again by Totó's place, and, according to whether the inside lights were on or off, he could deduce the activity of the old man whose boldness he so envied, or, from time to time, he could lure some tardy caller into his vehicle and drive away.

We commented on the fact that neither of us had living quarters of his own. At Enrique's suggestion we decided to rent an apartment together. He showed me a house—No. 42 Brazil Street—where some rooms were for rent. It was only a half block from the school of medicine, and, most important for me, it was close to the Department of Transit, which, in those days, was located in the

Santo Domingo Customs House and was invariably crowded with drivers applying for licenses or documents of some sort.

On the flat roof of the house there was an available room, furnished, with its own washstand. I signed the lease. Thirty pesos a month. The room was big enough for one bed only—not that we needed another—and, aside from the bed, one armchair, a console-table over which I hung a San Ignacio figure I had bought for ten pesos from Pepe Alcalde, and a folding screen. I had the screen made to order. It marked a stage, so to speak, on the route to the bed, and from behind it one could spy on whatever might be taking place there. A small window ventilated the room and gave us a view of Brazil Street down below. Enrique and I devised a signal whereby each could alert the other when the room was in use: a woven sash, left over from the perfervidly nationalistic décor of my first apartment, would hang in the window, visible from the street below. The one who saw it could spare himself the trouble of scaling the long flights of stairs. In such a spirit of cooperation we even worked out an exchange program: I passed my drivers and ticket-takers on to Enrique, and he reciprocated with the military cadets he managed to intercept chez Totó.

I invited Xavier, Delfino, and Montenegro to my new abode. No longer the Virgin of Istanbul's lover, Xavier had learned to procure for himself the little vagrant types that so attracted him. Around that time I began to be friends with Agustín Lazo, a nephew of Antonio Adalid. Antonio had told me earlier that he had "a terribly hypocritical niece" and that together we might be able to make her let down her hair. So one night I had the long-nosed, introverted young man as my guest. His hair looked as if it had been ironed into place; through his tightly buttoned suit he oozed culture and inhibitions. He was a painter of sorts, and he was up to the minute in literature and music. He insisted that we talk about art and the jokes told by his boisterous uncle made him blush profusely. Antonio observed him closely, goading me on in my efforts to lure his poor niece into a confession of sisterhood. I failed, but Agustín's relation with Xavier began on an immediate note of confidence. Less inhibited then, he and Xavier rented the empty room next to mine, and from his home Agustín brought fine velvet cushions to adorn it.

Enrique, being so timid, must have felt discomforted and threatened by the steady influx of friends who came to visit me in our room, not to mention the invasion of competitive tenants on the other floors. Xavier Villada Saviñón moved into a room which he tapestried in glowing colors, and Montenegro rented one of the others in the building—all of which inspired Enrique to dissolve our roommateship and set up his own headquarters elsewhere.

On the flat roof, aside from my room and the one occupied by Xavier and Agustín, there was one rented by a student from Veracruz and another where María the concierge lived with Jorgita, her ancient mother, Jorge, her brother, and a daughter named Carmen. All four of them were short and pudgy like identical dwarfs. After tidying up the rooms María would spend the rest of the morning hunched over the laundry basin scrubbing clean the little cloth towels and napkins from which, many years later, the blessed advent of Kleenex would liberate us. And then at night she would drag a simple cot halfway down the stairs. There she could stretch out and doze, getting up to open the street door when, at the most unwonted hours, one of the tenants came home and made his way hurriedly up the stairs, trailed by a furtive shadow.

TRES POEMAS DE *NUEVO AMOR*

1 La renovada muerte de la noche
   en que ya no nos queda sino la breve luz de la conciencia
   y tendernos al lado de los libros
   de donde las palabras escaparon sin fuga, crucificadas en mi mano,
   y en esta cripta de familia
   en la que existe en cada espejo y en cada sitio la evidencia del crimen
   y en cuyos roperos dejamos la crisálida de los adioses irremediables
   con que hemos de embalsamar el futuro
   y en los ahorcados que penden de cada lámpara
   y en el veneno de cada vaso que apuramos
   y en esa silla eléctrica en que hemos abandonado nuestros disfraces
   para ocultarnos bajo los solitarios sudarios
   mi corazón ya no sabe sino marcar el paso
   y dar vueltas como un tigre de circo
   inmediato a una libertad inasible.
   Todos hemos ido llegando a nuestras tumbas
   a buena hora, a la hora debida,
   en ambulancias de cómodo precio
   o bien de suicidio natural y premeditado.
   Y yo no puedo seguir trazando un escenario perfecto
   en que la luna habría de jugar un papel importante
   porque en estos momentos
   hay trenes por encima de toda la tierra
   que lanzan unos dolorosos suspiros
   y que parten
   y la luna no tiene nada que ver
   con las breves luciérnagas que nos vigilan
   desde un azul cercano y desconocido
   lleno de estrellas poliglotas e innumerables.

2 Tú, yo mismo, seco como un viento derrotado
   que no pudo sino muy brevemente sostener en sus brazos una hoja
       que arrancó de los árboles
   ¿cómo será posible que nada te conmueva
   que no haya lluvia que te estruje ni sol que rinda tu fatiga?

THREE POEMS FROM *NUEVO AMOR* (1933)

1 In the refreshened death of night,
   when we are left with only the brief glow of consciousness
   as we stretch out beside books
   from which the flightless words have fled, crucified in my hand,
   in this family crypt
   where each place and each mirror holds evidence of the crime,
   in whose wardrobes we left the chrysalis of those irremediable farewells
   we were to use for embalming the future,
   in the hanged men swinging from each lamp
   and in the poison of each glass we drain,
   in the electric chair where we lay aside our disguises
   to hide ourselves beneath the lonely shroud of death,
   all my heart can do is mark time,
   pacing about like a circus tiger
   close upon a freedom it cannot seize.
   We have all gone steadily to our tombs
   in good time, at the appointed hour,
   in ambulances comfortably priced
   or by natural and premeditated suicide.
   And I cannot continue plotting my perfect play
   in which the moon was to have a leading role,
   for now,
   all over the earth, there are trains
   to hurl their sorrowful sighs
   and then move on,
   and the moon has nothing to do
   with the swift fireflies that keep watch over us
   from a nearby but unknown blueness
   full of innumerable polyglot stars.

2 You, myself, dry like a defeated wind
   which only for a moment could hold in its arms the leaf
   it wrenched from the trees,
   how is it possible that nothing can move you now,
   that no rain can crush you, no sun give back your weariness?

Ser una transparencia sin objeto
sobre los lagos limpios de tus miradas
oh tempestad, diluvio de hace ya mucho tiempo.
Si desde entonces busco tu imagen que era solamente mía
si en mis manos estériles ahogué la última gota de tu sangre y mi lágrima
y si fue desde entonces indiferente el mundo e infinito el desierto
y cada nueva noche musgo para el recuerdo de tu abrazo
¿cómo en el nuevo día tendré sino tu aliento,
sino tus brazos impalpables entre los míos?
Lloro como una madre que ha reemplazado al hijo único muerto.
Lloro como la tierra que ha sentido dos veces germinar el fruto
    perfecto y mismo.
Lloro porque eres tú para mi duelo
y ya te pertenezco en el pasado.

3 Este perfume intenso de tu carne
    no es nada más que el mundo que desplazan y mueven los globos
        azules de tus ojos
    y la tierra y los ríos azules de las venas que aprisionan tus brazos.
    Hay todas las redondas naranjas en tu beso de angustia
    sacrificado al borde de un huerto en que la vida se suspendió por
        todos los siglos de la mía.
    Qué remoto era el aire infinito que llenó nuestros pechos.
    Te arranqué de la tierra por las raíces ebrias de tus manos
    y te he bebido todo, ¡oh fruto perfecto y delicioso!
    Ya siempre cuando el sol palpe mi carne
    he de sentir el rudo contacto de la tuya
    nacida en la frescura de una alba inesperada,
    nutrida en la caricia de tus ríos claros y puros como tu abrazo,
    vuelta dulce en el viento que en las tardes
    viene de las montañas a tu aliento,
    madurada en el sol de tus dieciocho años,
    cálida para mí que la esperaba.

To be a purposeless transparency
above the limpid lakes of your gaze,
oh tempest, oh deluge of long ago!
If since then I seek an image of you that was mine alone,
if within my sterile hands I stifled
the last drop of your blood and my tears,
if since then the world has been indifferent,
in wastelands endless, and each new night
has grown like moss over the memory of your embrace,
how then in the new day can I have any breath but yours,
any but your impalpable arms among mine?
I weep like a mother who has replaced her only dead son.
I weep like the earth which twice has felt the same perfect fruit
sprout within it.
I weep because you were destined to be my grief
and already now it is in the past that I belong to you.

3 This intense perfume of your flesh
is nothing more than the world which the blue spheres
of your eyes move and displace,
nothing more than the earth and the blue rivers
of veins imprisoned in your arms.
In your anguished kiss are all the round oranges
you sacrificed on the edge of a garden
where life for all time to come broke off from mine.
So remote was the endless air that filled our breasts.
I pulled you from the earth by the drunken roots of your hands,
and entire I drank you down, oh perfect delicious fruit!
Forever now when the sun touches me
I must feel the rude contact of your flesh
born in the freshness of an unexpected dawn,
nourished in the caress of rivers as pure and clear as your embrace,
sweetened in the afternoon wind
that comes down from the mountains to join your breath
and ripened in the sun of your eighteen years,
warm for me who awaited it.

Luis Cernuda

LUIS CERNUDA Y BIDON was born in Seville in 1902. He wrote his first poems in 1916, but his work remained unpublished until 1925, when his teacher, Pedro Salinas, arranged for nine poems to appear in *Revista de Occidente* under the title "Versos." His first book, *Perfil del aire,* appeared in 1927 to almost universal critical hostility or indifference. Bitter over this reception, Cernuda published little more poetry until 1936, when the first edition of *La realidad y el deseo* appeared. This work contained the revised poems of his first volume, now entitled simply "Primeras poesias," plus five new sections, including the surrealist poetry of "Un rio, un amor" and "Los placeres prohibidos." All of his subsequent poetry was included in successive editions of *La realidad,* and the third edition, in 1958, was immediately recognized as a landmark in twentieth-century Spanish poetry.

In 1937 Cernuda left Spain for Paris, thinking he would soon be able to return to his home. With Franco's victory this proved impossible and Cernuda began the wanderings that led him to Mexico. Exile provided the stimulus for his greatest poetry, beginning with the section "Las nubes" (1940), which, with "Como quien espera al alba" (1947) and "Con las horas contadas" (1952) would seem to constitute his greatest achievement. In "Las nubes" the influence of English poets, especially Blake, Wordsworth and Browning, begins to displace that of his earlier mentors, Aragon, Eluard, and Hölderlin. He translated poetry by Browning, Yeats, and Hölderlin, and his version of *Troilus and Cressida* is one of the best translations of any of Shakespeare's plays in Spanish.

After teaching at Glasgow, Cambridge, and the Spanish Institute in London, he moved, in 1947, to Mount Holyoke, Massachusetts. His experiences in England and Scotland intensified his feelings of "soledad," which for Cernuda was not merely "aloneness," but an ontological solitude, basic to the lives of all artists and all homosexuals. In 1949 he made his first trip to Mexico, which seemed to him the duplication of his native Andalusia and a refuge from the "grey Anglo-Saxon lands" in which he had been living.

It was not until 1952 that Cernuda moved permanently to Mexico, but that initial impression produced a volume of prose poems, *Variaciones sobre tema mexicano,* and some of the best poems in "Con las horas contadas." Also in Mexico he found what appeared to be the erotic ideal he had searched for throughout his life. This affair with a young man, though short-lived, produced the great series of love poems included in "Con las horas contadas," "Poemas para un cuerpo."

In the ten years before his death in 1963 Cernuda published little more poetry: a single volume, entitled *Desolación de la quimera,* appeared in 1962. This volume, after the calm of his previous work (even "Poemas para un cuerpo" are meditative rather than passionate), is a violent work, a settling of old scores, both aesthetic and personal, though for Cernuda the line between the two was often thin.

Although strictly speaking Cernuda is not a Latin American writer, he did live in Mexico during the last ten years of his life and considered it his new home. All but one of the Cernuda poems printed here are from this period. "Jealous Divinity," "Salvador," "With You," and "Life" are from Cernuda's great series of love poems, "Poemas para un cuerpo," written in Mexico to his male lover. "The Scandal" is from an earlier period.

All the Cernuda poems printed here are translated by Franklin D. Blanton. He has translated poetry and prose by Becquer, Aleixandre, Bousoño, González, Hierro, and others, and now lives in Austin, Texas.

CONTIGO

Mi tierra?
Mi tierra eres tú.

Mi gente?
Mi gente eres tú.

El destierro y la muerte
Para mí están adonde
No estés tú.

Y mi vida?
Dime, mi vida,
Qué es, si no eres tú?

SALVADOR

Sálvale o condénale,
Porque ya su destino
Está en tus manos, abolido.

Si eres salvador, sálvale
De ti y de él; la violencia
De no ser uno en ti, aquiétala.

O si no lo eres, condénale,
Para que a su deseo
Suceda otro tormento.

Sálvale o condénale,
Pero así no le dejes
Seguir vivo, y perderte.

WITH YOU

My land?
You are my land.

My people?
You are my people.

Exile and death
Are for me where
You are not.

And my life?
Tell me, my life,
What is it, if not you?

SALVADOR

Save him or damn him,
Because now his destiny
Is in your hands, abolished.

If you are a savior, save him
From you and from himself: calm
The violence of his not being one with you.

Or if you are not, then damn him,
So that by his desire
Torment will follow torment.

Save him then, or damn him,
But do not thus allow him
To go on living and to lose you.

EDITOR'S NOTE: It was common for Cernuda to address himself in his poems in the second person. This poem is nearly unique in that the "you" is Salvador, the poet's Mexican lover, while the poet himself appears in the third person, "him."

DIVINIDAD CELOSA

Los cuatro elementos primarios
    Dan forma a mi existir:
Un cuerpo sometido al tiempo,
    Siempre ansioso de ti.

Porque el tiempo de amor nos vale
    Toda una eternidad
Donde ya el hombre no va solo,
    Y Dios celoso está.

Déjame amarte ahora. Un día,
    Temprano o tarde, Dios
Dispone que el amante deba
    Renunciar a su amor.

LA VIDA

Como cuando el sol enciende
Algún rincón de la tierra,
Su probeza la redime,
Con risas verdes lo llena,

Así tu presencia viene
Sobre mi existencia oscura
A exaltarlo, para darle
Esplendor, gozo, hermosura.

Pero también tú te pones
Lo mismo que el sol, y crecen
En torno mío las sombras
De soledad, vejez, muerte.

JEALOUS DIVINITY

The four primary elements give
    Shape to my existence:
A body subject to time yearns
    For you forever.

Because the time of love, when man
    No longer goes
Alone, is worth all of eternity,
    God is jealous.

Let me love you now. One day,
    Sooner or later,
God arranges that the lover should
    Renounce his love.

LIFE

As when the sun shines into
Some corner of the earth,
Redeeming its poverty,
Filling it with green laughter,

So your presence comes
Over my dark existence—
To exalt it, to give it
Splendor, beauty, pleasure.

But then you depart,
Just as the sun does,
And the shadows of old age,
Solitude and death grow around me.

EL ESCÁNDALO

En las largas tardes del verano, ya regadas las puertas, ya pasado el vendedor de jazmines, aparecían ellos, solos a veces, emparejados casi siempre. Iban vestidos con blanca chaqueta almidonada, ceñido pantalón negro de alpaca, zapatos rechinantes como el cantar de un grillo, y en la cabeza una gorrilla ladeada, que dejaba escapar algún rizo negro o rubio. Se contoneaban con gracia felina, ufanos de algo que sólo ellos conocían, pareciendo guardarlo secreto, aunque el placer que en ese secreto hallaban desbordaba a pesar de ellos sobre las gentes.

Un coro de gritos en falsete, el ladrar de algún perro, anunciaba su paso, aun antes de que hubieran doblado la esquina. Al fin surgían, risueños y casi siempre envanecidos del cortejo que les seguía insultándoles con motes indecorosos. Con dignidad de alto personaje en destierro, apenas si se volvían al séquito blasfemo para lanzar tal pulla ingeniosa. Mas como si no quisieran decepcionar a las gentes en lo que éstas esperaban de ellos, se contoneaban más exageradamente, ciñendo aún más la chaqueta a su talle cimbreante, con lo cual redoblaban las risotadas y la chacota del coro.

Alguna vez levantaban la mirada a un balcón, donde los curiosos se asomaban al ruido, y había en sus descarados ojos juveniles una burla mayor, un desprecio más real que en quienes con morbosa curiosidad les iban persiguiendo. Al fin se perdían al otro extremo de la calle.

Eran unos seres misteriosos a quienes llamaban "los maricas."

THE SCANDAL

In the long afternoons of summer, after the doorsteps had been sprinkled, after the jasmine seller had passed, they appeared, sometimes alone, but usually in pairs. They dressed in white starched jackets and tight black alpaca trousers; their shoes creaked like a cricket's song and on their heads were tilted caps that allowed black or blond curls to escape. They walked, hips swinging, with feline grace, proud of something only they knew, and seemed to guard their secret, though the pleasure they found in it overflowed, despite them, to the crowd.

A chorus of falsetto shrieks, the howling of some dog, announced their coming even before they had turned the corner. Finally they appeared, smiling and nearly arrogant about the escort that followed them and hurled indecent nicknames. With the dignity of high personages in exile, they turned slightly toward the blasphemous retinue and let loose a witty obscenity. Yet, as if they did not want to disillusion the people, they swung their hips more exaggeratedly, tightening their jackets still more about their swaying, supple waists, at which the crowd redoubled their heckling and laughter.

Sometimes they raised their eyes toward a balcony where the curious leaned out to the noise and they had in their young, impudent eyes a great mockery, a contempt more real than that in those who with morbid curiosity went on persecuting them. Finally they disappeared at the far end of the street.

They were the mysterious creatures called "faggots."

"The Scandal" was written in the early 1940s, after Cernuda had left Spain but before he chose Mexico as his new home. *Ocnos,* the book in which the poem appeared, is devoted to an imaginative recreation of Cernuda's native Andalusia, and it was Mexico's resemblance to that land that, in the early 1950s, led the poet to settle there permanently.

Though this poem, then, does not refer to Mexico, its atmosphere and setting are similar to Mexico's and in view of Cernuda's later career, it seemed appropriate to include it in this anthology. "Street Queens," similar to those in the poem, are a noticeable feature of gay society in Latin America.

AMANDO EN EL TIEMPO

El tiempo, insinuándose en tu cuerpo,
Como nube de polvo en fuenta pura,
Aquella gracia antigua desordena
Y clava en mí una pena silenciosa.

Otros antes que yo vieron un día,
Y otros luego verán, cómo decae
La amada forma esbelta, recordando
De cuánta gloria es cifra un cuerpo hermoso.

Pero la vida solos la aprendemos,
Y placer y dolor se ofrecen siempre
Tal mundo virgen para cada hombre;
Así mi pena inculta es nueva ahora.

Nueva como lo fuese al primer hombre,
Que cayó con su amor del paraíso,
Cuando viera, su cielo ya vencido
Por sombras, decaer el cuerpo amado.

DESPEDIDA

Muchachos
Que nunca fuisteis compañeros de mi vida,
Adiós.
Muchachos
que no seréis nunca compañeros de mi vida,
Adiós.

El tiempo de una vida nos separa
Infranqueable:
A un lado la juventud libre y risueña;
A otro la vejez humillante e inhóspita.

De joven no sabía

LOVING WITHIN TIME

Time, mixing slowly with your body
Like a cloud of dust in a clear fountain,
Disarranges that ancient charm
And fixes me in silent pain.

Others before me have already seen,
And still others will soon see, how the lithe,
Well-loved form decays, reminding
A beautiful body how little glory is.

But we learn of life alone;
Always pleasure and grief offer
A virgin world to every man.
My coarse pain is new once more.

New as it was for the first man
Who fell with his love from paradise
When he saw, like a shadow-covered
Sky, the aging body of the beloved.

LEAVETAKING

Young men
Who were never the companions of my life,
Good-bye.
Young men
Who will never be the companions of my life,
Good-bye.

A lifetime separates us,
Insurmountable:
On one side, youth . . . free and laughing;
On the other, age . . . humiliated and unsheltered.

In youth I did not know

Ver la hermosura, codiciarla, poseerla;
De viejo lo he aprendido
Y veo a la hermosura, mas la codicio inútilmente.

Mano de viejo mancha
El cuerpo juvenil si intenta acariciarlo.
Con solitaria dignidad el viejo debe
Pasar de largo junto a la tentación tardía.

Frescos y codiciables son los labios besados,
Labios nunca besados más codiciables y frescos aparacen.
Qué remedio, amigos? Qué remedio?
Bien lo sé: no lo hay.

Qué dulce hubiera sido
En vuestra compañía vivir un tiempo:
Bañarse juntos en aguas de una playa caliente,
Compartir bebida y alimento en una mesa,
Sonreír, conversar, pasearse
Mirando cerca, en vuestros ojos, esa luz y esa música.

Seguid, seguid así, tan descuidadamente,
Atrayendo al amor, atrayendo al deseo.
No cuidéis de la herida que la hermosura vuestra y vuestra gracia
    abren
en este transeúnte inmune en apariencia a ellas.

Adiós, adiós, manojos de gracias y donaires.
Que yo pronto he de irme, confiado,
Adonde, anudado el roto hilo, diga y haga
Lo que aquí falta, lo que a tiempo decir y hacer aquí no supe.

Adiós, adiós, compañeros imposibles.
Que ya tan sólo aprendo
A morir, deseando
Veros de nuevo, hermosos igualmente
En alguna otra vida.

To see beauty, to covet it, to possess it;
In old age, I have learned of it
And see in beauty but a restless greed.

The hand of an old man stains
The young body when he tries to caress it.
The old ought to pass by
With a solitary dignity joined to belated temptation.

Fresh and desirable are the kissed lips.
Lips never kissed seem more desirable and fresh.
What can one do, friends? What can one do?
You know very well: nothing.

How sweet it has been
To live a while in your company:
To bathe together in waters by the warm sand,
To share food and drink from the same table,
To laugh, to talk, to stroll,
Observing nearby, in your eyes, that light and that music.

Continue, continue thus thoughtlessly,
Attracting love, attracting desire.
You did not care about the wound that your beauty and your grace
Opened in this immune passer-by who appeared before them.

Good-bye, good-bye, bundles of grace and charm.
Because I soon must go, trusting,
To where, the broken thread retied, I say and do
What here is lacking, what I did not know in time to say or do.

Good-bye, good-bye, impossible friends.
Alone now, I learn
To die, desiring
To see you again, equally beautiful
In some other life.

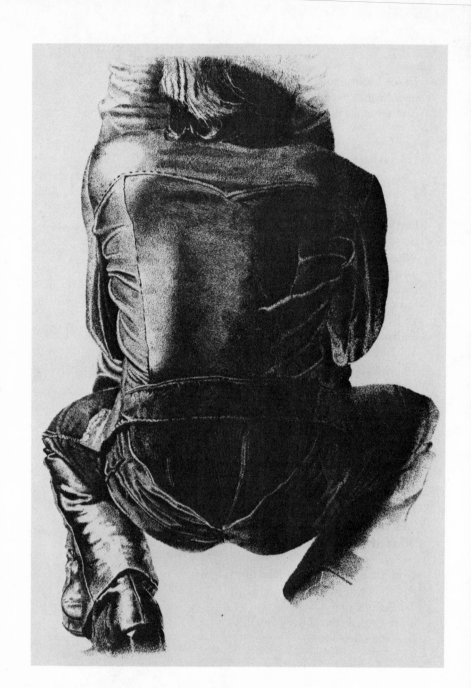

Boca (1974). Etching by Miguel Angel Rojas (Colombia)
Photo © by Oscar Monsalve

Xavier Villaurrutia

XAVIER VILLAURRUTIA was born in Mexico City on March 27, 1903, and died in the same city on December 27, 1950. He had his primary and secondary education at the Colegio Francés, after which he began to study law at the University of Mexico, but soon abandoned this career for literature. With Salvador Novo he edited the magazine *Ulises*. He was a member of the group "Contemporaneos" from 1938 to 1931. He studied dramatic arts at Yale University on a scholarship from the Rockefeller Foundation, and was professor of literature at the University of Mexico and director of the theater department of Bella Artes. His poetry on his favorite themes—love, night, and death—shows great verbal purity and emotional intensity. As a dramatist Villaurrutia began by translating Chekhov, Jules Romains, and Lenormand. His own three-act plays are *Invitación a la muerte* (1940), *La hiedra* (1941), and *La mujer legítima* (1942). With Gorostiza and Bracho he transformed dramatic art in Mexico. He was also an intelligent and subtle critic, writing prose of clarity and elegance which shows the influence of André Gide. His works (*Obras*) were published by El Fondo de Cultura Económica in Mexico City (1966).

Ernesto Bañuelos Enríquez

"MY PARENTS, Mexican migrant workers, were living in King City, California, just to the east of paradise, when I was born in 1948. Later, I was taken to Torreón, Mexico, to live with aunts. Torreón is where I learned to read, to play football, to look at men with pleasure, to masturbate. I spent my adolescence attending Catholic schools and tricking in movie-houses. I spent my adolescence, and then I wanted to be an actor, and I was an actor, and now I write whenever I want.

"My friends and I have problems very different now from those of childhood. Now we know all about love, loneliness, and the crisis that comes at age 30. Now we're interested in politics, and the Mexico City smog is smothering us, and Mario's dead now, and I don't live with Luís anymore, and things cost a lot more these days, and life almost makes me bitter at times, and—

"Tomorrow, maybe I'll wake up optimistic."

Xavier Villaurrutia

NOCTURNO DE LOS ÁNGELES

a Agustín J. Fink

Se diría que las calles fluyen dulcemente en la noche.
Las luces no son tan vivas que logren desvelar el secreto,
el secreto que los hombres que van y vienen conocen,
porque todos están en el secreto
y nada se ganaría con partirlo en mil pedazos
si, por el contrario, es tan dulce guardarlo
y compartirlo sólo con la persona elegida.

Si cada uno dijera en un momento dado,
en sólo una palabra, lo que piensa,
las cinco letras del DESEO formarían una enorme cicatriz luminosa,
una constelación más antigua, más viva aún que las otras.
Y esa constelación sería como un ardiente sexo
en el profundo cuerpo de la noche,
o, mejor, como los Gemelos que por vez primera en la vida
se miraran de frente, a los ojos, y se abrazaran ya para siempre.

De pronto el río de la calle se puebla de sedientos seres,
caminan, se detienen, prosiguen.
Cambian miradas, atreven sonrisas,
forman imprevistas parejas...

Hay recodos y bancos de sombra,
orillas de indefinibles formas profundas
y súbitos huecos de luz que ciega
y puertas que ceden a la presión más leve.

El río de la calle queda desierto un instante.
Luego parece remontar de sí mismo
deseoso de volver a empezar.
Queda un momento paralizado, mudo, anhelante
como el corazón entre dos espasmos.

NOCTURNO DE LOS ÁNGELES

for Agustín J. Fink

You could say that the streets flow softly in the night,
their lights not bright enough to lay bare
the secret known only to the men who come and go.
All of the men are in on the secret and nothing
would be gained by breaking it into a thousand pieces
when, on the contrary, it is so sweet to keep it whole
and share it with the chosen person.

If at any given moment each were to sum up
his thoughts in a single word,
the six letters of DESIRE would form a vast luminous scar
across the night sky,
a constellation older and brighter than the rest.
That constellation would be like a burning phallus
embedded in the deep body of the night,
or, better still, like the Twins that gaze into each other's
eyes for the first time and fuse in a fixed embrace.

Thirsty beings people the river of the street.
They stroll, linger, and stroll again.
They exchange glances, stares, smiles;
they pair off unexpectedly, at random.

There are bends in the stream and banks of shadows,
shores of indefinable deep forms
and sudden hollows of light that blind
and doors that yield to the slightest touch.

For a moment the street is lifeless, lonely.
Then it seems to gather itself into itself,
eager to flow again.
For a moment it is paralyzed, mute, panting
like a heart caught between spasms.

Pero una nueva pulsación, un nuevo latido
arroja al río de la calle nuevos sedientos seres.
Se cruzan, se entrecruzan y suben.
Vuelan a ras de tierra.
Nadan de pie, tan milagrosamente
que nadie se atrevería a decir que no caminan.

¡Son los ángeles!
Han bajado a la tierra
por invisibles escalas.
Vienen del mar, que es el espejo del cielo,
en barcos de humo y sombra,
a fundirse y confundirse con los mortales,
a rendir sus frentes en los muslos de las mujeres,
a dejar que otras manos palpen sus cuerpos febrilmente,
y que otros cuerpos busquen los suyos hasta encontrarlos
como se encuentran al cerrarse los labios de una misma boca,
a fatigar su boca tanto tiempo inactiva,
a poner en libertad sus lenguas de fuego,
a decir las canciones, los juramentos, las malas palabras
en que los hombres concentran el antiguo misterio
de la carne, la sangre y el deseo.

Tienen nombres supuestos, divinamente sencillos.
Se llaman Dick o John, o Marvin o Louis.
En nada sino en la belleza se distinguen de los mortales.

Caminan, se detienen, prosiguen.
Cambian miradas, atreven sonrisas.
Forman imprevistas parejas.

Sonríen maliciosamente al subir en los ascensores de los hoteles
donde aún se practica el vuelo lento y vertical.
En sus cuerpos desnudos hay huellas celestiales;
signos, estrellas y letras azules.
Se dejan caer en las camas, se hunden en las almohadas
que los hacen pensar todavía un momento en las nubes.
Pero cierran los ojos para entregarse mejor a los goces de su
    encarnación misteriosa,
y, cuando duermen, sueñan no con los ángeles sino con los mortales.

Then a new pulsation, a new beat,
casts new thirsty beings into the stream.
They wander back and forth, up and down.
They skim along the surface of the earth;
they swim on their feet, upright, so miraculously
that no one would dare suggest they aren't walking.

They are the angels!
They have come down to the earth
on invisible ladders.
They come from the sea, that mirror of the sky,
in ships of smoke and shadow.
They come to be fused and confused with mortal men,
to surrender their foreheads between the thighs of women,
to let other hands feverishly grope their bodies
while other bodies hunt out theirs until they come together
like the two lips of a single mouth.
They come to tire their mouths so long unused,
to set free their tongues of fire,
to sing songs and speak oaths and utter those dirty words
in which men have concentrated the ancient mysteries
of flesh, blood, and desire.

They all have phony names, short and simple—
Dick, John, Marv, or Lou.
Nothing except their beauty distinguishes them from mortals.

They stroll, linger, and stroll again.
They exchange glances, stares, smiles;
they pair off unexpectedly, at random.

As the elevators rise in their hotels they smile slyly,
remembering the slow, vertical flight of angels.
Their naked bodies bear celestial markings—
strange signs, stars, blueish letters.
They fall into the beds and sink into the pillows,
which for a moment remind them of clouds.
They close their eyes, the better to surrender themselves
to the pleasures of their mysterious incarnation,
and when they sleep
they dream not of angels but of mortal men.

Ernesto Bañuelos Enríquez

LA MÍA Y LA HISTORIA DE ALGUNOS AMIGOS EN ESTOS TROZOS DE AMORES COTIDIANOS

Y me empecé
a dar cuenta
de que era diferente,
cuando
en las caricaturas
ningún niño
se enamoraba
de su amigo.

+

Yo estaba chiquito
digo,
como de ocho años
y me gustaba ir a orinar
en el intermedio,
en el cine Nazas.
Digo,
me gustaba mirar a los lados
las pingas de los señores
ya con pelos y grandes.

+

Porque te agarré la pinga
me chantajeabas;
y por eso
tenía que comprarte
tres chicles "Motitas"
cada día.

+

Decían que daba dulces;
a mí no me gustaba él

ya por mayor y viejo,
pero
al fin,
un chocolate de los caros
no se desperdicia
y fui con él
a las cinco después de clases.

+

Yo me reía
y era feliz
con él
ahí
a mi lado
escribiendo, como yo,
No debo hacer peladeces
en el baño con mis compañeros
No debo hacer peladeces
en el baño con mis compañeros
No debo hacer peladeces
en el baño con mis compañeros

+

Ser joto
era pecado
y yo
vivía
dispuesto
a arrepentirme
si me confesaba
aquel cura
tan guapo.

THE STORY OF MYSELF AND SOME FRIENDS
IN THESE FRAGMENTS OF DAILY LOVES

And I began
to realize
I was different
when I noticed
that none of the guys
in the comic books
ever fell in love
with their friends.

+

I was little then,
I mean
about eight or so
and I liked to go peepee
between features
at the Nazas Theatre.
I mean
I liked to peep beside me
at the men there
with their cocks big
and hairy already.

+

Because I grabbed
your cock once
you blackmailed me
and to keep you quiet
I had to buy you
three pieces of
bubblegum every day.

+

They said he gave candy.
He was too big and old

and I didn't like him
but, well,
after all,
chocolate of the expensive type
isn't something you let
go to waste,
and so I went with him
at five o'clock one day
after school.

+

I was all giggles
and happiness
with him
there beside me
both of us writing
a thousand times each:
I must not do naughty things
with my classmates
in the bathroom.
I must not do naughty things
with my classmates
in the bathroom.
I must not do naughty things
with my classmates
in the bathroom.

+

It was a sin
to be queer
and I was always
ready to repent
provided that handsome
young priest
would confess me.

+

Fui solo al Matinée,
me senté junto a un muchacho
y poco a poco,
mientras
El Príncipe
le daba un baso
a La Bella Durmiente,
cerraba
mis ojos
con la esperanza
que tienen
los niños menores de siete años.

+

"Ese niño es joto,"
dijeron;
yo
sin preguntar
el significado
de aquella palabra,
llegué a mi casa
y entre las sábanas
con figuras de Walt Disney,
tuve
mi primera noche
de insomnio.

+

Desnudos
los dos solos
allá en el fondo
del taller
llamado
"Taller García,"
estuvimos
contentos y abrazados;
yo

de aquel mecánico
(amigo de mi padre),
él
con aquel chamaco
de la escuela "Benito Juarez."

+

Victor Manuel
era frágil y tierno,
Miraba a los compañeros
del salón
amorosamente.
Ellos
furiosos por esa mirada,
la patearon entre burlas
y amenazas.

Lo agarraron a golpes
por que se le caía la mano;
y yo asustado, aterrado,
miraba aquella escena
con una de las mías
en el bolsillo.

No sé que será de él,
pero antes cuando le pegaban,
lloraba.

Se quedaba
limpiándose la cara
sobre los pupitres del salón,
solo.

Y yo como los golpeadores,
me iba.

Yo asustado;
asustado de pensar que ellos
descubrieran el calor
de mi mirada.

+

I went alone
to the movies one afternoon
and took a seat
beside a boy there
and little by little
while Prince Charming
kissed Sleeping Beauty
I closed my eyes,
filled with the kind of hope
common to kids of seven.

+

"That kid's queer,"
they said.
Without asking
what the word meant
I went home
and under covers
printed
with Walt Disney characters
I spent
my first sleepless night.

+

Naked
the two of us alone
there in the back
of a shop
called "Garcia's Auto Repairs,"
all cuddled up
and happy—
me

with my mechanic
(a friend of my father's),
him
with his kid
from Benito Juarez
High School.

+

Victor Manuel
was delicate and gentle.
There was a tenderness
in the way
he looked at his classmates,
and they,
bothered by it,
kicked him, threatened him,
mocked him.

They beat the hell out of him
because he had a limp wrist.
Scared, terrified,
I looked on with my own hands
crammed deep in my pockets.

I don't know what
may have become of him,
but when they hit him then
he cried.

He stayed behind
cleaning up his face
among the desks
in the classroom,
alone,
and I like one of his tormentors
walked away.

I was afraid
they might discover the warmth
in my gaze too.

Ellos contentos de reprender
a un joto.

No sé que será de él.
Quisiera verlo cambiado,
quisiera posiblemente
que llorara otro poco
y que después con un cuchillo
matara a todas los golpeadores,
los hiciera trizas,
los regara por toda la Escuela,
en todos los salones,
y en la capilla
del "Sagrado Corazón"
que prohibe el crimen.

+

Cuando salí de la Primaria
mi papá me felicitó,
pero no dejó
que le diera un beso,
dijo
que ya no era edad
para besuqueos;
así
me quedé mucho tiempo
sin poder acercarme,
ni besar
ni sentir lo áspero
de una barba crecida.

+

Cuando tuvo novia
decía yo:
"Que bonita es ella,"
pero
lo miraba a él.

+

Y sólo porque te miré bonito,
me gritaste:
"¡Joto!"

+

Raúl
era
uno de esos muchachos
que con la mirada
te piden
que los beses,
que los toques por todas partes,
era
uno de esos muchachos
de los que con el tiempo
sólo te queda
su nombre:
Raúl.

+

Él era extraño,
callado siempre,
me miraba a los ojos
diciéndome: "Mi amigo";
un poco triste a veces
y alegre
con los chistes colorados;
ahora me he enterado
que se volvió marica.

And they were
proud of themselves
for having taught a queer
a lesson.

I don't know what
may have become of him.
I'd like to see him again,
changed a little.
Maybe I'd like to see him cry
a bit more,
and then, I think,
I'd like to see him
take a knife
and murder his tormentors
and cut them to shreds
and scatter the shreds all over
the goddamned school,
in all the classrooms,
and in the Chapel
of the Sacred Heart
which prohibits crime.

+

When I finished grade school
Dad congratulated me
but wouldn't let me kiss him.
The time was past
for playing kissy-kissy,
he said.
And so it was that
for a long long time
I couldn't draw near,
couldn't kiss,
couldn't feel·the wiriness
of a full-grown beard.

+

When he started
going steady I told him
how pretty she was
but
I always looked at him.

+

Just because
I thought you were cute
you had to shout
FAGGOT! at me.

+

Raúl
was one of those boys
who by their way of
looking at you
ask you
to kiss them,
to touch them all over.
He was
one of those boys
who
after some time has gone by
only the name
sticks with you:
Raúl.

+

He was always a little odd,
very quiet and reserved;
he looked me in the eyes
and called me his friend.
Kind of sad at times,
at times happy telling
his dirty jokes.
Just lately I learned
that he turned out gay.

+

Después de estar hablando
de muchachas
me dio un golpecito
en el hombro
y no sé cómo
bajó su mano hasta mi pantalón,
aquél de mezclilla
que tanto me gustaba
por desteñido y viejo,
la bajó y me agarro la verga.
Ninguno dijo nada,
los dos silenciosos
nos miramos a los ojos,
cuando
no sé qué pasó,
ni sé si pensé en lo que dicen
de los putos,
pero lo agarré a golpes
y la di una madriza,
y él también a mí;
bueno
nos peleamos.
Ahora que ha pasado tiempo
me pregunto por qué,
si a mí gustaba sentir
el peso de su mano
y lo que sea de cada quien,
Fernando
me caía muy bien.

+

Y tú,
aunque te burlabas
publicamente de mí,

soñabas,
y esto me lo decían tus ojos,
con mis nalgas.

+

Estábamos en la prepa,
y tú tan presumido
me dijiste aquella tarde:
"¡Yo la tengo asi!,"
después...
pasó todo aquello
por lo cual
ya no nos vemos.

+

Después de aquella borrachera
y el despertar
desnudos
en su coche,
me dijo:
"Sería mejor
no vernos más."

+

Era peluquero
y los muchachos
al pasar frente a la
"Ambos Mundos"
le gritaban maricón;
él
apretaba las tijeras,
respiraba hondo
mirándose en los espejos,
se imaginaba
llorar de rabia,

+

After a lot of talk about girls
he slapped me on the shoulder
and I don't know how
but he let his hand slip down
to my pants,
those jeans
liked so much
because they were old
and faded,
and he pulled them down
and took hold of my cock.
Nothing said,
both of us silent,
looking each other in the eye
until
I don't know what happened
I don't even know
if I remembered
all the things they say
about queers,
I don't know
but I let him have it
I really walloped him
and he slugged me,
I mean
we had it out.
Now that so much time
has passed
I wonder why,
why,
since I liked the feel
of the weight of his hand
and to tell the truth
I really liked Fernando.

+

And you,
although you made fun of me

in front of other people,
your eyes told me
how you dreamed
of my ass.

+

We were in high school
when you, so stuck on yourself,
told me one afternoon:
"I've got one this big."
Then all those things
took place
because of which
we don't see each other
anymore.

+

After that drunken binge
we woke up
naked
in his car
and he said:
"It would be best
if we don't see each other
again."

+

He was a barber
and some of the kids
used to yell queer at him
as they strolled by his shop.
He
would always tighten his grip
on his scissors,
breathe deeply
and stare off into the mirrors
for a moment,
imagining himself

y
seguía
su trabajo
con la tranquilidad
de siempre.

+

Era peluquero
y yo
al pasar frente a la
"Ambos Mundos"
me detenía y lo miraba;
él
apretaba las tijeras,
respiraba hondo
mirándose en los espejos,
se imaginaba
en la cama conmigo,
y
seguía
su trabajo
con la intranquilidad
de algunas veces.

+

Con sus ojos,
con esa mirada
con que se ven los cómplices,
me saludaba;
yo
no entendía
el por qué
de esa familiaridad,
hasta aquella tarde,
en que entré al baño de un cine
y lo vi separarse
precipitadamente
de un muchacho
y decirme

con su voz
hasta ese momento
desconocida:
"Echamos aguas
no seas cabrón."

+

Fui a la boda,
lo vi partir el gran pastel,
bailar el vals de los casados,
estar feliz con su mujer;
pero también
mirarme desde lejos
y recordar
mis brazos
abrazándolo.

+

"¿Cerraste la puerta?,"
dijo
y se quedó callado.

+

Que no le importaba,
que si por él fuera
nos dejaba hacer
todo
lo que quisiéramos,
que al fin y al cabo
era nuestro gusto;
pero que:
"Las leyes son las leyes";
nos dijo el policía
cuando yo
me cerraba la bragueta
y mi amigo
sacaba un billete
de los grandes.

crying with rage.
And then
he would go on with
his work
with the same composure
as always.

He was a barber
and when I strolled by
his shop I used to stop outside
and cruise him.
He
would always tighten his grip
on his scissors,
breathe deeply
and stare off into the mirrors
for a moment,
imagining himself
in bed with me.
And then
he would go on with
his work
with the same discomposure
as sometimes.

+

He always greeted me
with his eyes,
a special glance
like people exchange
when they share a secret.
I never understood the reason
for such familiarity
until that afternoon
when I went to the bathroom
at the movies
and saw him pull away
hurriedly
from a boy,
and then he said to me

in a voice
I had not heard until then:
"Don't act dumb—
go on and piss."

+

I went to the wedding,
saw him cut the cake
and dance the wedding waltz,
happy with his wife.
But at times I caught him
gazing at me
from across the room,
remembering my arms
and the way they held him.

+

"Did you lock the door?"
he asked,
and that was all he said.

+

He really couldn't care less,
I mean,
if it was left up to him
we could do
whatever
we damned well pleased,
since after all, really,
it was a question
of personal taste.
But the law is the law
the cop said
as I zipped up my pants
and my friend
fumbled for a bill,
one of those big ones.

+

Amaneció muerto,
a su lado
un frasco vacío
y una carta
dirigida a Pedro;
para nosotros,
sus padres,
el silencio
y la incertidumbre
de no conocer
a ese Pedro,
a quien en la carta,
abierta por nosotros
en un momento
de desesperación,
sólo le dice:
"Te amo."

+

Ahora
que estoy
perdidamente
enamorado,
me acuerdo
de que cuando nos miramos
por primera vez,
entablé con él
lo que se dice una conversación,
acto seguido
cojimos sobre la alfombra
de su casa,
después
de habernos conocido
en un camión
de la linea
Col. del Valle-Coyoacán.

+

Para ti
un pensamiento bonito
e imaginarte
guapo y fuerte,
ahora
que mi amor,
mi amigo al que quiero,
está lejos de mí,
ahora que regresará en la noche
un poco cansado,
queriéndome más,
diciendome
con o sin palabras
del encuentro entre ustedes,
y quedándose dormido
sobre mi hombro
antes de la hora
acostumbrada.

+

"Es un escándolo dicen
y hasta me maldicen
por darte mi amor";
escuchaba esta canción
en la radio,
cuando pensaba
en Luis
que tiene
29 años
y me ama.

+

Sencillamente
me encariñé con él,
paseamos juntos,
cogimos también juntos.

+

+

We found him dead
that morning,
a little bottle empty beside him
and a letter
addressed to Pedro.
For us,
his family
all the silence
and uncertainty of not knowing
who Pedro might be—
the Pedro
to whom in his letter,
which we opened
in a moment of desperation,
he said simply:
"I love you."

+

Now
that I'm
hopelessly
in love
I recall
the first time
we saw each other,
how I struck up with him
what might be called
a conversation
and a few minutes later
we fucked
on the carpet
at his house,
so soon
after meeting
on a bus
on the Valle-Coyoacan line.

+

Good wishes
to you,
imagining you
handsome and strong,
now
that my lover
the friend I love so much
is far away from me,
now that he'll be coming home
tonight
a little tired,
loving me even more,
telling me
with or without words
about the meeting
between you,
going to sleep
on my shoulder
before his usual bedtime.

+

"It's a shame, they say,
and they curse me even
for giving you my love"—
words from a song
I heard on the radio
while I was thinking of Luis
who is 29 and loves me.

+

I fell in love with him,
we were together a lot,
we fucked together.
It's as simple as that.

+

Adolfo Caminha

ADOLFO CAMINHA was born in Ceará, Brazil, in 1867. Orphaned at an early age, he was taken to Rio de Janeiro by an uncle who enrolled him in the Naval School there. As a naval cadet he visited many parts of the world, including the United States, about which he later wrote a book. In 1887 he returned to Ceará as a second lieutenant and began to take part in the intellectual and political life of that state. A passionate love affair with the wife of an army officer resulted in a scandal and his eventual resignation from the navy.

In 1890, as a public official in Ceará, he began his literary career. Two years later he returned to Rio, where he died of tuberculosis in 1896 at the age of twenty-nine.

Caminha's best-known work, *Bom-Crioulo* (approximate English equivalent: "Good Nigger"), was published in 1895. The theme of the novel—the overt sexual relationship between a mature black man and a boy of fifteen—provoked such a furor that the author was threatened with court proceedings. That theme gives Caminha a valid claim to the title of father of Gay Brazilian fiction.

Blending Romantic melodrama with the directness and honesty of Naturalism, the novel tells the story of Bom-Crioulo's love for Aleixo, the ship's boy. Back in Rio after the voyage during which they met, they settle into a room in a small boarding house owned by Dona Carolina, a Portuguese woman who has been a friend of Bom-Crioulo for many years. They live happily for about a year, until Bom-Crioulo is transferred to a battleship with new duties that no longer permit him to spend regular nights on shore. Aleixo soon forgets the man and enters into a relationship with Dona Carolina; in the meantime, tortured by his love for the boy and resentful of the circumstances that have separated them, Bom-Crioulo's health and mental stability begin to decline and his unruly temperament soon exposes him to a severe lashing that leaves him hospitalized. A broken man, abandoned by the boy he loves, he lives in constant agony, torn between his still-smouldering passion and his growing desire for revenge. When at last word reaches him that Aleixo and Dona Carolina have become lovers, he escapes from the hospital and makes his way, half-crazed, toward the boarding house. he encounters the boy on the street near the building and stabs him to death in the final scene of the novel.

BOM-CRIOULO

[The following excerpts from the first half of *Bom-Crioulo* present a condensed version of events leading up to Bom-Crioulo's seduction of Aleixo on board ship on the night before their arrival in Rio de Janeiro. This is followed by a section from the second half relating their life together on shore.]

THE THIRD PRISONER came next. He was a strong, husky black man, very tall and robust, a great savage-like figure whose formidable musculature stood as a challenge to the morbid pathology of a whole decadent and effete generation, and his presence there at that particular moment stirred up great interest and a lively curiosity among the spectators. He was Amaro, the looking man from the prow, known aboard ship as Bom-Crioulo.

"Step forward!" the commander said in an imperious tone, with much heaviness in his voice and face.

There was a sudden flurry of whispers, a light and timid murmur running through the ranks of the crew, much like the vague commotion that moves through the audience in a theatre during a change of scenery. Now things were taking a serious turn. Herculano and Sant' Ana, after all, were little more than rogues, poor sailors who could hardly endure the twenty-five lashes that had fallen across their backs. But now it was time to watch Amaro, the famous and terrible Bom-Crioulo.

The Code of Regulations was read again in a slow and cadenced voice, as if it were part of a religious ceremony, and the commander, fulfilling the just and noble task that had been placed upon him, asked Bom-Crioulo if he understood why he was going to be punished.

"Yes, sir!" Bom-Crioulo replied in a resolute tone, without flinching, as he boldly stared at the officer's golden medals. Though he stood there at attention beside the mast, his heels together and his arms falling stiffly at his sides, something in the line of his shoulders and the way he held his head nevertheless bore the stamp of a feline limberness and dexterity.

Bom-Crioulo, indeed, was not just a robust man, not just another of those privileged organisms who bear within their bodies the haughty resistance of bronze and can overwhelm with the sheer

83

weight of their muscles. The nervous energy inside him was an inborn quality that surpassed all of his other physical endowments, imparting a rare and unexpected acrobatic feeling to his movements. He had developed that natural gift through repeated drunken brawls with soldiers and boatmen on shore, for the truth was that from time to time Bom-Crioulo took his nips of liquor, sometimes going on binges that led him to do foolish things. He would arm himself with a knife and then stroll along the docks, completely transfigured, his eyes flashing fire, his cap tilted to one side and his shirt carelessly unbuttoned as if he were a madman. At such times anyone who got near him was behaving foolhardily, taking a terrible risk. The big black man looked like a wild animal that had escaped from its cage, and the other sailors and shoremen steered clear of him, wary of being attacked. Whenever there was trouble on the docks everyone assumed that Bom-Crioulo was there, at odds with the police again. A crowd would gather, with all the people who lived along the shore running out to the beach as if some great calamity had just taken place, and there they would take sides, some with the police and some with the Navy.

But now, aboard ship and out on the high seas, the reason behind Bom-Crioulo's detention was quite different, quite different indeed: he had dealt an unmerciful beating to a second mate who had dared to mistreat Aleixo, the ship's boy, a beautiful little sailor with blue eyes, much liked by all, about whom "certain things" were whispered.

Chained in the ship's hold, Bom-Crioulo had not uttered a word. In his normal state, away from the influence of alcohol, he was admirably gentle, and he had freely submitted himself to the authority above him, awaiting his punishment with resignation. He recognized his own offense and knew that he had to be punished. But once again he had proven that he was a man, and for that he was satisfied. Besides, he was very fond of Aleixo and now he felt sure that he would be able to win him completely, just as one conquers a beautiful woman, a bit of virgin territory, or a kingdom of gold.

The whip did not affect him; he had a back of iron to withstand it. In fact, he could no longer remember how many times he had been lashed before . . .

"One!" the voice called out. "Two! . . . Three! . . ."

Bom-Crioulo had taken off his cotton shirt. Naked from the waist up, exhibiting his muscles and his massive pectorals, his shiny black back with a deep smooth furrow running up and down the length of it, he did not even groan. It was as if his punishment were of the most trifling sort.

In the meantime, fifty lashes had already fallen. No one heard a sound from him or noticed the least contortion or any other sign of pain. All they could see were the marks of the whip on his broad back, one upon the other, purple and throbbing. They crossed each other like the strands of a great spider web, cutting the skin in all directions.

Suddenly then Bom-Crioulo shuddered and raised an arm: the full force of the whip had struck his loins and his lower stomach. It was a dreadful blow, dealt with extraordinary strength.

"One hundred and fifty!" the voice called out.

*   *   *

THE TRIUMPH of the abolition movement was still far away, very far away, when Bom-Crioulo, known simply as Amaro at the time, first appeared from no one knew where with a bundle on his shoulder, wearing cheap cotton clothes, a wide straw hat, and sandals made from raw leather. A minor then—he must have been eighteen—he knew nothing of the problems that confronted a colored man in a slave-based society. Naïve and determined, he had simply taken off without giving a second thought to the consequences of his flight.

In those days an "escaped Negro" had a fantastic capacity for terrifying the populace. The slave was hunted like an animal, with goads and firearms poised and ready, into the bush country and over precipices and rivers, up and down mountains... On their third page the newspapers carried the sketch of a runaway with a bundle on his shoulder, and beneath the sketch, almost always in bold type, a detailed announcement indicating the height, age, identifying marks, vices, and other characteristics of the fugitive. In addition, the "owner" always offered a generous reward for anyone who might apprehend the slave.

But Amaro, whose only fear was that he would have to return to the plantation, back into the bosom of slavery, managed to elude his pursuers. After spending the darkest night of his life hidden in a kind of cage with iron bars around it, he found himself trembling on the bank of a very wide calm river where boats were moving in all directions, some with sails, some spewing out trails of smoke...

That same day he went to the naval base, and as the ship pulled away from the quay with a sudden jerk, the new seaman felt his whole being awaken in a most extraordinary way; it was as if some mysterious fluid, delicious and fresh, had been injected into his African blood. The flat expanses of water singing against the prow of the cutter, the immaculate blue sky, the far-off profile of the mountains, the boats cruising from island to island, the motionless forms of the city back on the shore—the whole of the surrounding scene, in short, filled him with a sensation of life and liberty so strong that it was all he could do to keep from crying . . .

Military discipline, with all of its excesses, could not be compared to the burdensome work back on the plantation where his life had been governed by sticks and whips. Amaro was quick to earn the affection of his superior officers. At the beginning they could not restrain their laughter at the sight of a recruit so unaccustomed to the military way of life. Ungainly as a savage, with each step he took his ingenuous greenhorn manners provoked laughter, but after a few months had passed the general opinion was that "the black man was really beginning to shape up." During that first year of apprenticeship he never once had to be called up for discipline: his temperament was so mild that the officers themselves began to refer to him as "Bom-Crioulo." His only desire and concern was to go to sea in any ship whatever, to get used to life at sea and to learn, while he was still young, the customs of that life . . .

*   *   *

LIKE ALL GREAT AFFECTIONS, his friendship with the ship's boy was born unexpectedly, without precedents of any sort, in that fatal moment when their gazes first crossed. The indefinable stirring that simultaneously invades two people of opposite sexes, giving rise to the desire for mutual physical possession, that animal attraction that makes man a slave to woman and in all species urges the male toward the female—that was precisely the sensation that invaded Bom-Crioulo the first time his eyes met those of the boy. He had never felt such a thing before; no man or woman had ever produced such an exquisite feeling inside him. The fact is that the boy, a mere child of fifteen, had acted upon him with the force of a magnet, shaking him to the depths of his soul, taking possession of him and making him a slave again.

With a voice full of tenderness he called the boy to him and asked his name.

"My name is Aleixo," he answered as he lowered his eyes timidly.

"Listen now, my name is Bom-Crioulo, and don't you forget it," the man continued in the same tender and affectionate voice, without taking his eyes off the boy. "If anybody ever bothers you or does anything to you, I'm here to protect you. Okay?"

"Yes, sir," the boy replied, glancing up with an expression of gratitude on his face.

"Don't be ashamed. Just remember Bom-Crioulo, the lookout on the prow. All you have to do is call me."

"Yes, sir."

Bom-Crioulo frightened him at first, but soon he grew accustomed, without realizing it, to the man's affection and solicitude, and finally he felt a distinct warmth toward him. That was the beginning of a grateful and sincere affection.

It was then that the black man, enthusiastic about his newfound friendship, tried to show the boy how far that zeal could carry him by attacking the second mate who had mistreated him. The thought that Bom-Crioulo was willing to suffer for him made such an impression on the boy's spirit that he soon came to regard him as his selfless and disinterested protector, a friend to the weak . . .

* * *

THE EQUATORIAL CALM of the evening was followed, happily, by a cool refreshing breeze. It wrinkled the wide surface of the sea, swelled the sails of the ship, and lent a fresh look of good humor and joviality to all the faces on board. Everyone was overjoyed now at the prospect of soon reaching Guanabara Bay safe and sound. There in the harbor would be peace and plenty, there where life flowed smoothly, full of tranquillity, and each man could be near his family, just across from the city, free of all the cares and hardships that go with life on the high seas. And after twenty days at sea, out of sight of the land, working like dogs, it was time.

There was only one person who would like to have seen the voyage prolonged indefinitely, whose wish was that the ship might never arrive, that the sea would suddenly grow wider, swallowing islands and continents in its tremendous tide, and that only the old ship itself would survive the cataclysm, grand and indestructible, floating on and on, drifting through eternity. That man was Bom-Crioulo. Like a bird in agony his spirit struggled with a single idea—Aleixo, the ship's boy. The thought tortured him day and night and there was no room in his mind for anything else. He could have cursed the moment when the boy first set foot on board. Until then his life had unfolded as God willed it, more or less calmly, without troublesome worries. Sometimes he was sad, sometimes happy, to be sure, because nothing stays the same in this world, but at least his life had been moving along. And now, now there was no solution but to let things run their course.

When he was on duty and when he was on leave, whether it was raining or red-hot coals were falling from the sky, no one could take his mind off the boy. The thought pursued him from one moment to the next, a fixed, unshakable idea; his whole will relaxed and loosened, dominated by the desire to be united with the little sailor as if he were a member of the opposite sex, to possess him, to have him beside him, to love him and take his pleasure with him . . .

Bom-Crioulo could not remember ever having loved before, or, for that matter, ever having indulged in any of those adventures, so common during youth, which involve easy women. On the contrary he had always been indifferent to such things, preferring to make merry with the other men aboard ship, far away from the intrigues and deceits of women.

Why was it then that he no longer had enough strength to resist the impulses of his blood?

Boasting of how he was a man of the world, Bom-Crioulo was at first careful to flatter Aleixo's vanity by giving him a little cheap mirror that he had bought in Rio de Janeiro—"so that he could see how pretty he was." The boy looked at himself, grinned, lowered his eyes, and murmured something about how he had the face of a butcher. But still he kept the mirror, storing it away in the bottom of his trunk just as if it were some beloved object or a thing of great value, and every morning he went to look at himself after he had washed his face, sticking out his tongue and examining himself closely.

Bom-Crioulo understood the value of experience and set about completing the "education" of the little sailor. He taught him how to knot his tie, which, he told him, was not called a tie but a kerchief, and he advised him never to wear his cap squarely on his head because a sailor should tilt it gracefully to one side.

"And the shirt?"

"Ah, yes, always wear your shirt a little open to show the undershirt beneath it. The habit makes the monk, you know . . ."

The boy accepted Bom-Crioulo's advice much as if he had been the man's son, not bothering to look for motives behind his attentiveness. He saw other sailors who went about unwashed, poorly dressed and smelling of sweat, but they were few. On the other hand, there were some who even perfumed their kerchiefs and used oil on their hair.

Within the space of a few days Aleixo's whole appearance had changed and Bom-Crioulo looked upon him with the pride of a master watching the development of a disciple.

*   *   *

LISTEN NOW, you mustn't have anything to do with anyone in Rio de Janeiro," Bom-Crioulo told Aleixo, "because that city is a land of demons. Just don't let me catch you with anybody else, you hear . . ."

The boy absent-mindedly bit the corner of his dark blue cotton kerchief with its little white designs, listening to the man's promises and dreaming of a rose-colored life there in the Rio de Janeiro he had heard so much about, there where there was a great mountain named Sugarloaf and the emperor had his palace, a beautiful mansion with walls of gold . . .

Being a sailor on his first voyage, he let his imagination exaggerate everything out of proportion. Bom-Crioulo had promised to take him to the theatres, to Corcovado (another mountain from which you could see the whole city and the sea), to Tijuca, to the Passeio Público—in short, he had promised to take him everywhere. They would live together in a room on the Rua da Misericórdia, a comfortable little room where two wrought-iron beds would fit, or, if not, one large wide bed would do. He, Bom-Crioulo, would pay for it all from his own pocket.

*   *   *

THE WIND WAS STILL STRONG.

The scene on deck looked like an encampment of nomads. Numb from work, the crew had fallen into a deep sleep, scattered about here and there in the open air with a general disorder like that of gypsies who are not choosy about the land they lie on. The damp floor, the blowing air, colds, beriberi—they were little concerned with such things now. It was much more crowded and cluttered down below where sailcloth hammocks, hanging one over the other from iron rods, as dirty as kitchen towels, swayed in the

weak and dying light of the lanterns and vague half-naked bodies
moved about in the cavernous darkness. The hold had the nauseous
odor of a jail, a bitter stench of human sweat mixed with urine and
tar. With their mouths open, snoring heavily, the black men there
twisted and tossed in the unconsciousness of sleep. Naked torsos
embraced the floor in indecorous postures cruelly revealed by the
light. From time to tie someone would begin to mutter unintelligible
things in his sleep, and once a stark-naked sailor got up from the
midst of the others, his eyes transfixed, filled with fear, and screamed
something about someone trying to kill him. It turned out that he
was the victim of a nightmare, nothing more, and then silence
settled over the scene again.

Bom-Crioulo was off duty. All that afternoon his spirit had been
in turmoil, plotting schemes whereby he could triumph in the coming battle with Aleixo and fulfill, at last, the strong desires of a man
tortured by Grecian carnality.

On several occasions he had made an effort to sound out the
boy's feelings, trying to convince him through physical stimulation,
but Aleixo always brushed him aside, gently rejecting the Negro's
advances much as a courted girl might do. "Come on, Bom-
Crioulo," he would say, "stop making jokes . . ."

But that day Priapus swore to bring the struggle to an end. Victory or death! Either the boy would consent or their friendship
would be no more. "The whole matter" had to be resolved.

"What matter?" the boy asked with astonishment.

"Nothing really . . . I just don't want you to be angry with me,"
Bom-Crioulo replied, and then he hurriedly asked Aleixo where he
was going to sleep that night.

"There on the prow, because of the coolness."

"Okay, we'll talk about it then."

At nine o'clock when Bom-Crioulo saw Aleixo headed toward
the prow he grabbed his hammock and hurried after him. It was
then that the others saw him slip past with the bundle under his
arm, graceful as a cat.

As soon as he lay down beside the boy and felt the warmth of his
roundish body, the gentle tepidness of that flesh, so desired and yet
still undefiled by impure contacts, a savage appetite cut off his
speech. The light stopped short of the nook where they had taken
refuge and they could not see each other. Instead, they sensed each
other, guessed each other's presence beneath the blankets.

After a cautious but brief silence Bom-Crioulo whispered some-thing in the boy's ear and moved closer to him. Aleixo remained still, without breathing. Hunched up, his eyelids instinctively clos-ing with sleep, he lay with his ear against the deck and listened to the splash of the waves against the bow of the ship. As if in a dream he saw Bom-Crioulo's thousand and one promises parade before him: the room on the Rua da Misericórdia in Rio, the theatres, the strolls . . . And then he remembered the punishment that the black man had endured for his sake. But he said nothing. A deep feeling of well-being settled over his whole body, and in his own blood he began to feel urges he had never felt before, something like an inborn longing to yield to the man's whims, to abandon himself to the other's desires . . .

"Go ahead," he murmured quickly as he turned over.

PART TWO

THE SHIP'S CLOCK marked a quarter of six, and the city, sub-merged in the gathering dusk, seemed to doze off slowly, fall-ing bit by bit into a quietude like that of an abandoned plaza, taking on the melancholy silence of a remote village.

The lights came on and the crowds along the Largo do Paço thinned out quickly, leaving only occasional groups of lingerers standing about in the shadows and a few individuals with parcels under their arms getting off the tramcars in front of the docks . . .

Bom-Crioulo turned to the left, walking beneath the arcade, and headed for the Rua da Misericórdia, arm in arm with the ship's boy, smoking a cigar that he had bought at a stand in the street. In the vicinity of the War Arsenal they paused in front of an ancient-looking building with blinded windows and two balconies of worm-eaten wood on the ground floor, which was occupied by a family of blacks from Angola. At that moment their voices could be heard coming from the dark interior.

"This is the place," Bom-Crioulo said, recognizing the house and disappearing into the unlit entranceway. Aleixo trailed along be-hind him in silence, hugging the wall as one does when entering a strange place for the first time.

"Come on, silly!" Bom-Crioulo said as he grabbed him by the arm. "What are you afraid of?"

Cautiously they made their way up a bleak, abandoned staircase with steep steps that threatened to collapse beneath their feet. The black man tugged at a cord hanging beside the door and in the dining room inside a bell responded with a dull ring. At first there was no answer and Bom-Crioulo pulled the cord more vigorously a second time.

"Who's there?"

"It's me, Dona Carolina. Open up . . ."

"Coming, coming . . ."

A moment later the sailor threw himself into the arms of a round-ish, fat, middle-aged woman, clutching her tight against his chest and even lifting her off the floor in spite of her weight, all with the understandable joy of old friends meeting again after a long ab-sence.

"Tell me everything that's happened to you, Bom-Crioulo. Come in, come in . . . And who's the little one?"

"The little one? It's all because of him that I'm here. I'll tell you about it later . . ."

And they hugged each other again, laughing with joy, she still in her apron, looking very plump, her hair parted in the middle with two braids down the back, and Bom-Crioulo at his most jovial be-havior, showering her with affectionate exclamations, telling her she looked fatter, prettier, and more girlish than ever.

*   *   *

FROM THE FIRST NIGHT spent in the house Bom-Crioulo began to feel a very intimate sort of delight, something like a deep spiritual joy mingled with a love for the dark life of that house fre-quented now by almost no one. For him it was the beloved retreat of a seaman on leave, offering sweet rest for his voluptuous soul. He could not even dream of a better life or a more ideal living ar-rangement; the world for him now was summed in what he had: a little room on the upper floor, his Aleixo, and nothing more. As long as God might grant him health and good judgment he would want for nothing more.

The room, off to itself with a window opening toward the back of the building, was a kind of garret eaten up by termites and smelling strongly of phenic acid. A young Portuguese man, soon after his arrival in Brazil, had died there of yellow fever. But Bom-Crioulo, though he lived in dread of such fevers, was not bothered by the fact; instead he tried to forget the whole matter and make himself at home in the place once and for all. All the money he could get his hands on went to buy furnishings and rococo knickknacks—

little figurines, ornaments, and other baubles, often brought from aboard ship. Little by little the tiny room took on the appearance of a Jewish bazaar, overflowing with trifles, piles of empty boxes, common seashells, and other decorative accessories. The bed was of the folding type, covered with canvas, and already well-used. Each morning when Bom-Crioulo got up he took pride in spreading a thick red coverlet over it.

For months he led a calm life, rigorously methodical and measured, carrying out his duties on board ship and coming to shore twice a week accompanied by Aleixo. Never once did he expose himself to discipline or punishment. Even the officers were puzzled by the change that had come over him, and they adopted an admiring attitude toward his good behavior.

"It's all just a thing of the moment," Lieutenant Souza suggested. "Before long you'll see him drunk and unruly again. He always used to have a stubborn disregard for the rules of life—as gentle as a lamb one day and as wild as an animal the next. That's part of the African character, you know."

The boy, for his part, lived in a state of perpetual happiness like one who had never known worries and cares. Whether aboard ship or on shore, he had nothing to complain about. He was always clean, and no one ever saw him lying around on the deck or getting soiled with pitch up on the prow. Fortunately for him, the first mate, recognizing him to be a well-behaved, clean, obedient, and hard-working young man, selected him to take care of the ship's ropes and cables, and so it was that Aleixo could rarely be seen among the other sailors. His favorite spot was the bridge, or astern, where he repaired the flags and pennants and learned other duties which his job entailed. Sometimes he would get into long chats with the officer on watch, telling tales about the provinces and the time when he was the simple son of a fisherman, just a poor boy growing up beside the sea. The other sailors would look on with envy, making malicious signs of jealousy among themselves. A certain midshipman, well-mannered and democratic in spirit, occasionally gave him money for cigarettes. Then he would go to Bom-Crioulo and show him the coins that "his midshipman" had given him. Everybody on ship treated him affectionately; even Agostinho the custodian, usually so brusque and severe, was kind to him, with a tone of tenderness in his voice. Aleixo, in short, had it made.

And ashore, in the room on the Rua da Misericórdia—it goes without saying that his life there was idyllic. They lounged about in their drawers there, he and Bom-Crioulo, wallowing about to their hearts' content on their old canvas bed which provided a cool relief from the heat. Alone, a carafe of liquor within reach, they could laugh and talk for hours in complete freedom without anyone coming to disturb them.

Only one thing annoyed the boy: the libidinous whims of the black man. That came about because Bom-Crioulo, not content with possessing him at any hour of the night or day, always wanted much more and so obliged him to indulge in excesses. He made a slave of the boy and used him as one might use a cheap woman, proposing any extravagant whim that came to his mind. It was on their first night there that he insisted the boy take off all his clothes and stand stark naked in front of him so he could see his body . . .

The dull light of a tallow candle pervaded the room.

"Ah, there's nothing to see," Aleixo protested with a whine but no tears.

"Sure, there's something to see . . ."

And so the boy, meek and submissive, unbuttoned his flannel shirt and then his trousers, placing his clothes piece by piece on the bed.

Bom-Crioulo's desire was fulfilled, for Aleixo soon emerged in his full and exuberant nakedness, very pale, with the rounded, callipygian* forms of his body standing out in the voluptuous half-light of the room, in the caressing shadows of that lewd and neglected sanctuary of inconfessable passions. He was the beautiful image of an ephebe such as Aphrodite's Greece might have immortalized in strophes of limpid gold and in statues of strong and sensuous workmanship. Sodom was reborn then in a sad and desolate room on the Rua da Misericórdia, where, at that hour of the night, everything had subsided into the sweet quietude of a far-off wasteland.

"You can look now," the boy murmured, standing firm on his feet.

Bom-Crioulo was ecstatic! The full and milky whiteness of that tender flesh sent shivers through his body, stirring his nerves in a strange way, stimulating him like a strong liquor, thoroughly captivating and enrapturing his heart. Never before had he seen male forms so beautifully molded . . .

* * *

---

*Callipygian: having beautifully proportioned buttocks. —*Ed.*

BOM-CRIOULO'S SHORE LEAVES became more and more frequent. Always hard-working and quick to carry out orders, fulfilling his obligations with the same patience as in those earlier days when the future held the smiling promise of a better life, he more than compensated, in the eyes of others, for his misbehavior on previous voyages. The first mate granted him special favors, always reminding him that he should be careful and go easy on the liquor.

Any dedicated and disciplined sailor could consider him a friend, a father almost. It was merely a question of behaving correctly, "like a human being," as Bom-Crioulo said. And Bom-Crioulo, aware of the respect others had for him, did his best not to betray it. Whenever there was a job to be done, he did it cheerfully and willingly, thinking of his next shore leave.

Every second day now you could find him in his room on the Rua da Misericórdia taking a good rest, completely free of duties and annoyances.

Soon he seemed to be losing weight, and he even felt a sensation akin to weakness in his chest. Whenever he worked a lot or exerted himself too much a deep drowsiness would come over him, accompanied by a desire to stretch out on a soft, fresh bed and relax his nerves. Even his shipmates noticed a change in his appearance.

"You're getting thin, Bom-Crioulo."

"Me, thin? Do you think I'm sick maybe?" And he would pass his hand over his face to examine it.

"Maybe you've got a girl on shore, eh?"

"A girl! Come on now!"

One day he asked Aleixo if he too thought he was losing weight. Aleixo felt that he was but told him it was "nothing to worry about."

That put his mind at ease and he continued to lead an unworried existence, now on the ship, now ashore. With great peace of mind he watched Aleixo grow up beside him, witnessing the early development of certain organs as the boy passed into a new stage of life. He observed, like someone studying the evolution of a rare flower.

His feeling for the boy was no longer lascivious and fiery as it had been before: it had changed into a calm friendship, a shared affection without all the fevers and jealousies of passionate love.

Nearly a year of living together was enough to lead him to identify completely with the boy and to feel that he knew him thoroughly. Now he was convinced that Aleixo would not betray him by going away with any trickster who might try to gain his confidence. The certainty that he commanded the boy's respect gave him a smug peace of mind like that of a happy husband or a zealous capitalist who carried his money tucked away where thieves could never find it.

Almost a year slipped by before the sturdy thread of that mysterious friendship, nourished in an upper room on the Rua da Misericórdia, suffered even the slightest strain. The two sailors lived for each other, each fulfilling the other.

Gasparino Damata

GASPARINO DAMATA is the pen name of Gasparino da Mata e Silva, born in 1918 in Catende, state of Pernambuco, Brazil. He belongs to a family of traditional sugar-cane planters (paternal side) and intellectuals (maternal side). He completed his elementary and high school education in Recife, the state capital. As a young man he was an office boy, a junior soccer player, a singer and sailor. During World War II he worked as an interpreter for American soldiers serving in Recife. In 1943 he began service as an official in the U.S. Transportation Corps. The end of the war found him in San Juan, Puerto Rico, where he began work on a novel. He soon returned to Brazil and worked as an interpreter on the docks of Rio de Janeiro and Santos (the main harbor of the city of São Paulo).

In 1949 Damata started his career as a professional journalist in Rio de Janeiro, and the following year he published his novel *Queda em Ascensão,* which was well received by Brazilian critics especially for the freshness of its language. He chronicled his sea life in this novel as well as in the collection of short stories *A Sobra do Mar.* He also published a second novel, *Caminhos da Danação.*

Damata has been the chief pioneer in the publishing of gay literature in Brazil: he organized and edited the first gay anthology of fiction to be published in Brazil, *Histórias do Amor Maldito* (1969). This work included short stories by several authors (Aguinaldo Silva, Edilberto Coutinho) included in *Now the Volcano.* Shortly thereafter Damata co-edited with Walmyr Ayala a companion anthology of Brazilian gay poetry, *Poemas do Amor Maldito.* There followed in 1976 a collection of gay short stories written by himself, *Os Solteirões.* The two stories translated in *Now the Volcano* are taken from this last volume.

Damata also worked for some time as special assistant to Raimundo Souza Dantas (the first Brazilian black ambassador) in the Brazilian Embassy, Ghana, Africa. In 1978 he was one of the founders of the gay cultural newspaper *Lampião,* and remains one of its editors. He currently lives in Rio de Janeiro.

REVENGE

Male homosexuality, as practiced by young men in underdeveloped countries, is a problem of the stomach, and therefore a social problem. Most of its victims are the sons of separated or divorced parents from the middle class, people whose buying power has diminished considerably, as well as boys from the less favored class, who practice it with a certain naturalness, and, unlike the others, without dramas of conscience, simply as a means of supplementing their low income.

THE BOY STEPPED INTO the dentist's waiting room with the same decided air that a patient with an appointment might have: he took a seat, first picking up a well-worn magazine from the corner table to distract himself; ahead of him there was only one elderly woman waiting her turn, and so he seemed satisfied. His appearance was not particularly impressive; he was wearing blue velvet pants, already quite frayed, with a label from a well-known purveyor of masculine fashions in Copacabana, scuffed shoes that had not seen a polish for at least a week, and an Italian shirt of a style that was very fashionable at the time, though his already showed signs of wear. The shirt was the last gift he had received from a woman he met there in that same room, with whom he had lived until a month or so ago when she kicked him out for another boy who was perhaps not as handsome but who—as she had told him to his face during a violent argument—was much better in bed because he was more of a man.

From time to time he glanced up impatiently ("Fuck! I wonder if he's shut himself up inside there with some other boy") and looked at the door to the office, and then he would go back to his magazine, thumbing through it absent-mindedly, biting his nails. In his eagerness to get the matter settled in a hurry he had called from the street several times in an effort to speak with Ferreira, but the phone that afternoon was always busy. Finally he had had to borrow a slug from a man he knew who was also waiting to make a call; he dropped it into the machine, listened to the busy signal ("Shit! Still busy!") and then tried again, and that time he managed to get through to the dentist, who told him to come up to the office. But when he tried to explain his reason for calling the man seemed impatient and cut the conversation short.

He thought that Ferreira would attend to him immediately, even before the patient who was waiting there, just as he had done on so many other occasions with him and with other boys. But a middle-aged woman with dyed hair soon emerged from within and asked his name; immediately then she told the elderly woman to step inside and closed the door behind her. Silence, and the hum of a fan, and more waiting. When she appeared again, a half hour later, she had a message for the boy.

"Dr. Ferreira asks if you could wait just a while longer and then he'll be with you," she said with the smile of an employee who knows everything about the private life of her boss.

Not annoyed, but impatient because of the delay, he tried to thumb through all the magazines within his reach, thinking that might make the time pass faster. Each time he turned a page his eyes, heavy with sleepiness and fatigue, wandered off at random and focused on the details of the waiting room that had changed but little since the time when he lived with Ferreira: the same red carpet, now visibly worn, reproductions of engravings of English country scenes, a painting by Franz Crajcberg which he'd never understood, a lamp with a base made from a big bottle, a corner air-conditioner that ran only during the summer—in short, all the things he had once been very familiar with and which, in a certain way, still had a familiar look about them. Nothing exaggerated, nothing flamboyant, because Ferreira, unlike many of his kind, avoided anything that might give him away—superfluous queenery, as he used to say. On several occasions—one of them in the apartment of Tito Saldanha, who was known to his intimate friends as the Baroness of the Acacias—he recalled Ferreira's emphatic denunciation of such things.

"I hate to see people making a public spectacle of themselves," he often said. "Let your hair down, but only at home, or at least between four walls."

The boy felt forsaken, at a loss as to what to do, and in addition to that he was hungry. He had left the boarding house early, with only a cup of coffee, to pay a visit to an aunt of his who lived in Cascadura There he had hoped to borrow some money to pay his share on the rent of a room where he lived with three other young men, but his aunt's house was shut up tight and a neighbor said that she was away on a trip to Juiz de Fora.

He had no idea how Ferreira would receive him, though he had not forgotten the dentist's bitter words, weeks ago, in the West-

falia Bar where they had gone for their nightly snack after closing
the office and he had announced that he was going to move in with
Elvira Sodré. He knew how much Ferreira hated Elvira, a middle-
aged secretary who liked young girls but would take in a handsome
young boy from time to time to cover up. She was a declared
enemy of the dentist. But the boy had no choice but to look for the
man now, though deep inside he felt little hope; Ferreira was not
the type of man to forgive a betrayal so easily. And to make matters
worse, the boy had been suspended for a month from the soccer
club with a fine of fifty percent to be levied on his earnings because
he had twice failed to show up for training and had missed a match
in Volta Redonda, a city near Rio.

His life with Ferreira during the first few months had been a bed
of roses in one sense, for the dentist had showered him with gifts,
taking him out to expensive restaurants, to the theatre and to good
movies; but, on the other hand, it soon became routine and boring,
suffocating, intolerable at times, an elegant prison, because Ferreira
never allowed him a moment to himself and had even had other
boys follow him around and report if they saw him talking to
another queen, visiting other apartments, or meeting girls on the
beach. He had no friends that he could talk with and was always
alone because Ferreira, so experienced and callous, knew that it is
usually friends who lead a boy astray and corrupt him by putting
ideas into his head and opening his eyes to certain aspects of the
situation, or by taking him to meet other people, who then promise
him the world and great wealth but never come across with the
goods once they've gone to bed with him, and then one fine day,
disgusted with the whole scene, the little bird flies away . . .

Usually he got up late, around eleven in the morning, gulped
down a loaf of French bread with four fried eggs and a liter of milk,
put on his pants and then headed for the beach; at three he would
go back home, eat lunch, dress leisurely, and then go back out to
catch the bus to his lover's office. There he would stay in the waiting room, so well dressed that one could take him for a patient
with an appointment, and read magazines, always with one eye on
the women but always without forcing the point because one of
them might get annoyed and complain to Ferreira. He was happy
with the life he led—a life which, if on one side it had its disadvan-
tages, was rewarding in other ways because it gave him a feeling of
well-being, of having taken a step forward, of belonging to a social
milieu that he had never expected to be a part of.

After the dentist closed for the day they would leave together and go directly to the Westfalia Bar on the other side of the street. There Ferreira usually joined a small group of friends, all of them gay. They would have a few rounds of draught beer and chat until later, when they would go for dinner at a very famous Hungarian restaurant downtown. Immediately after dinner they would go to the movies or to the theatre, where the boy met intellectuals, artists, and some very pleasant but aging women who, he learned later, were lesbians.

On Saturday night (Ferreira spent his Sundays on the estate of a friend in Petrópolis) the dentist almost always played cards with some gay acquaintances. With nothing to do, the boy amused himself in an adjoining room by reading *Grand Hotel* and dirty books he had bought from the Italian at the newsstand on Constante Ramos Street, stretched out on the sofa in a pair of shorts, exhibiting his beautiful thighs, so smooth and well-molded, and his bulging genitals, much like a prized pet kept in the house so it cannot roam the streets and mix with others of inferior breeding. In the smoke-filled living room, around a table made of jacaranda wood, smoking constantly, their silence broken only by coughs and the clearing of throats, speaking only at the end of a round, Ferreira and his three partners played until late in the night, leaving the boy to himself, with no thought of him, just as if he were a package that one could leave in a corner and pick up later, certain that no one had tampered with it or touched it in the meantime.

He would almost always wake up with Ferreira shaking him affectionately ("Wake up, boy, and let's go to bed"), a cigarette holder between his sound teeth and his eyes gleaming, while the irritating sound of a record by Ella Fitzgerald came from the phonograph, low enough not to bother the neighbors. Still drowsy and groggy, he would catch a glimpse of a couple dancing in the middle of the well-lit room as if it were a nightclub, hugged close together, whispering things into each other's ear and then pausing to kiss on the mouth. On one occasion, which he remembered well, he was lying as usual on the sofa reading his dirty books while Ferreira and his friends played cards. Ferreira had to go to the bathroom and they suspended the game; he stayed away for some time and his friends began to talk in hushed voices mixed with low laughter, and suddenly the boy realized that they were talking about him. With his heart pounding, almost in his throat, he put the book aside and listened carefully, catching a bit of conversation between the two who had danced and kissed the previous Saturday. The third, a bald man named Felipe, kept quiet, his attention fixed on the cards spread out over the table, ignoring the conversation of his more talkative friends.

"A real knockout, don't you think?"

"A knockout, no, but he's handsome, Not my type, though."

"What do you mean he's not your type?"

"Just that: he's not my type. I like boys that are more masculine, more of the macho type, with hair on their chest and legs . . ."

"I know what you're hinting at . . ."

"You know what?"

"Well . . . I know . . ."

"If you know, then say it."

"Say what?"

"Oh, come on . . . Do you mean you haven't noticed?"

"Noticed what?"

Laughter.

"You really haven't noticed?"

"That he's half-queer himself."

"Huh? Him . . . ?"

"Stop it, you dumb queen. You're not blind, are you?"

More laughter.

"Do you think he has a big cock?"

"You mean you haven't noticed?"

"I'm not like you, my dear, who can't keep your eyes off him."

"Well, it is, honey. One of the biggest in creation."

"And how do you know?"

"Because Ferreira said so . . ."

"Do you expect me to believe that Ferreira would talk about such things with you?"

"Well, he did. He told me himself."

Laughter.

"But there's one catch: it only gets hard when—"

"When what? What?"

"When you stick your finger up him."

"Oh no, I just don't believe it!"

"But it's the truth."

"And how do you know, you old whore?"

More laughter.

"How do I know? Because Ferreira told me . . ."

"You have to be joking."

"It's no joke, my dear. He can only get hard with a woman."

"With a woman? Come on now . . ."

"At least that's what he told Ferreira . . ."

"He told Ferreira that? And you believe it? Come on!"

"Well, whether he can get it up or not doesn't matter in the least for Ferreira, sweetie. You know what Ferreira's real thing is . . ."

"What?"

"Fucking, of course, not getting fucked!"

The boy felt like jumping up from the sofa and raising hell with the two of them to show them that he was a real man and not what they said he was and then throwing them out of the apartment. But he weighed the consequences since, after all, they were Ferreira's guests, and he tried to control himself. With his heart still beating wildly, unable to forget the insult, he stared toward the room where he could only see them partially, watching the smoke from their cigarettes climb in spirals up to the ceiling and then spread out toward all the corners with no way to escape. Later that night when the dentist came to wake him he turned abruptly toward the other side of the bed, visibly digusted. Ferreira realized that something was wrong and began to question him. The boy told him the whole story, leaving out no details, his eyes flashing and his voice half-broken, and then he buried his face in the pillow and cried.

"That's just a professional risk you have to run," the dentist said simply, disturbed by the incident, his face suddenly gloomy. "Forget it now, and tomorrow I'll see what can be done about it."

The following day was Sunday, and they went as usual to Petrópolis to visit Ferreira's friend, a retired diplomat, quite wealthy, and a personal friend of President Vargas in the time of the *Estado Novo*. They went in the van that the dentist kept stored in a garage, driven by César, one of Ferreira's former boys—because the present one didn't have a license—who was supposed to sleep that night with Hilário, the owner of the estate. The fourth passenger was Leonardo, a gray-haired man with something of the gallant about him, who had no boy of his own. Ferreira's boy enjoyed the trip and the house itself, located in an elevated part of the city, with a magnificent swimming pool, a volleyball court, a ping-pong table on the porch, hammocks for relaxing, a stunning view, and an orchard full of fruit trees sloping up to the foot of the hills. But the second time that Ferreira took him there he went against his will, pretending that he felt a cold coming on; he had to be dragged almost, sulking and pouting, as if he were being taken to the most disagreeable corner of the earth. Bothered by the boy's reluctance, by his sudden ill feeling toward the house and its owner, Ferreira asked why he felt that way, but he always avoided any real explanation of why he had come to hate those excursions to Petrópolis.

"Has Hilario done something to you? Did he try to seduce you?"

The boy shook his head no.

"Then why such a long face?"

They sat down at the table for lunch, he and Ferreira on one side, César and Leonardo on the other, with the host at the head of the table. Everything was very formal, which the boy disliked immensely. A waiter appeared, impeccably dressed in a white uniform and gloves, and placed four butter dishes beside the plates, a saucer with two slices of sandwich bread, arranged the silver service, and put the glasses of Czechoslovakian crystal in place. Then he glanced at his boss and hurried back to the kitchen in search of something he had forgotten; a moment later he returned and began to serve the meal. In front of each person he placed a plate with a simple filet and two boiled potatoes, decorated with a large leaf of lettuce and two very thin slices of tomato; then he took a pitcher of orangeade and filled each of the crystal glasses just above the halfway mark. There was no sign of any fine wine, and the boy thought it would come later with the second course. He thought nothing of it when he saw César and Ferreira look at each other with strange expressions on their faces. He was dying of hunger, and he gulped the food down in the bat of an eye and finished off the orangeade in two swallows, thinking that was the first plate, the beginning of the meal and nothing more, but he was soundly deceived. That was all there was, except for a tiny orange pudding for dessert. He got up from the table just as he had sat down, dying of hunger, and he and César, both very silent, headed for the orchard (Ferreira and Leonardo stayed on the veranda with Hilário, talking about a mutual friend in São Paulo who had just died of leukemia). As soon as they reached a part of the orchard sheltered from view, they looked back to be sure and then stooped over and picked up some oranges that had fallen to the ground; they peeled them with their fingers and began to suck the pulp in an effort to forget their hunger, to see if they could fool their stomachs, which were growling for food.

"Shit! Did you eat enough?" he asked César, spitting the seeds as far as he could.

"Eat? Man, what was there to eat?"

"If I'd known it was going to be like this I wouldn't have come."

"That guy has a reputation for being the stingiest queen in all Rio. He's famous for his habit of starving people to death. That's why he can't get a boy to come here."

"And why in the fuck did you come if you knew he was that way?"

"Why did I come? Because I owed Ferreira the favor. The old fellow has always played it straight with me, and so I couldn't say no, even knowing that . . . . . ."

"Goddamn! That fucker would eat shit if it weren't for the smell!"

"And he's got money coming out of his ass. You know how many apartments they say he owns? Forty-two, and that's just in Copacabana, because the son of a bitch has others scattered around in other parts."

"Does he have a boy?"

"A boy? You've got to be kidding! All the guys run from him like the devil from the cross."

"And him with so much money . . . ?"

"He doesn't like to pay, and when he does it's so little that it makes you want to tell him to stick it up his ass."

"But you came to sleep with him, didn't you?"

"Yeah, but Ferreira will settle the account with me later."

"And Leonardo, is he rich?"

"He used to be, but now he ain't got shit. He blew it all gambling in Las Vegas."

"He seems like a nice guy."

"Of all of Ferreira's friends, he's the one who behaves best. He never meddles in other people's business—a genuinely nice guy. They say he once was the handsomest boy in Brazil, with women clamoring all over him, and that he was even Lana Turner's lover for a while."

"Whose lover?"

"Lana Turner's. You know—that old blonde American movie star."

"Ah yeah, now I remember," the boy said as he set to work on his tenth orange.

"And why didn't Leonardo marry her? Didn't it work out?"

"Why didn't he marry her? What a silly question, man. You must still be new to this whole scene."

"I've noticed that he can't keep his eyes off my thighs."

"Okay, there's the answer to your question. That explains the whole thing, right?"

When they returned Ferreira and Hilário were still on the porch. By that time they were talking about an exhibit by Roberto Burle-Marx, who was furious because he hadn't sold a single painting in spite of the weight of Jaime Mauricio's review in his art column in the *Correio da Manhã*. Mauricio had done what he could to help but had failed to convince the public and the collectors that the well-known landscape painter was an artist of any great worth, to be ranked with Portinari. Later, when they went for a drive downtown at Ferreira's suggestion, the boy told the dentist he was going to buy some magazines, and then, with César, he had a quick snack because they were still dying of hunger. It was then that César told him that Hilário did not care for him and even felt that his arrangement with Ferreira wasn't going to last, that it was just a whim on the part of the dentist, who often let his daydreams get the best of him. The whole affair, according to Hilário, was a waste of time and money, and all for a boy who wasn't even good-looking.

To tell the truth, he wasn't really handsome and never had been, not even in his better days when he first appeared on the scene. He was never the beauty that Ferreira, in the heat of excitement and completely hooked, had talked about constantly in his circle of friends, rattling on and on much as if he were the first boy he had ever had. Stout, healthy, with enormous hands, a shock of hair falling across his forehead, and the half-mocking smile of someone who would turn down any advances, he was no different from dozens of boys his age who came from the provinces or lingered on in Rio to try their luck in the city after finishing their military service and ended up wandering back and forth through the busy streets of Copacabana during the day, often hungry, with nothing but a cup of coffee for breakfast, stationing themselves night after night in front of the Mercadhino Azul and the Alcazar in search of sex, decked out in expensive clothes stolen from an apartment where they had spent one night but would never return. He didn't have a really fantastic body either, not the type to make an old queen's mouth water—nothing like Belini, for example, that prime specimen of manhood, so handsome that all the rich faggots sighed for him and were ready to pay whatever he asked to get him in bed. He did have smooth well-made thighs that attracted attention, a pleasant face, dark-complexioned, and a certain attractiveness of the kind that some boys have without even being aware of it, and which often makes them more appealing than the really beautiful types. It was precisely that quality that made him so attractive to Ferreira, that special something that can be sensed at times but not explained.

"Okay, I agree with you—he really isn't handsome," Ferreira would sometimes say, changing the record when his friends could no longer stand it. And then, to arouse their envy, he would close his eyes and add smilingly, "But he does have his charms. There may be others just as good in bed, but I promise you there's no better one in the whole of Rio."

Finally the door to the office opened. Ferreira was still wearing his white dentist's outfit, with a cigarette holder between his teeth. Very calmly he stood listening to his elderly patient who was complaining about sharp pains in her upper left jaw and frequent attacks of neuralgia. He glanced at the boy, said goodbye to the woman, who made an appointment with the blonde assistant for the following Friday, and then he closed the door again. Once more the boy was left staring at the four corners of the room, bored and annoyed because he had already read all the magazines on the table. Soon the assistant appeared again, placed her purse on a chair, pulled up her skirt and casually adjusted her hose, getting ready to leave for the day. Then she turned around, opened the office door, said goodnight, smiled, closed the door again, and left glancing hurriedly at the clock. Once again he was left alone, biting his nails, worried, hungry, wishing he had a cheap sandwich or whatever.

Suddenly the dentist appeared in the waiting room, ready to leave, and looked at him coldly. "How are things going, kid?" he asked, "and what's on your mind?" Very calmly he turned out the lights, locked the office, put the key in his pocket, and headed toward the elevator. The boy followed close behind him, silent, gnawing what was left of a fingernail; like any boy who is physically appealing, he kept hoping that Ferreira, after giving him a good lecture, would welcome him back and forgive him. But the elevator, apparently stuck on one of the upper floors, took some time in coming, and all they could do was stand there in the hall waiting, and there the boy realized that the dentist was looking at him in a peculiar way, examining him with a cold distant gaze, and that he had changed completely. But since he was hungry and had nothing to lose, he decided to go along with the man anyway and take the situation for whatever it was worth.

Past forty already, of moderate height, with straight black hair combed back on his head, a little gray at the temples, an American cigarette in a short holder in the corner of his mouth, a half-blasé air about him, Ferreira always wore a coat and tie, attractive suits of dark or light cashmere made for him by the best tailors in town, shiny black shoes, and white or beige shirts with French cuffs and gold cuff-links. In his own eyes he was quite elegant, though his enemies said behind his back that there was nothing elegant about him (there was always someone, more gossipy than the rest, who would run to him and tell him what the others had said), that he was simply pretentious and that wearing expensive imported clothes didn't necessarily make anyone elegant, not even Didu de Souza Campos, who year after year was at the top of the "ten best" list. Nevertheless, Ferreira ignored all such comments, and every three months or so he would buy a new wardrobe. He wasn't really wealthy but he had two jobs that paid well—one as assistant professor of odontology on one of our more respected faculties, and then his dental practice itself, well established, with a roster of well-heeled patients. But he was never really happy, not even when he had a boy living with him. His friends often said that he felt some kind of compulsion to flagellate himself, to make himself miserable and unhappy, and once in a moment of crisis he confessed to Hilário, one of his closest friends—snubbed by the others because of his stinginess—that the worst misfortune of his life was his inability to enjoy himself sexually, that ordinarily he could not reach an orgasm.

He had only two special loves in life. The first was dark-skinned boys, fairly tall, between eighteen and twenty years of age, preferably fresh from the provinces because those who spent their lives treading the sidewalk day and night around Cinelândia and Copacabana were already corrupted and no longer worth the trouble. It was foolish to place any hopes on any of them, for all of them were beyond redemption. When Ferreira went out cruising and happened upon a boy he liked, one who still seemed moldable, he approached him discreetly and invited him for a snack or a cup of coffee; then he would ask him where he was from or where he had come from, how long he had been in Rio, and after examining all of his documents and making sure that he was acceptable, Ferreira would call a taxi and head for his apartment on Rua Raul Pompéia. Once there, he would immediately send the boy to the bathroom, telling him to pull off all his clothes and bathe carefully from head to toe. He would always tell him to leave the bathroom door open or ajar, and then Ferreira would stand there watching to see if he used enough soap, if he washed his privates well, especially his rear, and if he had a big cock or a small one; and if by any chance it happened that the boy had phimosis, he was unconditionally dismissed, no matter how much Ferreira liked him or how eager he was for sex, because a boy with phimosis, even if he were as handsome as Tony Curtis, was something that neither Ferreira nor his friends could accept.

In Ferreira's way of seeing things, every boy had a price, and that business of hanging onto one boy all one's life, even after marriage to a woman, was sheer nonsense, a habit that Americans had, for aside from being rather expensive, such a relationship brought nothing but headaches. But if the boy was good-natured and caused no problems, he might stay with Ferreira for three months or so, maybe even longer; then he would try to arrange the boy's life for him—that is, to help him find a job so he could support himself and get along in the world—or sometimes he would send him back home, just send him away summarily, with no regrets, but in such a way that they would part as friends, not as enemies, the boy leaving with a suitcase full of good clothes, money in his pocket, and the hope of coming back to Rio and staying as a guest in Ferreira's apartment until he could find a job and arrange things for himself.

In questions of love Ferreira believed only in bought pleasures— that is, only in boys who fucked exclusively for money or material gains, who knew how to make the best of the situation, all with as much sincerity as possible, with no hypocrisy, so that nobody would get hurt at the end. No "I love you" or nonsense of that sort. A boy who got emotionally involved was no good because he was a queen on his way out of the closet ("And I know enough queens already . . .") and would turn over on his stomach without a struggle. Though Ferreira's real bag was fucking, he couldn't stand a boy who flipped over as soon as they crawled into bed; on the contrary, he preferred one who gave in less readily, who at the beginning would hold back out of pride, because such reluctance increased Ferreira's pleasure in the situation and that increase was important since he was usually incapable of achieving complete satisfaction in the act itself. But if the boy suited his tastes, if he was adaptable and "well-behaved," as Ferreira had the habit of describing them, then he took him out and fitted him with a whole new set of clothes, made him presentable, and then proceeded to teach him how to behave in the company of others, at home and in public places and in the office. At first he would create an aura of mystery around the boy by hiding him from his friends and refusing to introduce him to anyone, while at the same time praising him extravagantly. That way he made everyone curious and terribly eager to meet his "new beauty." After a month he considered the period of initiation over and then would take the boy to meet his friends, who would either approve of him or find fault with him.

Ferreira's second love was modern painting, but only oils, which he considered an excellent investment (he had, in fact, already resold a few paintings when he found himself short on cash). It was a great pleasure for him to see the works of Brazilian painters hanging on the walls of his tasteful apartment with its light-brown carpeting and its furniture by Oca, all bought at a good discount because one of his patients was Maralti, a partner in the firm, in whose apartment Ferreira played cards on Wednesday nights. His collection consisted of a Portinari, which everyone thought very fine; a large Pancetti, really striking, that depicted a muddy stream in Campos de Jordão, and, by the same painter, a small seascape, also quite good, that he would not sell for anything; a madonna by Volpi; a fine Djanira, from her Bahía period; a reasonably good Di Cavalcanti; a head of Christ by Inimá, received in payment for some dental work he had performed on the artist; and three pictures by Franz Crajcberg, a new young painter ("'You like that? Well, I think it's a lot of crap!'") generally felt to be quite talented and promising, which he had bought at Jaime Mauricio's insistence.

He didn't care for drawings, not even drawings by Portinari, whom many people considered better at drawing than at painting; nevertheless, in the bedroom just above his bed he kept a watercolor by Roberto Burle-Marx, considered quite good, which portrayed a naked mulatto sitting on the edge of a double bed with his legs spread apart, showing an enormous erect penis, and a second figure, apparently female, undressing in the middle of a room lit only by the sparse light of a candle. It was from a series that the famous painter of gardens had done and distributed among his friends, calling the series "Male Prostitution in Bahía." In it he documented a certain all-male whorehouse in Salvador, much frequented by people from Rio and by local personalities.

The elevator was full since it was time for everyone to be leaving the offices in the building; as he and the boy stood side by side

Ferreira watched him from the corner of his eye and noticed that he had lost a lot of weight, that his skin was covered with splotches, with kiss-marks on his neck, and that he had lost completely the boyish carefree appearance he once had. He noticed too that the clothes he was wearing were obviously not his own, and worst of all, that he smelled like one of those boys that you pick up on the street and take home with you, and the first thing you do is tell them to take a bath and scrub their feet, which usually stink, to wash their behinds and get themselves in a proper condition for sex. He was no longer even a shadow of the unkempt little boy that Ferreira had picked up one night in front of the Mercadinho Azul. Then he was wearing good clothes but had not had a bath for days, and he was so hungry that the first thing he asked Ferreira was whether the man would be willing to buy him a meal. Ferreira took him that night to a more discreet place and asked him what he would like to eat. Without thinking twice he said he'd like a steak with French fries, and then, to start off, he gulped down a roll with butter and drank two glasses of beer. Suddenly he became very talkative, babbling about how he wanted to be a parachutist, and after he had eaten the steak and potatoes, along with another roll and another glass of beer, he told Ferreira the story of his life—that he was seventeen, had been born in Juiz de Fora, that he had a mother but no father and that he hated his stepfather.

Tonight they went across the street to the Westfalia Bar, frequented almost exclusively by foreigners—Germans and Austrians mostly—and a few gay people who were friends of the manager. The bar served the best French and Swiss cheese in town, homemade rye bread, good draught beer in ceramic mugs, and a first-rate whiskey sour, better perhaps than those served in the bars of many luxury hotels. Ferreira made his way to the back of the bar and found Felipe there, known to the crowd as "the Gringo," more bald, stooped, and skinny every day. Lost in thought, he was playing with his whiskey glass as if for some time he had been waiting for someone and now felt that he was about to be stood up. His ability to drink without ever getting drunk was enviable and impressive. No one had ever seen him drunk in the bar or anywhere else. Ferreira approached, pulled up a chair with a gesture of displeasure, greeted him quietly, and sat down. The boy said he had to go to the men's room, and Ferreira kept his eye on the door, expecting him to return at any moment. When he delayed for some time, Ferreira immediately jumped to the conclusion that he had met someone inside and was making an appointment for that night.

Ferreira had known Felipe since their university days, when he always made high scores on his exams. They were always together then, and since they were never seen in the company of the opposite sex, they were signaled out as pederasts, queers, but the rumors could never be substantiated. In part they had been motivated by spite, since Ferreira and Felipe were at the head of the class academically. Once a classmate who was fond of kidding rubbed his hand against Felipe's buttocks. Felipe took offense and a fight broke out, but those who gathered around soon leaped into action and separated the two fighters. Much later the two friends had had a misunderstanding over a boy of Felipe's who said that he had spent a night in Ferreira's apartment, but it turned out that the boy was lying. The two made up, but their friendship was never the same again; after that they always treated each other with a certain distance and reserve.

Ferreira turned and motioned for a beer. A young waiter appeared who looked like a German immigrant fresh off the boat, with little command of the language and great difficulty in expressing himself. He asked what they would like to eat and drink. Ferreira ordered a dark beer for himself and a light beer for the boy, who was just returning, along with a cheese sandwich plate and an extra plate of slices of rye bread with a wedge of Roquefort. The boy sat down, glancing back uneasily toward the bathroom, and then Ferreira introduced him to Felipe, who greeted him with the peculiar gesture of silently lowering his cheese. By force of habit, not because he was suspicious, Ferreira asked if the two already knew each other, and Felipe casually said that they had seen each other at the Fluminense Soccer Club but nothing more. The boy quickly finished off the two sandwiches that the waiter brought, sneaked a bite of Roquefort from Ferreira's plate, which he didn't like, and then asked if he could order something else. The dentist ignored him at first, repentant for having brought him to a place where things, aside from being fine, were also rather expensive.

"You can ask for as many sandwiches as you'd like," he answered a little caustically, not finding much charm in the boy's suggestion. "Go ahead and kill your hunger."

He watched as the boy ate the two extra sandwiches that the waiter placed in front of him, his thoughts supposedly on other matters. He watched as if he were not aware that the boy had always been a hearty eater, a monster of sorts in that respect, that he ate from the moment he set foot in the apartment, leaving the refrigerator bare, that he ate on the street whenever they went out together, and that even while asleep, in the middle of a nightmare, he had once asked the maid where she had hid a liter of milk. Felipe, in the meantime, was drinking silently, so delicate and unobtrusive that one would hardly think he was there. Turning toward him, Ferreira began his story, like the main actor in a Greek tragedy who suddenly speaks a line not in the text, an accusation drawn from deep within himself in a moment of despair, working it admirably into the play. His voice was slow and calm, his gestures measured; his posture and the manner in which he spoke bore the mark of an ageless feeling that has lived in the heart of nearly every human being since time immemorial and is the point where love and hate fuse.

"This is the famous Laércio," he said, "the one I told you about once, remember? The handsomest and most coveted boy in Copacabana and maybe in the whole of Rio de Janeiro. Well, he left me to live with a female tramp. A woman without any trace of class. The result is what you see here before you now . . .

"I think you met her," he continued. "An Elvira so-and-so, who was a patient of mine. After that she started turning up at my apartment with a young woman named Sonia, who was maybe a little interesting. You know who she is but you don't remember. Well, do you want to hear the rest of the story? This Elvira, I learned afterwards, is a lesbian, one of those who from time to time have to have a boy in the house to cover up and throw people off the track. But even that doesn't work and sooner or later everybody in Rio finds out that she really goes for women. And don't think this idiot here knew what was going on; he just fell into the trap . . ."

Surprised by the attitude of Ferreira, who had never forgiven him, and who on several occasions had sent him angry reprimands by other boys from the Soccer Club, none of which he had taken seriously or thought of as more than a joke, Laércio lost control of himself, blushed, and stopped chewing; he glanced with suspicion at Felipe, who kept his head cautiously lowered, turning his glass of whiskey sour between his long fingers, with no desire to get involved in a matter he had already heard discussed at length. Then he glanced at Ferreira, who was smoking nonchalantly, as calm as a great landlord gazing out over his vast domains. The truth was that Ferreira saw no reason to forgive him, that he still felt humiliated by the way the boy had deserted him, and very resentful of it; and, as if losing the boy had not been enough, all of his friends pounced on him at the time and for days the phone did not stop ringing. His bad luck was all they could talk about, and everyone, it seemed, was laughing at his expense, taking delight in his predicament. In desperation he phoned Elvira's apartment and sent her to hell, demolishing her with words, and then he launched into details of the boy's private life, telling her all sorts of unsavory stories about him. At that point his friends took up the case, telling him that he had lost the game, that his phone call was an unfortunate mistake, and so on, and so on. For several weeks Ferreira stayed shut up in his apartment and was never seen in his usual haunts and hangouts; he then took a vacation and hid out in Hilário's house in Petrópolis. Even so his acquaintances continued to gossip about him, to pick him apart, and though the boy had his glaring faults, they ended up taking his side against Ferreira, and whenever the subject came up a chorus of voices would declare that Ferreira deserved what he got.

Laércio felt a knot in his throat where a wad of bread and cheese, wet with saliva, had gotten stuck on the way down and would not move forward or backward. With a sticky sensation in the roof of his mouth and an expression of surprise and displeasure in his shining brown eyes, he felt much like a servant who after years of work in a house realizes that he is about to be fired and replaced by another because of some unpardonable mistake which he did not consider particularly serious at the time, or simply because he is no longer needed.

"Oh fuck, Ferreira! So you're going to start that again, are you?" he blurted out forcefully, his mouth still full of food, and then he began to chew again, his arms crossed on the table, his gaze turned aside.

What Ferreira had wished for most during all that time was to get even with Laércio, to humiliate him in the presence of a friend, to take his revenge, because what he had told Elvira Sodré on the phone that time was not even half or a third of what he had to say. But unfortunately the boy had disappeared from circulation at the time and Ferreira had no more word of him, no idea of where he hung out or where he could be found, because the boys from the Fluminense Soccer Club simply vanished and no longer dropped by his apartment. Later he learned that they had signed a contract to play as professionals on teams in Salvador and the state of São Paulo. But now, when he least expected it, luck had smiled upon him and delivered the victim into the hangman's hands. Starving and with no place to turn, in a moment of extreme hardship, the stupid kid had remembered him and come running to him, convinced that his mere presence was enough and that with a whisk of a sponge he could wipe the past clean and take up where they had left off.

If by any chance the boy thought Ferreira was still in the dark, that he was not fully aware of what had happened, then he was deceiving himself completely, for just as each day's newspaper reports the previous day's robberies, assaults, crimes of passion, and suicides, so news travels through gay circles and sooner or later— or immediately—everyone knows. It is part of the homosexual's character not to let such happenings drift by without comment. One learns something and then he tells another, who tells another, and so the news spreads. Laércio's case was no exception, and hardly a week had passed before the news got back to Ferreira when he happened to run into a gay former classmate whom he had not seen for a long time, in front of the Metro Moviehouse where he was about to get in line to see a rerun of *Gone with the Wind*.

"Listen," Amaral—the former classmate—said during the course of the conversation, lowering his voice and glancing cautiously to both sides, "have you seen that boy lately that left you to live with that woman—what's her name?—ah yes, Elvira?"

"No, I haven't seen him for several months," Ferreira answered, half annoyed by the question. "As far as I know he went back to Juiz de Fora."

"What? You think he went back? I saw him on the street the other day... and in such a mess that I felt sorry for him. That woman of his kicked him out, you know, but I guess there's nothing more between you and him, right? Of course you knew that she's a lesbian?"

Ferreira showed no inclination to discuss the matter and Amaral, noticing his reluctance, said goodbye with a friendly but formal smile and a feminine gesture that Ferreira always found annoying, and then he went on his way, satisfied with himself for having conveyed a bit of valuable information to a less fortunate friend. Ferreira was so bothered by that inopportune conversation that he was about to forget the movie and leave, but then, in front of the ticket window, he resolved to go ahead and see the film, which he had missed the first time around because he had been in bed with the mumps.

Amaral could be quite charming at times, with stories so funny that he left people convulsed with laughter; but it was best to hear them at home, in private, because he was something of a suspicious character, much too flamboyant, and for that reason everyone tried to avoid him in the streets, even Ferreira, to whom he was distantly related. In Amaral's opinion there were two kinds of boys: those who are worthy of respect, who say as little as possible and fuck because they need the money and then end up getting married, without ever trying to hide from their wives the fact that they've lived off queens, who have no hang-ups about the whole matter; and those who at first seem to be very serious and not at all inclined to talk, but later, when they've lost their bashfulness, are worse than the queens themselves, dancing in public with their "spouses," always on the make, drinking and talking madly without giving much thought to what they're saying. Laércio himself was one of the latter, and when Ferreira had introduced him to Amaral during a dinner party that he gave in his apartment, Amaral's comments were much to the point: when Ferreira had cornered him in the kitchen and asked him what he thought, he had said, "If you want my sincere opinion, he's no good." He was the type of boy who would spend the whole week in the house reading comic books and watching television, going out to the beach from time to time, without ever opening his mouth—unless it might be to brag about something or to say something stupid—until one would finally get fed up with him and send him back to hell.

Well aware that at any moment Laércio might burst into speech, shiowing off as it was natural for insecure boys like him to do, perhaps to impress Felipe who until then had known him only by sight, Ferreira had waited silently for the right moment to attack, ready to take him apart and finish him off once and for all. He rolled his king-size American cigarette between his fingers to soften the tip, which he then inserted into his short holder; he lit up, crossed his legs, glanced to the left, and then, remembering that he had an appointment to meet Valdo by the Amarelinho Bar at seven on the dot, he tried to hurry the matter along.

"What have you been doing lately?" he asked the boy.

"Oh, just hanging around . . . I got suspended from the team at the Fluminense but I'll be going back at the end of the month. The position is mine . . ."

"You look like you've lost some weight."

"Yeah, from a cold I caught, but I'm over it now."

"And how's Elvira these days? What's she doing now?"

"Oh, she's okay ..."

"Give her my regards."

He paused for only a moment and Laércio, more sure of himself now, launched into a story about a weekend he had spent with some friends in Paquetá at the house of somebody named Botelho, a really far-out guy, loaded with money, who didn't give a shit about anything, and on he went, exaggerating as usual, forcing the point, with the phony masculine air of a boy who talks about women but is ready to roll over for any man who wants him. He had never seen such a house in all his life, he said; it had more rooms than you could count, two swimming pools—two swimming pools, goddamn!—and more food and drink than you knew what to do with, and all you had to do was just help yourself—I mean, why was there any need to ask for permission? And if you didn't like what was going on, all you had to do was put on your pants and head for the beach, with all the blue, blue water, or you could slip on a pair of shorts and lie out by the pool drinking whiskey and listening to music. And if you felt like fucking, well, all you had to do was grab a girl and take her inside, anybody except Ilsa, that is, Botelho's girl, who wasn't really pretty anyhow, but let me tell you, she's got a pair of legs you wouldn't believe! But you have to keep hands off, especially when it's a nice guy like Botelho, and anyway, as I was saying, if you wanted to fuck all you had to do was grab one of the chicks and ...

"Stop it!" Ferreira broke in. "Just cut it out, okay?"

The boy stopped, taken aback, and after a brief pause Ferreira took up the attack again, with the whole situation now in his hands, just as he had wanted it.

"Come on, kid, where did you get your girlfriend? Up until now the only girl you mentioned was Ilsa, Botelho's girl. Now where did the other one come from?"

If looks could have killed, Ferreira would have fallen dead there on the spot, as if struck by lightning. Caught in his lie, Laércio turned pale and swallowed hard, fumbling about for a place to put his hands; he turned to Felipe with the anguished look of someone caught in a nightmare, begging somebody else for help because he's about to drown in a swollen river or on the verge of falling into a deep dark well. He still tried to fish around for some shred of an explanation, but Ferreira would not let up.

"Damn it, Ferreira, you're a real ass," the boy protested, transfixing him with a gloomy gaze.

Without flinching, still in calm possession of himself, Ferreira stuck another cigarette into his holder after sucking on it to clean it, his freshly shaven face—he had shaved before leaving his office—beaming with satisfaction. Immediately he turned toward Felipe with the proud air of someone who knows he is in charge of the situation, and he noticed that the gringo, visibly annoyed by having to take part, however indirectly, in something that was unpleasant to him and which he did not approve of, seemed to want to disappear from view, to take cover under the table. Unwavering in his intention to unmask the boy and humiliate him, but careful to place him first in as difficult and as discomforting a position as possible, to subject him to as much pain as possible, Ferreira moved his attention back to Laércio, who was still pale and temporarily out of action, certain that he had put his foot in his mouth and exposed himself to Ferreira's attack.

"Listen, Laércio," the dentist continued in an impersonal tone. "I've known your friend Botelho much longer than you think. And do you want to know something? He's never touched a woman in his life. Boys are his thing, boys just like you, of just about your age. And do you want to know something else? Botelho likes to screw his boys, and anybody who says anything to the contrary is a liar."

Laércio averted his eyes, shook his head, and wiggled about restlessly in his chair like a person whose only desire at the moment is simply to be left alone.

"Damn it, Ferreira! You don't let anything slip by you, do you?" he exclaimed, grimacing, lost in thought, his dark face suddenly gloomy and his beautiful dark-brown eyes still shining. On his lips, chapped by the sun on the beach, there appeared a forced smile as the boy, disgusted and repentant, thought what a fool he had been to mention Botelho. He could not stop thinking about what a silly mistake he had made, he who had put himself out for Ferreira and other faggots like him, all of whom, in the end, were nothing more than a mean, stingy, vindictive bunch of pederasts. He had deceived himself, and he couldn't imagine what he had been thinking of when he decided to look up Ferreira and try to make peace with him, to see if at least he could spend a few days in his apartment until things worked out with the Fluminense, or until he could get transferred to some other club, or until he could go back home to Juiz de Fora.

It shocked him to see how well informed Ferreira was, how much he knew about what had been going on, and for that reason he didn't try to contradict the man anymore; he just kept quiet and listened. The dentist began to tell the whole story, a rundown of Botelho's life: he was a likable scoundrel, loaded with money, with an engaging gift of gab that could lure any boy in; he had pull with the police because of a brother-in-law who was a district police chief, and if that wasn't enough, he had an uncle who was a general, and if the man didn't approve of his nephew's crazy habits and bizarre life-style, at least he didn't disapprove of them, and anyway, anybody who has a general for an uncle can relax and breathe easy, knowing that he's covered from behind. It was true, he said, that Botelho spent his weekends in his house in Paquetá, but the house, although very comfortable, was not as impressive as Laércio had described it. He always went with a few friends and with Ilsa, who screwed with anybody who wanted her and was paid to serve as a camouflage and to keep things moving. Botelho's technique for attracting boys, though naïvely simple, was quite productive: he would invite a crowd for the weekend, telling them they could do as they pleased, that he had a wife, and everybody fucked, and what kind of boy after all wouldn't be happy to spend a weekend that way, telling his friends later that he fucked and ate and drank and all for free, without it costing him a cent?

On the first visit things would go more or less as Botelho promised, except that the girls he mentioned would for some reason not arrive; but anyway there was Ilsa, and though she was supposed to be Botelho's mistress she would fill in as best she could, sneaking off with some and distracting the others with food and booze. But the second time the set-up would be different, with a whole new script; the only woman around would be Ilsa, already tired, drunk, and unwilling to fuck, and the excuse would be that the girls somehow hadn't been able to make it but that there was still a chance they'd show up later, and anyway, there's food and drink for everybody and you can change clothes and do as you please, just make yourself at home . . . And by that time, let's face it, who's going to complain because the girls haven't shown up and there's no woman to fuck? Only an idiot would think of leaving, especially with it being so difficult to get to and from Paquetá. No, the thing to do by now is stick around and enjoy the day, taking advantage of the pool

and the sea, listening to good music, going for rides in the boat—
and then Botelho decides to make his play. And what kind of boy,
confronted with so much refinement and such a good life, all for
free, with so much to gain—easy money included, because I can
assure you that Botelho isn't the stingy type, and he's generous with
his grass too—what kind of boy isn't going to give in?

Ferreira's information came largely from Paulo, a very pleasant
student and ex-lover of Marcondes, a patient of Ferreira's who had
a house in Paquetá which he later sold when he moved to Belo
Horizonte. He wanted to take the boy with him, but he lived with
his parents and couldn't go. Once when Marcondes was away on a
sudden trip to Brasília where he had to settle some matters, Paulo
was invited by a classmate to spend the weekend at Botelho's house
in Paquetá, where, he said, they could have their fill of women.
Since Paulo felt a longing for the island and was terribly horny at
the same time, he didn't even bat an eye; he took his classmate's
offer and they caught the first boat over. They didn't find the girls
that the classmate had mentioned; the only woman there was Ilsa,
supposedly Botelho's girlfriend, a really groovy girl as far as they
could tell, but ugly as sin, and not in the mood for fucking. It wasn't
long before they were ready to leave, but Botelho, in that nice way
of his, with all sorts of coaxing, convinced them that they should
stay; it turned out that they had a good time, and Paulo, always
smart and alert, ended up in bed with Botelho, who had had an eye
on him for some time. Botelho took a strong liking to the boy and
they became lovers, and it wasn't long until Paulo was buried under
gifts—a gold Swiss watch, a motorcycle, expensive clothes, and all
sorts of things that he had never seen during his time with Marcondes, who was a nice guy but rather stingy.

"So, Laércio, don't try to tell me you fucked with a girl in Botelho's place, because girls are just what was missing there. If you
fucked, it had to be with a man," the dentist concluded with a slight
smile on his face, and then he put his cigarette in his mouth unhurriedly in a majestic gesture of triumph, like a fighter who has just
won a very hard victory.

The boy did not attack him then and there because the bar was
not the place for a fight, and anyway there was Felipe, who had
nothing to do with the whole matter or with Ferreira's perverse-
ness; he was an educated man, peaceful and harmless, a genuinely
nice guy, and there was no reason to cause trouble in his presence.
But what Ferreira deserved was a good beating, a fist right in his

face, something to teach him not to be such a bastard, always thinking he was better than the other queens. With a sad gloomy look on his face he turned his gaze toward Felipe, much as if he were somehow obligated to explain his life and actions to the man since he was the only person in a position to hear his side of the story and judge it objectively.

"You know," he said, venting his anger, "since the day I set foot in Rio de Janeiro I've been surrounded by faggots and buggers and the only goddamned thing I can hear is, 'God! Look at that boy! Isn't he something! Get a load of those thighs, and what an ass, what a cock . . .'"

Felipe laughed somewhat awkwardly and asked him where he was from. He said he was from Juiz de Fora and then continued his monologue.

"Shit! Not a single day has gone by since I came here—I mean, not a single day—without some ass making a pass at me. If it's not on the street it's in somebody's apartment or in the club—I mean, they just won't leave me alone. I don't think there's a fucker in Rio that doesn't want to get up my ass. Somebody comes up to me on the street and asks what time it is, and you know immediately what's going on—it's either a queen who wants to get fucked or some bastard who wants to screw you. I tell them to fuck off, but do you think that helps? No, that's when they really start flocking around you . . . Even there on the island, goddamn, I mean even there on the island . . . Shit, it makes me want to laugh . . . I mean, how could the guy . . . just listen and tell me how . . ."

He stared defiantly in the direction of Ferreira, who was biting the nail on his little finger, distant, pretending a complete lack of interest, but without missing a word or a detail, and then he moved his chair closer to Felipe and, with one hand covering the side of his mouth, asked in a low voice if he could order a sandwich. He motioned to the waiter by holding up two fingers in the V for victory sign, and then he immediately hid his hands under the table, satisfied with himself, and with a certain degree of shamelessness, not caring about anything anymore.

"Well, man, I went in to change clothes," he continued, "and another guy came in behind me. I didn't know where in the fuck he came from. I didn't pay any attention to him because he looked like a regular guy, you know, a hundred percent man, one of those who go for women and wouldn't be caught dead fucking around with men, not even for money . . . Well, would you believe that the bastard got all worked up when he saw me take off my clothes and put on my bathing suit? 'Hey, you guys!' he shouted in a loud voice so everybody could hear, and everybody came running to see what was wrong. It was disgusting. And you know what the bastard said when everybody was gathered around? 'Look at that ass!' he said. They all burst out laughing, shit, and it was a big joke for them . . . It made me feel really shy and self-conscious, and I called Botelho and told him I was going back to Rio, but he said that would be silly and finally he talked me into staying . . . But that was a lousy thing to do, really, and the rest of the day all the guys kept rubbing it in, and I wanted to get even with somebody but finally I decided to take it as a joke and not let it bother me . . ."

He smiled at Ferreira, who was still silently biting his fingernail, as if unaware of what was being said. The boy picked up the second sandwich, wiped the corner of his mouth with the back of his hand, and began to chew again without taking his eyes off the dentist. In his corner of the table, almost invisible, Felipe was turning his sixth glass of whiskey sour between his fingers, apparently enjoying himself, amused by the whole affair, if one could judge from the expression on his hairless face, which by now was a little sweaty and terribly flushed.

"I know I'm handsome," Laércio continued in a provocative tone, "and that I have feminine features, but I'm a man, goddamn it. And what's more, if I wanted to live the rest of my life off a queer, I wouldn't have to spend another day working. But I'm a man, a real macho, and whether you want to believe it or not, I've only got mixed up with a queer once, and then it was because I was so hard up I didn't have any choice. What I like is women—I mean good pussy, understand?"

"Okay, kid," Ferreira broke in, offended because Laércio's last words were undoubtedly directed at him, "would you please shut your mouth and stop talking nonsense?"

"What do you mean, nonsense?"

"Just cut it out, will you?"

". . . but I *am* a macho . . ."

"A macho, hell. You know perfectly well that you're just as queer as any of us," Ferreira came back angrily. "You know that you lived with that woman all that time just because you wanted to prove you're a man and don't try to tell me any different. And all along you knew that she was lesbian, or would you try to deny that too? Come on, answer me: did you know it or didn't you?"

Laércio knew he had lost the bout, and like a dog that's just been kicked and shrinks gracelessly into a corner, he turned his eyes away and began to pick his teeth with the greasy toothpick that had held his sandwich together. Through his head, with the brilliance of a lightning flash, passed the savage words that Elvira hurled at him that day when they fought: "A macho who lives with a queer ends up queer himself, or maybe you already are . . ." His hatred for her doubled, for in addition to deceiving him, making a fool of him, she had tried to belittle him in front of her friends and turn him against Ferreira, for whom, in spite of everything, he had always felt a deep respect..

"Goddamn it," he said, "I think I'm going crazy . . . I mean, I don't know what in the fuck I am anymore . . . whether I'm a man or a queer . . . I just don't know anymore . . ."

And turning to Felipe, who seemed to be there against his will, he asked the man's opinion. Ferreira broke in without giving Felipe time to answer.

"You're a homosexual!" he shouted hysterically, banging his fist on the table. "You're a homosexual, and it's time for you to stop playing the big macho!"

Ferreira noticed then that they were the last customers in the back room and maybe in the whole bar, for in the main room there was nobody to be seen. Everybody had already left without their noticing. Tired, leaning against the counter with the sleepy face of an old Saint Bernard who had lost the scent it was tracking, the waiter was waiting only for them to finish up and pay their bill. In front of the cash register a middle-aged German, the short squat brother of one of the owners of the place, stood with a bored look on his face, waiting for them to clear out so he could close up for the night.

But Ferreira still did not feel like leaving; he crossed his legs and continued smoking, with a distant look in his eyes, thoughtless and blank. At his side, silent as a stone, Felipe played with his glass of whiskey, demonstrating his phenomenal resistance to hard liquor. And in the other chair, completely silent, Laércio yawned from time to time and stretched himself.

At such moments no one could guess what was going on inside Felipe's head, so shiningly bald and pinkish that it could be seen even in the dark. As an inconspicuous figure in a group of brilliant and successful homosexuals, the gringo was generally thought of as dull and boring, but almost everyone envied him his incredible luck; without even trying, he managed to lure the best boys in Copacabana into his hands. On more than one occasion, learning that such and such a boy whom he himself had lusted after had been seen entering Felipe's apartment or riding beside him down Atlantic Avenue, Ferreira had grown exasperated and exclaimed, "I know he's lucky, but that's really too much!" At other times Felipe could be seen in the company of poorly dressed boys whom everybody had had and nobody wanted anymore, the type who will go with anybody for a few cruzeiros and a double milkshake to stave off hunger.

Ferreira never tired of insulting him behind his back, for aside from being irksomely lucky, it seemed that fate had chosen him to witness many of the most dramatic moments in Ferreira's love life, principally his squabbles with his boys. During his first serious misunderstanding with Laércio, which came about because of a girl who spent the whole day phoning him, Felipe had been present, and then that particular night, when Ferreira entered the bar, there he was again.

Laércio cleared his throat and shuffled his feet, about to break the silence, which by that time had become oppressive.

"Okay..." he said, standing up immediately and clearing his throat again. Then he extended his hand toward Felipe, who shook it nonchalantly, with a slight grin on his lips, and then he turned toward Ferreira and asked meekly if he could stop by his apartment later. Without acknowledging the question Ferreira continued smoking calmly, eager for him to go away because none of the many boys that had already passed through his life had ever caused him as much trouble as Laércio had caused him in so few months, and worst of all, Laércio had left him for a woman, a fact that he could not forgive, though Elvira, to tell the truth, was not exactly a woman...

"What about it, Ferreira?" the boy insisted. "Can I stop by or not?"

"You can go to hell, Laércio," Ferreira answered harshly without bothering to look up at him.

Ferreira nonchalantly made his way out of the bar and strolled toward Cinelândia, flanked by Felipe, who showed little sign of having drunk so much. He wanted to keep his appointment with Valdo, who had phoned him in his office to say that he had "something new" to introduce to him. But before they reached the Amarelinho Bar Felipe suddenly took his leave in a somewhat suspicious manner, with no explanation and no indication of where he was going. Ferreira, however, did not attach much importance to the matter. Restless, the dentist headed toward Rua Alcinde Guanabara, stopped on the corner, and Valdo soon appeared with two kids that Ferreira had already seen around before, the type it would not do to turn your back on; Ferreira called Valdo aside, scolded him and quickly got rid of him, greatly annoyed because whenever he needed money or dental work he never failed to come around.

Ferreira then walked to the corner, signaled a taxi, and told the driver to take him up to Santa Teresa where he could pick up a painting he had left in Pascoal Carlos Magno's house. He had been on the verge of buying it earlier but at the last minute had decided against it. The taxi stopped in front of the ambassador's house and he told the drive to wait; moments later he came back with the picture under his arm, climbed back into the taxi, and told the driver to leave him in Flamengo, a little beyond the Hotel Glória, that is, by the building where Maralti lived, for every Wednesday Maralti had a group of friends over to play cards.

When he entered the Count was on the phone; he put the painting on a little marble table in the entrance hall and went into the living room where he indulged in light conversation with Hilário and Lula Sabóia, an almost unbeatable pair when it came to cards. The Count kept up a shallow conversation with someone, one of those that go on forever; time after time, with the charming voice of an Italian speaking Portuguese, pronouncing each syllable clearly, he repeated, "What? A real beauty, eh? Well, why don't you bring him here? No, my dear, that's not important at all. Oh, so you'd rather go straight home with him? I understand. Yes, yes, I understand perfectly!" And then he broke into a long healthy horselike laugh that Ferreira found somewhat contagious; but he showed no sign of hanging up the phone, and whenever Ferreira thought he was about to finish, Maralti would let loose another horselike laugh and the conversation would continue, apparently interminable.

With nothing else to do, annoyed because there's nothing in the world worse than listening to someone talk for hours on the phone, he decided to kill time by leafing through a book that Maralti had left open on top of a table in the reading room. He turned it over and looked at the jacket—*Travels in Western Africa,* by Nino Soloni, ex-Commissioner of Italian Commerce to the Gold Coast. He read a bit from a page marked with a red ribbon: "The thing that most

draws the attention of the white traveler on a journey from Cou-
tounou to Allada, the ancient capital of the tiny kingdom of Ardra,
is the remarkable number of wooden and stone phalli which he sees
displayed in small sanctuaries in front of the house. Generally the
sculptures are modeled on a scale two or three times that of any
normal human member. Afterwards I learned through Pierre Le
Dix, a professor of anthropology and a distinguished Africanist,
who happened to be visiting Dahomey at the same time, that among
certain groups in that region the phallic cult is . . ."

Just then he heard Maralti's melodious voice. "Do excuse me,
my dear," the man said, embracing him, "but I was talking with
Felipe and . . . anyway, let's have a drink, okay?"

He took a seat beside Maralti, his partner in the game, and asked
Lula Sabóia if he wanted to deal. Lula put his cigarette aside, shuffled
the deck, put it on the table, and asked Hilário to cut the cards;
Hilário cut them, and Lula shuffled again and began to deal. Ferreira
picked up his own cigarette and stuck it in the corner of his mouth,
inspecting his own excellent hand, and then suddenly his mind
turned back to the conversation between Maralti and Felipe only
minutes earlier; he thought of the mysterious way in which Felipe
had said goodbye to him on the street, with no mention of where
he was going, and then he thought of Laércio, who was in the
market for a good meal . . .

"But . . . but what are you laughing at, Ferreira?" Maralti asked,
breaking into the dentist's train of thought, gazing at him with an
astonished expression.

Gnawing his cigarette holder and still smiling, with no intention
of explaining his laughter, Ferreira played a golden ace and won the
round. After all, an explanation of his laughter would not help
matters in any way; if Felipe wanted to latch on to Laércio, or if he
merely wanted to spend a night with the boy, what difference did it
make to him? It was their problem, not Ferreira's. That night his
luck was running incredibly high, and if his opponents had not been
Hilário and Lula Sabóia (who during a coffee break admitted the
possibility of defeat), he and Maralti, for the first time, would have
come out on top in a fascinating series of plays whose outcome
was not clear until the last hands were drawn, and which, unlike
their earlier engagements, went on until dawn.

WALL OF SILENCE

He went out with his father one day to hunt deer and witnessed a memorable scene. In a clearing two males were fighting fiercely over a doe. At last the strongest won. In an attitude of submission the loser lowered his head and the winner mounted him from behind.

HE RAN INTO THE MARINE as he left the downtown movie-house where he had gone to kill time. He had gotten up in the middle of the film, bored with Frank Sinatra who, in spite of his balding head and wrinkles, was playing the role of a young man, tough and merciless toward his enemies. His heart was beating heavily but he did his best to show no surprise or any trace of emotion that might betray him and let the boy know that he was acting out a drama, that their meeting was not by chance. He would not be able to bear it if the marine ever learned that he had already been pursuing him for several weeks, leaving his office a little early for that purpose, stationing himself, without the least results, wherever he might pass or happen to be.

Without even a casual greeting he took the boy forcibly by the arm, as the police in the movies do with suspicious characters, and led him into the vestibule of the Mesbla department store. They followed a group of people who were trying to get in out of the rain. They had barely gotten inside when the rain and the wind grew worse; the trees along the Passeio Público twisted violently in the gusts, and an airplane passed by so low that one would have thought it took off from the top of the Serrador Building. A chubby-cheeked middle-aged man ran after his Tirolean-style hat and was almost struck down by a Ford Galaxie driven by a lady. A branch fell from a tree on the other side of the avenue, and suddenly half of the street was left in darkness.

At first the marine seemed puzzled, but soon he recovered from his initial fright. He did not react in any way, as the man had expected, and he showed no sign of hostility. He merely glanced rapidly at the man out of the corner of his eye and smiled faintly. Then he took a handkerchief from his pocket and passed it slowly over his wet forehead and neck, venturing a second quick glance. But since the man remained stationed in front of him, expression-less, like someone demanding an explanation (which he would never get), and since the tense atmosphere of distrust and bewilderment had eased somewhat, he turned toward a store window and began to examine the merchandise on display in it. The rain was still coming down heavily.

It must have been around eight thirty, and since the marine was in civilian clothes and had his folder with him, the man assumed that he must have been returning from the house of a rather mysterious sister of his who lived in Cruz Vermelha. He was wearing the same light wool pants, bought at one of the permanent clearance sales in some store on the Rua da Alfándega, the type that the less demanding soldier wears and then throws away (usually they are very vain and insist that everything be first class, especially clothes), and the same flowery-print shirt, now missing many buttons, which he had brought from the Dominican Republic. His shoes too were the same pair, light brown with buckles, that the man had given him the previous Christmas.

He had always suspected that the mysterious sister was actually a female trick of the boy's, one of those secret affairs that almost all handsome boys of his age have. Or maybe she was an old sweetheart, or even a married woman, one of the type, available by the hundreds, who like to fuck with fresh young boys. Sister, she wasn't; the man was convinced of that. If he had wanted to he could have sent someone to check the matter out (there's always someone willing to handle such things) but he never really felt inclined to bother. After all, what the boy did when they were not together was of no great concern to him; he simply wasn't interested in his private life, who he ran around with or had stopped running around with. It was his feeling (much to the distaste of many of his friends, who considered him cynical and lacking in self-esteem) that a woman, even a whore, neither harmed nor hampered a relationship, provided, of course, that the boy could handle the affair in a way that did not create tensions. He was not one of those men who, consumed by jealousy over any silly little incident, never allow their boys to flirt with women or to take a step away from their watchful presence.

People kept filing into the hall, and if it continued that way it wouldn't be long until nobody would be able to move about in the place. It wasn't really hot, though the temperature had begun to climb as a result of the strong lightning and the thickening crowds of people. The floor was completely wet, dark with water, and soon it turned into a layer of mud that made him feel uneasy, eager to get out of the place however he could and as quickly as possible. His eyes were sullen and flushed with anger, which gave him the look of someone ready to kill or to destroy things with his bare hands, and the marine avoided looking him in the face, unable to bear such a confrontation. But from all appearances he was undisturbed, calm as always, just as if nothing had happened or as if it had been only yesterday or barely a week ago when they had last seen each other.

For the time being the man had only one desire: to grab the marine by the neck and strike him. But he restrained himself. He was a gentleman, as the boy knew, but once he lost his temper he acted like a wounded animal without worrying about the consequences. It was in his house, alone, where they would settle the matter, not there in front of so many people. He could not bear scandals, and there was no place better than home for handling such affairs. And after all he would be the one to come out with the short end of the deal; the marine had nothing to lose, for he was the victim and he would always be right. Still the man was entitled to an explanation; all he demanded was that the boy say why he had disappeared, that he come up with a reasonable excuse. Once again the blood rushed to his head and he felt an urge to slap him, to make him suffer, and once again he had to get hold of himself and let his reason prevail. He could not run the risk of losing the boy now that he had him in his hands again, and if he acted rashly he might end up losing him forever. But at the same time he wasn't sure whether he would have the courage to send him away, to get him out of his life once and for all if such steps should be called for. He was simply not prepared for such a possibility and he could not pretend that he was.

He had never underestimated the boy, though during their two years of nearly perfect friendship he had proved to be almost always docile and submissive (he was punctual too, and for the man that meant a lot). He never forgot that he was dealing with a person who had an extremely difficult and rather peculiar temperament, one of those boys who, when they say "not today," can never be coaxed into changing their mind. At other times, though, when he had decided that the night was going to be a waste and expected nothing more to come of it, the boy would suddenly come to him and give himself without the least insistence on the man's part, and then they would spend the rest of the night awake. The following day, exhausted, the man would hardly be able to work, and he would tough it out as best he could, with a headache, eager to get back home and go to bed. On the other hand, if the truth must be told, he never really managed to control the boy, to tell him what he should do and what he shouldn't do, as had been the case with the others who had passed through his hands. And since he never interfered with his life (in that respect he knew only what the boy freely told him when he decided to open up and talk), he could never guess what the boy's real thoughts and plans were or when he was really content and happy. In spite of his being young and healthy, physically healthy at least, he was by nature a closed secretive type who talked little, one of those people who mean yes when they say yes and no when they say no, with whom insistence gets you nowhere.

The heat inside the hallway had become choking, suffocating, and outside in the street the rain was still falling, stronger than ever, with no indication that it would let up anytime soon. Flashes of lightning split open the sky and the peals of thunder were loud enough to be disquieting. It was enough to give the impression that the buildings were falling down and the mountains that surround Rio were crumbling. The water had already reached the curb and soon would cover the sidewalk, and then no one would be able to leave unless he was willing to get soaked and to battle his way through the currents. Some people passed with newspapers on their heads, and from the doorway others tried in vain to catch the attention of a taxi, making urgent signs to the passing cars. Two boys from one of those gangs of slum kids that hang around the streets began to shout at a friend who had lingered behind. They were drenched, but it didn't seem to bother them and they paid no attention whatever to the rain. With his back to it all the marine took no notice of what was going on around him and much less of what was happening outside. When he turned back around and looked at the man meekly, with a slight smile flowering on his wet lips, the man's anger had subsided somewhat. Another kind of emotion had taken hold of him now, an undefined desire which could have been either a dark urge to get even with the boy or a need to forgive him and get back on the good side with him as quickly as possible.

"Why did you disappear?" he asked.

He never forced the marine to talk more than was necessary, for he never opened himself completely even during those moments of greatest intimacy, not even when they lingered in bed after sex, one's leg over the other's, both of them physically satisfied, apparently thinking about nothing. That would be like asking the boy to take responsibility for some job that many sergeants could only handle with considerable difficulty, or like asking a five-year-old child with no special gift for mathematics to work a problem with decimal fractions. Generally it was left up to the man to do the talking and to make plans for a future that included the two of them. The boy never let himself be carried away by facile praise, and he wasn't vain like all the others; whenever someone told him that he had a good physique, an athlete's body, he would merely smile. He had only one source of obvious pride: his set of strong perfect teeth. More than once he had been caught in front of the mirror examining them carefully. He wasn't particularly fond of classical music (the man usually listened to one of the composers he liked best while he bathed) but, unlike the others, he would never ask to change the record to one by Roberto Carlos. Instead he would take out one of the historical comic books that he carried with him in his folder and read until it was his turn in the bathroom. He always took a leisurely bath, a half hour or more, using up more than half a bar of soap in the process.

The man wanted to repeat the question but decided it was best not to insist. There were two possibilities: either the boy did not want to answer, or he had not heard clearly because of the thunder. And later he came to the conclusion that the boy would never tell him the reason why he suddenly stopped phoning, why he had disappeared as he did, with no warning and no explanation. He recalled that weeks before he disappeared he had begun to behave strangely, like someone who wants to say something but doesn't have the courage to say it. He would linger in front of the television, silent and glum, as if he were marking time before undertaking some disagreeable task that he was obliged to finish. Not even the comedy shows on TV could get him excited or make him laugh. Still, somehow, he at the same time had not really changed; he was still docile and very considerate, always ready to fuck as often as the man wanted, and with the same willingness that he had shown the first time they went to bed together. That was what the man could not understand.

Restless because they couldn't leave, and progressively more excited by the presence of the marine, whose leg was positioned against his own, the man breathed with great difficulty, experiencing an extreme discomfort, a tightness in his chest that made him gasp for breath. Suddenly he closed his eyes and saw himself in bed with the boy again, remembering how he had kissed so freely ("Did you know your mouth has a strange taste of nicotine and okra?"), only to confess afterwards, as a matter of pride, that he had never been kissed by a man before. He could hardly budge in either direction, blocked on one side by a fat woman with full breasts and on the other side by a couple who necked through the whole thing, pushing him against the marine. A sudden desire came over him, so violent that he had to stick his hand quickly into his pocket to restrain his member. His reaction was quick and subtle, lasting only a few seconds, but even so the boy noticed it. The man tried to shift his position; he laughed lightly, as if the incident had helped him to overcome the constraint and the violent desire that continued to torment him. If he delayed one more day in satisfying his desires he would end up in desperation, completely mad. His need to possess the boy doubled in intensity, becoming even more burdensome. With a half-smile on his lips the boy turned back toward the display window to examine once more the little battery-operated radios and the tiny tape recorders. He remembered how he had gone on a spree in the bar of the Hotel El Caribe and blown all of his savings on one of those machines, including what he had set aside to send back to his mother in Pernambuco. Without worrying any more about the heavy-breasted woman, who seemed to be watching him, the man put his mouth up against the boy's ear and asked the same question as before—"Why did you disappear?"—and, as before he got no answer.

They left, sheltered by the marquees, as soon as the rain had slackened somewhat, and got as far as Lapa. They didn't delay more than a couple of minutes, hurrying on to save time. Aside from the fact that he lived far away, the marine could not stay out late that night, as just by chance he was on duty the following day and had to be at the barracks early in the morning. They climbed up to Santa Teresa in a single breath, turned around the old colonial mansion on the corner, and reached the first streetcar stop at the old bridge. The man felt wobbly at the knees, his breath short, due to the exertion. They were in luck: a streetcar had just pulled up, and since he lived only a short distance from Curvelo Station, in fifteen minutes more, at most, they would be at the door of his house. They were alone in the shelter except for an elderly inspector dozing in the corner and a white-haired dog, apparently ownerless, that came to lick the man's hand and had to be chased away. But the streetcar showed no sign of starting, and the man began to fear that his scheme would not work out as planned. He turned an anxious, fixed gaze on the marine; his round face, with its heavy beard, closely shaven, like a dark blueish shadow on each cheek, bore traces of hope and at the same time a fear of loss, and his heart beat more forcefully. But he was determined to take the boy to his apartment, whatever the consequences might be, and for that reason he tried to behave more pleasantly, to show him that although he had been offended he bore no grudge, that he was ready to forget what had happened, to take up again where they had left off. He asked the boy if he was tired and he said simply that he was, without pursuing the matter any further, and the man concluded that he knew he had a debt to settle and that nothing else interested him for the moment.

The streetcar was already stuffed with people and they couldn't find a seat. The seats were all wet and most of them were facing backwards. So they had to ride standing up, squeezed once again between a couple who had a foreign look about them and a gentleman with a goatee, loaded with bundles and books. With all the jostling about inside the streetcar as it climbed, the man's body rubbed against the boy's, and that fierce uncontrollable desire rose up in him again. But this time he did not reach for his cock; at such close quarters it would be almost impossible for anyone to notice unless he just happened to be unlucky. He slipped one arm around the boy's waist while the streetcar lurched and bounced about like a small tugboat, still holding fast to the railing above him with the other hand. When he felt that warm bulky thing brushing his thigh the boy glanced back and smiled; the man smiled too and clasped him tighter around the waist. On a sharp turn the streetcar jerked to the side and then took a dip that brought from the tracks a strident sound of iron against iron, throwing the passengers one against another. The man put his mouth against the boy's ear and asked him something, but, since the boy did not understand what he said and glanced at him immediately with a sharp questioning gaze, the man repeated the question.

"Okay now," he said, "why did you disappear?"

But just at that moment the streetcar pulled into Curvelo Station and they had to get off. They lingered for some time then in the station, wondering what they should do next. The weather was still bad. The other passengers went on their way protected from it by raincoats and umbrellas. With nothing to shelter them, they had to take to the street again to avoid the fine rain blown about by the wind, stepping around the puddles of water that the downpour had left on the muddy pavement. Halfway along they decided to try the sidewalk even though it looked slippery and dangerous in the dim light. That was the only way to avoid the loose stones left at random by the workmen who had started repairing the old colonial streets several days before. When they reached the entrance of the building the man had to stop and rest; he noticed that the sky had cleared somewhat, though it was still full of low, dark clouds, and a great beam of light was dividing in half the waters of the bay.

They hurried up the stairs without worrying about the neighbors, and then the man's first act, as soon as the door closed behind them, was to envelop the boy in a long and almost irrational embrace. But the boy remained totally indifferent to it, for when he had decided to go along with the man he had resolved to let himself be possessed sexually for one last time and then never again, neither with him nor with any other man. When he tried to kiss him the boy turned his pale face aside and pushed him back. The man made two more attempts, both with the same results; the boy proved stubborn in his resolve. Annoyed, the man pulled him tight against his chest as if he wanted to crush him, to melt their flesh together, embracing him with such force that their bones cracked. By that time the man was no longer in control of himself, and suddenly he let loose a deep strangled sigh, and his body stiffened and then went limp; he had to hold to the boy to keep from falling. Seconds later he felt the sticky, still-warm liquid trickle down his leg and turn into a cold uncomfortable paste between his shin and his sock. A pleasurable sensation of release invaded him, a delicious fatigue, and still embracing the boy he slept that heavy dreamless sleep which, though it lasts only a few seconds, leaves one with the feeling that it lasted much longer.

He went to the bathroom to pull off his pants, wet with semen, and changed into a pair of shorts, taking time to wash himself. Back in the living room he found the boy sitting in his underwear on the edge of the couch. He was leafing through one of those magazines with color photos of men and women engaged in intercourse which an old friend from the university, now a diplomat, had sent him from Denmark. He sat down beside the boy, who continued to look calmly through the magazine, and surrounded him with a strong, nervous embrace; his arms were trembling slightly and his heart was pounding with such force that it seemed about to leap out of his chest. Soon he relaxed the embrace and let his nervous hand ramble over the boy's body, from his sweaty back down to his flanks, and from there over his smooth round buttocks and back up to his fine waist, like that of an athlete, where it came to rest. His heart beat faster and faster, while his temples throbbed, warm and sweaty. Calm, without betraying the least trace of constraint, the boy continued looking at his exotic pictures with the certainty of someone who knows beforehand what he must give and what he will receive in return and so can take his time about it. When he realized that it was time to begin he put the magazine aside and turned toward the man with a smile and offered him his mouth, all with no great enthusiasm. It was not until then that the man noticed that he had lost a molar and now had a small scar in the corner of his upper lip. He forced him to stand up, and, beside the couch, still mouth to mouth, he began to undress him, nervously pushing down his shorts with his one free hand. When he was about to lead him toward the bedroom the boy tapped him lightly on the shoulder with the tips of his fingers, indicating that first he had to go to the bathroom to piss or to use the john. Immediately the man let go of him, suddenly remembering (though it was already too late) that at the most inappropriate moments the boy had the bad habit of asking to go to the bathroom or insisting that he was terribly thirsty and had to get up to get something to drink.

"Is there any water in the refrigerator?" he asked, adding that he had had a few drinks at his sister's house and that had left him with an awful thirst.

"There's some cold water from the filter," the man said in a slightly hostile tone of voice. "The damned refrigerator's been out of order for days now and the repairman still hasn't showed up to fix it."

He wasn't satisfied with just one glass, not even a big tumbler filled to the brim, and he asked for another. Frowning, the man went back for a second glass, visibly annoyed. Then he stood in the middle of the room waiting for the boy to finish it, hiding his great impatience only with some difficulty. But the marine, without the least sign of any hurry, savored the water gulp by gulp like a thirsty mule that happens upon a spring after a long time out in the sun and sets about killing its thirst. Each time a swallow of liquid passed down his throat it made a dull gurgling sound like that of a bubble of air rising from the muddy bottom of a pond. And the boy drank slowly, taking his time. Once again the man's desire became so exaggerated and obsessive that it could have been compared to a pain that had been bothering him for days with no remedy to deaden or allay it. It was all he could do to keep from snatching the glass from the boy's hand and smashing it against the wall. When at last the boy had quenched his thirst he turned toward the man, who, still annoyed, motioned him toward the bedroom with his hand. His heart was pounding wildly, and a horrible headache which he always got when things did not go his way was threatening to set in. Suddenly the boy grabbed the pillow and hid his face, just as if that were the first time he had done such things and he felt ashamed, or as if he wanted to play hard to get and be begged. Furious, the man seized him by the shoulders and forced him to turn over on his stomach, and when he saw that he was going to put up no resistance, that his reluctance had been nothing but a silly game, he crawled on the boy's back and screwed him. His tan face was pushed against the mattress, his mouth half open, twisted by the pressure, while one arm hung over the edge of the bed. He slept, or pretended to sleep, through the whole thing. Still not satisfied, the man fucked him a second time, more violently than the first, as if he were determined to leave the boy's sweaty flesh marked indelibly with a strong memory of himself.

After they finished the marine slept deeply and peacefully for a quarter of an hour or so with his forearm curved beneath his head, his legs together, while his throbbing stomach, lightly covered with hair, rose and fell with the same rhythm as his breath, low, healthy, almost inaudible. At one point the man felt an urge to bend down and kiss him on the navel, but, afraid of waking him, he had to be satisfied with a light caress, watching him as he slept. Suddenly then he felt like going to the bathroom to piss and to get a cigarette for himself, but he decided to stay put, to leave that for later since there was no particularly urgent need for him to do either. He wanted to stay beside the boy as long as he could because he had come to the conclusion that, in coming to the apartment with him, the boy had made a concession somewhat against his will and that once he left this time he would never come back, that this was his way of saying goodbye.

The man felt tempted to keep the marine beside him in bed for some time still by engaging him in a long conversation. He needed to speak his mind, to get things off his chest as soon as possible, and the occasion would never be more favorable. But he realized that he would get nowhere, that the boy would never tell the truth, and so he desisted. When the boy woke up he would launch into a sort of routine, an unpleasant ritual such as a person completely devoid of imagination might engage in, and only with great effort would the man be able to put up with it. He would get up, go to the bathroom, return, begin to dress immediately, and then, once he was ready, he would pick up his folder, look at the man with a soft lingering gaze, and tell him in a low voice that he was leaving. No one, then, could make him stay a minute longer. He would do it all without a superfluous word, everything perfectly timed, and though he would make an effort not to show it, he would be visibly in a hurry to leave. It always happened that way, except on those occasions when he came prepared to spend the night. Then the schedule of events was different: they would have dinner and then watch television until late in the night, preferably old movies with actors whose names the boy barely knew or had never heard mentioned; last of all, they would have a snack and go to bed.

In an agile, almost catlike movement, the boy woke up and slipped his leg across the man's satisfied body and stood on the floor, barefoot and naked, heading off immediately toward the bathroom. As usual he lingered in the bathroom for some time. When he returned he stood for a minute or more in the middle of the room with his gaze fixed on nothing in particular, like someone about to make an important decision; then he reached his arms above his head, stretched his whole body, and yawned.

"Do you have any cigarettes?" he asked.

"Over there. Look for yourself," the man answered casually.

He had bought a pack of Hiltons before going to the movies and had not even opened it. In all the commotion he had left them in the pocket of his coat, which he had thrown across the sofa as he entered the room with the boy. He didn't feel inclined to get up and go back to the living room just to get a cigarete, and so he didn't move. If it were something else, medicine for example, he would have moved, but not for a cigarette. When the boy saw that he was going to stay put, he got up and went off lazily toward the living room. He had not dried himself well and his long muscular back had an opalescent sheen along the curve of the spine and a little below the shoulder blades. He sat back down with the pack of cigarettes in his hand, opened it quietly, took one out and stuck it in his mouth without bothering to offer one to the man. It wasn't until then that he remembered that he had no matches, but there was a lighter among some papers on the little table in the corner. He reached out his hand, took it between his fingertips and lit the cigarette. He had hardly taken one puff when he raised his hand to his mouth and gave two short yawns, one after the other, which served as an advance notice that it was time for him to get dressed and go home. Nevertheless he remained seated with the cigarette between his teeth. He was bluffing, and behind all of his actions there was a hidden purpose. At the very least he was waiting to see if he could get a little more money than the man usually gave him when he brought him to the apartment. But he was deceiving himself. The man's patience suddenly ran out, reached its limit, and he felt a need to make the boy suffer, to humiliate him. He stretched out his arm and turned off the radio. Acting as if he understood that the man intended to provoke him, the boy continued smoking calmly, his gaze wandering distractedly about the corners of the room. The man was left with no choice but to play the role of the scoundrel and try to hurl some degrading insult in his face, something that would hurt him and belittle him.

"You have somebody else, right?" the man said.

"Somebody else? What do you mean?" the boy asked in a soft voice.

"Somebody new. Come on, you know what I mean. Are you trying to play innocent with me?" he added with a vicious smile.

"I don't know what you're talking about," the boy said without changing his expression. "I really don't know what you mean."

"I mean that you've got another man," he said in a biting tone. "You're not going to try to tell me that—"

"So far I've been with only one man," the boy said with an air of certainty which always disoriented the man, "and I have no intention of going with any other."

"Then why did you disappear?" the man asked once more, raising his voice.

"And who said I disappeared? I was sent to Angra dos Reis for some training and I didn't have time to let you know . . ."

"Do you really expect me to believe that?" the man said mockingly as he tossed the sheets aside.

"Believe whatever you want. Have I ever lied to you before?"

The boy's excuse, intelligent and much to the point, left no doubt whatever but the man continued to believe that he was lying, that he had not gone for any training in Angra dos Reis or anything of the sort. That story might fool someone else but he couldn't be taken in by it. Then the urge to know why the boy had disappeared and whether or not he was living with someone else came back to him with an obsessive insistence. But once more he managed to control himself. The thing that intrigued him most about the whole situation, something he would never be able to understand, was why, if the boy really intended to break off the relationship and call it quits, he had not taken advantage of the time, about three months back, when his girlfriend had moved in with him. Could there have been a more propitious moment or a better excuse? But still the boy had continued to seek his company, phoning him punctually every week to have sex with the same enthusiasm as always, just as if there were no woman in his life and the girl did not exist. A possible explanation suddenly occurred to him: maybe the boy had begun to change with the birth of his child, when he had become a father, and the man, too self-centered and concerned with his own affairs, had failed to notice the transformation. The boy's only alternative then would have been to disappear, to drop out of the picture, or to continue leading a double life which was probably very distasteful to him. But all of that was nothing but a hypothesis, a supposition, and the man needed some objective concrete facts if he were not to be left forever with that nagging doubt, never really knowing whether the marine had lied to him or not.

"And how's your wife?" he asked, trying to change the subject.

"She was pretty sick last week, but she's doing better now."

"And the kid?"

"He was sick too with diarrhea, but he's already over it too."

"Can he talk yet?"

"Ah no, not yet. It's much too early for that," the boy said with a weak smile.

"Someday soon you'll have to take me over for a visit. I'd like to see the kid. And am I still his godfather?"

"Of course, why not? Unless you don't want to be anymore," the boy said with no great conviction.

"Sure I want to be! It's up to you to set a date for the baptism. What about next Sunday?"

Suddenly the man felt rather tired, with no desire to get out of bed for any reason whatever. But he decided to get up in spite of himself, and in a second he was on his feet. He looked for his sandals, put on his pants, went to the closet, took a bathrobe from the racks and slipped into it. He spent five minutes or more in front of the mirror combing his hair until at last he was satisfied with it. No one could say that he was vain, but at the same time he was not one of those people who love to lounge around the house, reading, watching television, or listening to music. With the air of a child who likes to catch visitors by surprise he smilingly moved back toward the bed and threaded the four fingers of his right hand like a comb through the boy's thick black hair. Still not satisfied, he took the cigarette from the boy's mouth (his second) and put it in his own mouth just as lovers do in the movies; he took a deep drag, let the smoke filter out slowly through his nostrils, and then returned the cigarette to the boy. Taken aback, the marine glanced up at him quickly, gave him a forced and rather graceless smile, and then lowered his head and continued smoking, his round smooth buttocks pressed against the edge of the mattress, which yielded to the weight of his body. Suddenly the man felt an unpleasant sensation, that familiar hissing in his chest when he breathed, but he did not allow himself to be affected or frightened by it. He went to the bar, poured himself a half glass of whiskey and drank it at one shot. There was no better remedy for the chronic asthmatic allergy that returned to plague him at that time every year, whenever he exerted himself in any way or whenever he got his feet wet and then delayed changing socks and shoes, as had happened not long ago. That time he had spent a wretched night. Most of the time on such occasions he would finish off half a liter of whiskey and then he would not be able to go to sleep until around dawn. When he went back to the bedroom the marine was quietly thumbing through the magazine of nude women that a short while earlier, against his will, he had been forced to lay aside in order to satisfy the man's wishes. Seen in profile, he bore an even greater resemblance to Jairzinho the soccer player. He no longer looked like the boy, contradictory but passionate, apparently free of hang-ups, who in those weekly festivals of pleasure always assumed a secondary role of a not very honorable sort, either for money or for the pure and simple joy of surrendering himself to another man, whichever the motive might be. Now he gave the impression that nothing had happened, that it was something remote, not worth remembering, and that once he stepped out of the apartment it would be completely forgotten, consigned forever to the past. When he had decided to go home with the man that night he had acted out of gratitude and nothing more, in recognition of the great deal or little that the man had done for him during the last two years, feeling at the same time that he should leave with a clear record, owing nothing, free of all obligations, like a weak beam of light disappearing bit by bit from the dusty floor of an empty room, leaving no trace. He wanted to leave nothing behind him, however insignificant, of which he might be reminded later.

"What about a drink?"

"I'd rather have a glass of water," the boy answered.

"You mean you're still thirsty?" the man asked with some surprise.

He went to the kitchen and selected one of those big cheap tumblers, the type that servants use, filled it to the brim and set it on a tray. Then he decided it was best to carry it in his hand to avoid spilling any water on the carpet. When he returned to the room the marine got up quickly, throwing the magazine aside, and took the glass. He had already put his jockey shorts on again. As before he gulped down the contents of the glass in one long swallow, with the greediness of a thirsty animal, making the same curious gurgling sound as the liquid flowed down his throat. As soon as he finished he began to get ready to leave, with no rush, as always, though he knew that it was already late. Two things were on his mind at the same time: what excuse he was going to give his friend in the barracks now that the end of the month was drawing near and he had not gotten the money he needed to repay him, and his son, who for lack of a cradle had to sleep in the middle of a big double bed with pillows at each side to protect him. Seated on the edge of the bed, his legs crossed, a glass of whiskey in his hand, the man followed the boy's slow silent movements with the knowing, paternal smile of a father watching his rebellious son getting ready to leave home. It was strange that the marine had come only once in his uniform, and then the man found it more becoming than civilian clothes. He had never forgotten that seventh of September (it had been raining rather heavily in the morning but later in the day the sun came out) when he went to watch the parade, or rather to watch the marine march past with his rifle on his shoulder, sweating profusely in a sumptuous red outfit, hot and heavy, that could have been taken off some dead soldier in the days of the Empire. At that point he became aware of how he was trying to store away in his memory the slender long-lined figure of the boy and whatever else he could of his personal traits and characteristics: his slow calm movements, the color of his skin, his smile, his manner of looking, his coarse tone of voice, his sudden silences. But why try to deceive himself, if within the space of a year or less he would remember nothing, if everything would be reduced to a memory of a memory and that too would soon fade away? When he finished getting ready, the boy picked up the folder and positioned himself calmly in the middle of the room, waiting for the man to get up and open the door for him. But the man didn't budge or even uncross his legs. With his eyes fixed on the boy standing there motionless in front of him, he raised the glass to his lips again, drunk but still in control of himself, and recalled with a feeble smile the last time he had seen the boy, just before his unexplained disappearance. He remembered clearly the day and the hour, the music that was playing when he came into the apartment and turned on the radio, the special perfume of the antique hardwood furniture, the sickening smell of wash-water coming from the underwear that the maid had washed that morning and left to dry in the bathroom. He had stayed in his office until late that day taking care of some papers and when he was about to leave the marine phoned ("Could I speak to Dr. Sampiao, please?") to say that he urgently needed to see him. He left immediately and went to wait for the boy at the usual spot. He was somewhat apprehensive, expecting the worst, for after all that was not the day on which they always met, and to make matters worse the boy showed up an hour late. They headed for the station, took the streetcar, and it was not until they were halfway home that the boy announced that his baby had been born.

"Have you named him already?" the man asked.

"Yes, Leandro."

"Who does he look like, you or his mother?"

"Some people say he looks like me, but others say he looks like his mother," the boy said with a laugh.

"Is he pretty?"

"Pretty! A newborn baby is never pretty," he said, laughing again.

The birth of the child had apparently changed nothing, and nothing could be expected to change from one moment to the next. That, at least, was what the man told himself. And if things did speed up and take a quick turn, heading off in another direction, it was something that he could never have presupposed. It took him by surprise. That night, in violation of his usual habits, the marine drank whiskey with soda water and smoked heavily. And then he stayed later than usual. Deep inside he was happy. At one point he began to talk about his plans for the future, already behaving like a man loaded with obligations, the father of a large family, with a long task ahead of him. He wanted to spend only one more year in the military, he said, and as soon as he got out of uniform he would go to work as a partner on an estate that his father-in-law owned in

Campo Grande. It was a small farm, but the soil was rich and very productive, with lots of good sugar cane and bananas, corn, and many other crops. And its yield could be increased considerably; it was just a question of putting your heart into it, with your shoulder to the wheel. One of his sergeants wanted to get into the deal as a partner (assuming that the father-in-law was willing, of course) and their idea was buy a truck and take their produce directly to the market. It wouldn't have to be a new truck; one of those used trucks would do, since a new one would cost a fortune and their capital was very limited or nearly nonexistent. He wanted to build a new house too on the spot where the father-in-law lived because the old house, in terribly bad condition, was not safe anymore. A good downpour and the whole thing might come caving in. And aside from that he was going to dig another well. The one already there was a mess too, full of mud. They would raise pigs, at least five or six head, along with thoroughbred chickens, and they could supplement their earnings by selling eggs and young roosters at the door of the house. He didn't expect to get rich but he did want to get by, like his elder brother-in-law, who was a taxi driver, and he wanted to have enough to furnish the house with everything that a family really needs, even when they're poor. Radio, refrigerator, a gas stove, a good TV set. And later, a car, even if it had to be second-hand. Since he had never gone beyond elementary school, he wanted to give his kids a good education. Wasn't that the kind of life he should try for? That night the man didn't have the nerve to suggest they go to bed, and at last it was the marine who started undressing. Then they moved into the bedroom. On his way out that night the boy had suddenly turned back and kissed the man tenderly on the cheek for the first time.

"Leaving already?" the man asked in a husky voice.

"Yeah."

"And when will you be coming back?"

"I'll give you a call."

"Okay, you know the number, don't you? Or have you forgotten it already?"

He put the whiskey glass on top of the little table, got up, smiled at the marine as he followed close behind him, and headed toward the living room. He picked up his pants, removed the wallet that he always carried in his back pocket and took out two ten-cruzeiro bills, the new type that had just recently been put into circulation. But to his great surprise the boy refused them, pushing them back with his hand. Annoyed, the man told him, almost in a shout, that they were to buy a gift for the baby, and then he reluctantly accepted them. After he had opened the door for the boy to leave, listening to his measured steps as he descended the stairs, followed by the dull thud of the street door, which he must have closed in anger, the man went to the kitchen and put a kettle on the stove to brew some coffee. Whenever he felt too drunk, or whenever he was bothered by something, he always tried to make himself a pot of strong coffee as quickly as possible. There was nothing better; it hit the spot like nothing else could. Suddenly then an unexplainable euphoria came over him, an urge to sing and laugh at the same time like someone who had just had a narrow escape in an accident and felt a need to celebrate his new lease on life. Back in the living room he put on a recording of Paganini's violin concerto, low enough not to bother the neighbors, returning immediately to the kitchen to serve himself a mug of coffee to drink while he listened. but soon, without understanding why, he had had enough of the music and he turned the stereo off. He got up and went to the back room, which had a beautiful view of the Bay of Guanabara, and there, to his surprise, he noticed that the sky was full of stars, completely clear, and that the moon, huge and brilliant, had just risen. He felt like having more coffee but resisted his desire, to avoid having to go back for the cup that he had forgotten to bring with him. With his arms crossed on the windowsill he stood for some time calmly gazing at the city down below. During all that time there were few things that caught his attention: a plane landing at Santos Dumont, and, minutes later, another one taking off (maybe they were the same), a small night watchman, with mixed Indian and black blood, who blew his whistle several times from different streets, a black tomcat and a tannish she-cat noisily making love on top of a wall, and the flat thud of an avocado as it fell from the solitary tree in the garden. It was almost dawn when his eyes grew heavy and he began to feel sleepy. He closed the window to shut out the chill and went to bed.

Caio Fernando Abreu

CAIO FERNANDO ABREU was born in 1948 in Santiago, Rio do Sul, Brazil. He began writing at the age of six ("It's a natural thing, a manufacturer's defect perhaps—the impossibility of living life without inventing things on top of it") and had his first story published in 1966 while he was still a student in Porto Alegre. In 1968 he moved to São Paulo and two years later won the Fernando Chinaglia Prize for his volume of short stories *Inventário do Irreme-diável* (Inventory of the Irremediable). In 1971 he moved to Rio de Janeiro where his novel *Limite Branco* (White Boundary) was published. In 1972 he returned to Porto Alegre and then, in 1978, moved to São Paulo, where he currently lives. His collection of short stories *O Ovo Apunhalado* (The Dagger-struck Egg) appeared in 1975 and received an honorable mention in the National Fiction Awards. His fourth book, *Pedras de Calcutá* (Stones of Calcutta) was published in 1977. Translations of individual stories by Abreu have appeared in Germany and Spain, and one of his stories— "London, London, or Ajax, Brush and Rubbish"—was made into a film in Europe.

About a recent vacation he writes: "The sunsets were very pretty. I spent the best summer of my life.... Loved a lot and did yoga beside the sea, very thankful for being alive and having traveled through all the placed I've traveled through, for having lived everything that I've lived, and for being exactly what I am."

VISIT

I WOULD LIKE to have stayed there forever, standing on those decrepit stairs, feeling the shadows thicken in the garden behind those steps I was now treading, reaching back to the little rusted gate that only moments ago I opened, hearing the noise of the street filtered through dense foliage, gazing at her aged, sweet face, her hair tied over the nape of her neck and an old cameo hanging against her lace collar, an antique look about her, as if she would like to play the piano at dusk, sipping something light like jasmine tea while the shadows on the stairs moment by moment grew denser until the cries of the children began to sound numb and suddenly she would realize she'd been left completely in darkness, in spite of the street lights reflected with cold splendor in the dusty crystal of the cupboard, and then.

Then she looked at me with her kind eyes accustomed to the shadows and maybe she could not quite make out my form against the still-sunlit street, but I stood perfectly still until I saw that her lips were parting amiably, as if with a smile, an antique smile, one of those beamed at a photographer taking an anniversary photograph, and in order not to bother her I said simply that I'd like to see his room, and it was difficult for me to say anything at all, and I can't remember if I really spoke or if I just put my hand in my pocket and showed her a crumpled newspaper clipping, without saying anything, and then if her smile broadened, understanding but still cautious, and if she stepped back slowly consenting to my request and after that if she led me through the silent carpeted hallway and if I saw the portraits of old dead relatives aligned on the wall and by combining the eyes from one, a wrinkle from the corner of the mouth of another, a stray lock of hair from a third, the solitary mien of a fourth—and before she paused at the foot of the stairs, the fingers of her left hand touching the white railing, a little surprised by the way I lingered behind—but before that I had had enough time to compose his likeness, feature by feature, from the portraits of his dead relatives, and like a harsh claw memory gripped me and to keep from suffocating I glanced back at the little parlor with its wicker furniture and saw the piano in a corner with the cup of jasmine tea and a fine thread of steam rising from it, and.

And then if I smiled at her, kindly too, and slowly climbed the stairs, matching my steps to hers, looking down at her thick-heeled shoes, then turning my gaze away, toward my own hand, as white as the railing on the stairway, and that harsh claw caught my throat again and I thought, then: I thought of his fingers, every day, so long ago, trailing along the same dusty railing, smelling the same vague scent of mold arising from all the corners, and if I stopped again, weighed down by it all, and again if she drew close to me at the door of the room, telling me in a low voice, so low that I try to recall whether she really said anything at all: that this is where he lived: and if she pushed the door with her slow way of moving and turned on the light, and then.

Then I seemed to catch from her eyes a fugitive glimmer of tears too often held back, and before going in I paused to consider once more, fiercely almost, that I could still turn away and run back down those stairs, without touching the railing, could still make my way back through the hall without glancing up at the gallery of portraits, could go back through the worm-eaten door, back across the garden, and open again the little rusted gate and step back into the street, warm with sun and life, but.

But doing none of those things, moving away from her fragile body and stepping inside the room and realizing, then, that I could no longer turn and run away, and.

And inside the room, looking at the books scattered about on the shelves, the bed with its sheets all in a mass, as if only a short while earlier someone had gotten up from it, and some reproduction or another on the wall, maybe a twisted figure by Bosch that I would later look at more closely, touching things maybe, maybe I'd touch the yellowed papers and smile thinking of all the monsters he carried about inside himself without ever showing them to her, she who said she'd touched nothing, dressed all in black, just that ivory cameo around her neck, and for a moment I had wanted to take hold of her until with fingers the color of the cameo she stroked the hard veins in the door and said nothing, as if everything around us were growing dark and suddenly just that movement of her fingers over the hard veins in the wood of the door had life, though it was dead, and also that thing called loneliness which we must feed with trifling rituals lest memory dissolve like an old tapestry exposed to the wind. She is no longer smiling.

All she says is that it's best for me to be alone, for me to close the door, and then she leaves, leaving me entangled in a movement that I'm compelled to choose, because it isn't possible to remain enthralled forever in the middle of the room, attentive only to the swift and chaotic unwinding of memories. But I do nothing. I remain standing in the middle of the room and the door closes behind me. And I look out at the roof where we used to throw breadcrumbs for the little birds, hidden to keep from frightening them off, until they came, but they never came, it was difficult to seduce winged things, we knew even then, but still we continued throwing out crumbs which, untouched, dissolved in the rain. It was easy to imagine him there, to hear him climbing the stairs two steps at a time, to imagine him opening the door and standing there looking at me without saying anything, and then we would embrace and as before I would feel his stray locks brushing my face like a harsh claw, and then I no longer knew how to see anything, to hear anything, and then I shifted my body from the middle of the room toward the bed beneath the window and buried my head in the tangled sheets hunting for some kind of warmth immune to time, immune to moths and dust, and I hunted his scent in all the corners of the room, and I called to him by the name he once bore, and I found nothing because everything slips away and the blowing winds carry the sheets of paper far away, out beyond the windows opened onto the roof where there are no longer any breadcrumbs for the birds that never came. But I hold back my tears, even though all at once I am down on the floor, looking for the mark of his shoe, a bit of thread or a hair, his hairs were always falling out, he dropped them out the window onto the roof, in the afternoons, and we believed that one day we'd be important, though we were satisfied with little daily joys that we didn't share, both afraid that our modesty would be ridiculous to the other, for we wanted to be epic heroic romantic undisciplined suicidal, because it was hard in the outside world to pretend that we were like other people, but in the corners of that room we had strength, blood, sperm, fever perhaps, as if we had malaria and were deliriously journeying through the same hallucination that the icy iron bed doesn't bring back, because that is all gone now and it's useless to continue here, looking for what I'm not going to find, among books that I don't dare to open for fear of finding his name, the name he bore, and proving to myself that life is nothing but this, mine, and that I didn't exchange it for another one made of dreams, of inventions, of fantasies, though still I hear him say that he unerstands that others must have felt the same sorrow, and they endured it, but that this sorrow is his, and that he would not endure it and realizing that all that has slipped away like the warmth in the cup of jasmine tea forgotten on the piano, and.

And then to grow hard to think that everything happened in a kind of dizziness, and to deny the painful testimony of memory and the same purple light of dusk falling through the greenery and the windowpanes to cast misshapen shadows on the white wall, and to shake off my shoulders as if all the dust on them were real, almost able to see the tiny shining atoms dancing a moment in the air before settling onto the carpet, the books, the unmade bed, and then.

Then to turn off the light and descend the stairs once more, without looking at my fingers almost lost against the whiteness of the railing, and to go back through the parlor and talk to her without her seeing me and back through the hallway, her beside the piano, and back to the door and through the garden as if I could forget everything that I didn't see, but to look back just before opening the gate and it would be, then, like seeing her so diluted that I would not know if she were really there and would ask her something in a voice so loud that the people in the street would stop to look and I'd be certain that she hears me, that she isn't seated beside the piano in the dark purplish room with her cup of tea getting cold, in a voice so loud that I would oblige her to turn around and face me and say firmly yes, no, that all of this isn't true, that all of us, she, he, I, and all the steps and all shadows and all the portraits are part of a dream dreamed by someone else, not by her, not by him, not by me.

A STORY ABOUT BUTTERFLIES

ANDRÉ WENT CRAZY yesterday afternoon. I should add that maybe it's a little arrogant of me to put it that way—*went crazy*—as if I were perfectly certain not only of my own sanity but also of my capacity to judge the sanity of others. How should I say it then? Maybe *André began to behave in a strange manner,* for example. Or *André seemed a bit disorganized* or even *André appeared to be much in need of a rest.* Be that as it may, after a while, soon, and so slowly that it was until yesterday afternoon that I decided something to be done about it, André—excuse my boldness or arrogance or haughtiness or whatever you want to call it—André went completely mad. I thought of taking him to a clinic, for I vaguely remembered having seen on TV or maybe in the movies a green place full of very calm people, all withdrawn and a little pale, with gazes that had nothing to do with this world, reading or cutting out paper dolls, surrounded by nice, helpful nurses. I thought André would be happy there (and I must say, in spite of all I've had to suffer lately because of him, I would still like very much to see him happy). But one glance at the balance in my checkbook was enough to tell me that a clinic was out of the question. Then I decided on the hospital. I know, it seems rather harsh to say it that way, in such a matter-of-fact manner: then-I-decided-on-the-hospital. Words are treacherous and misleading. To tell the truth, I didn't exactly "decide." The fact is (1) that I had very little money and André had even less, or rather none at all, since he stopped working when the butterflies began to emerge from his hair, and (2) a clinic is very expensive and a hospital is free. Furthermore, those places like the one I saw in the movies or on TV are always very far away (in Switzerland, I think) and I would not be able to visit him as often as I'd like. And the hospital is right nearby. So, having clarified the matter, I repeat: I decided on the hospital.

André didn't put up the least resistance—sometimes I think he's always known that in one way or another he'd have to end up that way. So I helped him into a taxi, and then we got out, walked across the courtyard, and at the main entrance the doctor on duty didn't ask many questions. Just name, address, age, whether he'd been there before, things like that—André kept quiet and I had to supply all the answers just as if I were the crazy one instead of him.

Never for a moment did the doctor doubt my word. It even occurred to me that if André were not really crazy, and I just said he
was, that would be enough to keep him there for a long time. But
his appearance left no doubt, the way he just stood there, without
saying anything, his eyes fixed and his hair all in a mess. When the
two male nurses were escorting him in I wanted to say something
else but couldn't. He stood there in front of me, looking at me. No,
not exactly looking at me because it had been a long time since he
really looked at anything—his eyes seemed to be turned inward, or
sometimes it was as if they actually gazed through people and things
and saw, deep inside them, something that even they did not know
about themselves. His way of looking even gave me the creeps,
because it was a very . . . to be honest, a very wise gaze. Completely
insane, but extremely wise. And it's not very pleasant to be subjected to such translucent gazes all the time, especially in your
own home. But suddenly his eyes seemed to blink (they shouldn't
have blinked because—let me explain—a blink, for me, is a sort of
comma that the eyes insert into a conversation when they want to
change the subject). Without blinking then, his eyes blinked just
for a moment and returned from that world André had moved to
without leaving a forwarding address, and then they looked at me.
Not at something about me that even I didn't see, not through me,
but toward me in a *physical* way, I mean, toward that pair of gelati-
nous organs located between the forehead and the nose—toward
my eyes, to speak more objectively. André gazed into my eyes as he
had not done for a long time, and it surprised me and I felt like
telling the doctor on duty that the whole thing was a joke, that
André was perfectly all right, since he was looking at me as if he
actually saw me, since he had recovered the polite and almost
friendly expression of the André that I knew and lived with, as if he
understood me and did not hold it against me for having taken him
there, as if he were forgiving me, because it was not my fault, nor
his either, that he had gone mad. I wanted to take him back home
with me, to undress him and lick him all over as I used to do, but
there was that stack of papers all signed and full of Xs in the little
boxes beside the words *unmarried, male, white,* and so on, and the
nurses standing beside him, fidgeting a little already—all of this ran
through my head while André's gaze lingered on me.

"You can only fill a glass to the brim," his voice said, quoting
from Lao-tse, "and then not a drop more."

Then I left. The nurses seized him by the arms and led him

inside. There were some other crazy people watching it all through a window. They were ugly, dirty, some of them toothless, their clothing streaked, soiled, smelly—it frightened me to think I might return one day and find André like them, ugly, dirty, toothless, his clothing streaked, soiled, and smelly. I thought the doctor was going to put his hand on my shoulder and say *Courage, my good man,* as I had seen in the movies. But he did nothing of the sort. He lowered his head over the stack of papers just as if I were no longer there. I turned half away without saying any of the things I had wanted to say—for them to take good care of him, for them not to let him climb out on the roof or spend the whole day cutting out paper dolls or picking butterflies out of his hair as he had the habit of doing. I walked slowly across the courtyard full of sad madmen, stopped for a moment by the iron gate, and then decided to go back home on foot. It was late afternoon and the streets were awful with all the cars, the distracted people, and the sidewalks full of shit and filth—I felt bad and very guilty. I wanted to talk to someone but I had withdrawn from everyone since André began to go crazy, with that look of his tearing me apart inside, and I had a feeling that my own way of looking had become like his, and suddenly it was no longer just a feeling: when I realized it, I was looking at the people around me as if I knew something about them that even they didn't know. Or as if I were gazing straight through them. They were unsavory types, pale and dirty. When I looked through them I saw what they had been before—and what they had been before was a thing without color or form, and I could let my eyes rest in it because they felt no need to worry about naming it or giving it a color or an appearance—it was smooth and calm white. But that smooth, calm whiteness frightened me, and when I tried to turn back I began to see in people what they did not know about themselves, and that was the most terrible thing of all. What they did not know about themselves was so alarming that I felt as if I had violated a tomb that had been sealed for centuries. The curse would surely fall upon me, and no one who knew that I had been so daring would ever forgive me.

But something inside me was stronger than I was, and I could not help but see and feel behind and beyond those pale, dirty types, and then I realized that all of them there in the street and in the city and in the country and in the whole world knew that I was seeing exactly in that way, and suddenly it was no longer possible to pretend or to flee or to beg forgiveness or to try to go back to that earlier way of looking—and I was sure that they all wanted vengeance, and at the moment when that certainty came over me I stepped up my pace to escape, and God, God was by my side: there was a taxi stand on the corner, I climbed into a cab, told the driver to drive straight ahead, threw myself into the seat, closed my eyes, breathed deeply, and dried my sticky palms on my shirt. After a while I opened my eyes to look at the driver (discreetly, of course). He was keeping a close watch on me through his rear-view mirror. When he saw that I was looking he turned his eyes quickly away and switched on the radio. *Ladies and gentlemen, it's now six in the afternoon,* a voice on the radio said. *Please tighten your seatbelts and prepare your minds for the takeoff. In just a moment we'll be leaving on a long voyage with no return. Attention now, we're beginning the countdown: ten—nine—eight—seven—six—five . . .* Before the voice got to *four* it dawned on me that the driver was one of them. I told him to stop, paid the bill, and got out. I don't know how, but I was right in front of my house. I went in, turned on the light in the living room and sat down on the sofa.

The house was quiet without André. Even with him it had been quiet recently: he always stayed shut up in his room, cutting out paper dolls or sitting against the wall, his eyes staring in that peculiar way of his, or sometimes in front of the mirror searching for the butterflies that emerged from his hair. First he would rummage around with his fingers, pushing his locks aside, and then he would find a butterfly exactly as if it were a louse. Proceeding very carefully, he would take hold of it by the wings, between his thumb and his index finger, and then he would throw it out the window. *That was one of the blue ones,* he'd usually say, or some other color. Immediately then he'd climb out on the roof and repeat a lot of things that I couldn't understand. From time to time a black butterfly would turn up. Then André would undergo violent crises, would get all alarmed, would weep, break things, and accuse me of all sorts of wrongdoings. It was when the last black butterfly appeared that I decided to take him to one of those green places, and later, to the hospital itself. He broke all the furniture in the room, then tried to bite me, saying it was my fault, that it was I who put the black butterflies into his hair while he slept. That was not true at all. Often while he slept I would just move close to him to watch him. I liked to see him that way, oblivious to the world, the light-colored hairs on his chest rising and falling over his heart. Then he was almost like the André I had known earlier, the one who used to bite my neck furiously in our sweaty nights of long ago. Once I happened to trail my fingers through his hair. He woke up abruptly and glared at me in horror, seized my wrist roughly and said that now I could no longer pretend that it wasn't I, that he had caught me redhanded in the exact moment of treason. It was some time ago that he came to be that way. I was very tired, too tired to understand any longer.

But now there was no André in the house. I went to the bath-room with its heaps of soiled clothes, its drippy faucet, to the kitchen where the sink overflowed with dirty dishes and pots and pans that had been there for weeks, with dusty curtains on the window and the sweet smell of grime in the corners. After that I resolved to gather up my courage and go to his room. André wasn't there of course. Just his magazines scattered all over the floor, a pair of scissors, and paper dolls among the pieces of broken furniture. I picked up the scissors and began to cut out some paper dolls. I invented stories as I clipped, gave the dolls professions, pasts, presents, futures too though that was harder to do, but also I gave them some sorrows and a few dreams. It was then that I felt something like an itching in my hair. I went to the mirror and looked. It was a butterfly. One of the blue ones, I was happy to discover. I took it between my thumb and index finger and set it loose at the window. It fluttered about for a few seconds, hesitating in a perfectly natural way since that was the first time in its life that it had found itself over a roof. When I saw its hesitancy, I climbed up on the windowsill and stepped out onto the roof-tiles to advise it.

"That's the way things are," I said. "The world out beyond my head is made up of windows, roofs, clouds, and lots of those un-pleasant white creatures that you see there below. Don't spend much time close above them or you'll run the risk of piercing them with your gaze or seeing in them things that even they can't see, and that would be as dangerous for you as it is for me, that violating of the tombs of centuries, but you, being a butterfly, can avoid them without much problem: all you have to do is flutter above their heads and never light on them, because if you light on them you'll run the risk of getting tangled up again in their hair and being reabsorbed into their swampy brains, but in case you can't avoid it, due to bad luck or a moment's carelessness, you mustn't torment yourself too much, it wouldn't help in the least—just try to slip inside those brains of theirs as smoothly as possible or you may be cut to shreds by the edges of their thoughts, all of which is quite natural, just don't be too afraid—try only to preserve the blue color of your wings."

My advice seemed to calm and reassure it, and it livened up and headed off toward the sunset. When I was about to turn around and climb back into the room I noticed that my neighbors had been watching me. Without giving a second thought to them I went back to my paper dolls, and soon the same thing began to happen again: a bubbling sensation, the mirror, the butterfly (a violet one this time), the window, the roof, the same advice. And then the neighbors and back to the paper dolls. And so on for some time.

It was no longer afternoon when the first black butterfly appeared. As soon as my thumb and index finger touched its viscous wings my stomach contracted violently and I screamed and broke the object nearest to me. I don't know exactly what, I only know there was a noise from the fragments I made, all of which leads me to suppose it was a china vase or something similar (at that moment, I think, I remembered a sound from the nights of earlier times: the fringes of the shawl on the wall falling over the strings of André's violin as we rolled out of bed onto the floor). I tried to break more things and to scream even louder, to cry too, if I could, because I had nausea, and never more—when I heard the sound of footsteps in the hall and a number of people invaded the room. I think I looked at them first in the way I used to look. I managed to recognize some of the neighbors who had always watched us, the man from the bar down on the corner, the gardener from the house across the street, the driver of the taxi, the resident manager of the building next door, the whore with the white shawl. But immediately everything expanded and I couldn't keep from seeing them in those other ways, even though I didn't want to, and the only solution was to close my eyes, but when I closed my eyes my vision turned inward into my own brain—and in it I discovered an infinitude of black butterflies nervously fanning their sticky wings, clamoring all over each other in a rush to sprout through my hair. I fought for some time. I still had some hope, though the hands that seized me were many.

At dawn today they got the best of me, and then they called a taxi and brought me here. Before getting into the taxi I tried to suggest some place with a lot of green, with friendly, helpful people, all of them withdrawn and a little pale, some reading books, others cutting out paper dolls. But I knew they would not allow it: anyone who had seen what I had seen was unworthy of forgiveness. And besides all that, I had completely unlearned their language, the language that had also been mine, and though with some effort I might be able to recover it, it was not worth the trouble, it was a language so loaded with lies, so full of ambiguity, each word meaning several things in several other dimensions—I could no longer hold myself, like them, in one dimension, every word billowed outward and invaded so many kingdoms and so many kingdoms that in order not to get lost I chose to be silent, attentive only to the bubbling up of butterflies inside my brain. When they went away, after filling out a stack of papers, I stared at one of them in the same way that André had stared at me.

"You can only fill a glass to the brim," I told him, "and then not a drop more."

He seemed to understand. I saw how he was disturbed and tried to say something to the doctor on duty but couldn't say anything, observed the way he lowered his eyes to the stack of papers and the indecisive manner in which he walked across the courtyard and stopped in front of the iron gate, glancing to both sides, and how he then went away, on foot. With no more delay then the men brought me inside and threaded a needle into my arm. I tried to fight back but they were very strong. One of them held me down with his knee on my chest while the other jabbed the needle into my vein. I sank into a deep well padded with whiteness.

When I awoke, André was looking at me in a completely new way. Almost the way he used to look at me, but with much more intensity and calm—as if now we shared the same kingdom. He smiled. Then he reached his right hand toward my hair, joined his thumb to his index finger, and very gently extracted a butterfly. It was one of the green ones. Then he lowered his head. I reached my fingers toward his hair and pulled out another butterfly. It was one of the yellow ones. Since there were no roofs nearby, they fluttered about the courtyard while we chatted together about those very things—me about his butterflies, him about mine. We stayed there for a long, long time, until I, without meaning to, pulled out one of the black ones and we began to fight. I bit him many times, drawing the blood from his flesh, while he sank his fingernails into my face. Then the men came, four of them this time. One of them held each of us down with a knee against the chest while the other two stuck needles into our veins. Before falling back into the well padded with whiteness we managed to smile at each other and stretch our fingers toward each other's hair, and then, with our index fingers and thumbs joined, at the same time, with very great care, we each extracted a butterfly. That one was so red that it seemed to be bleeding.

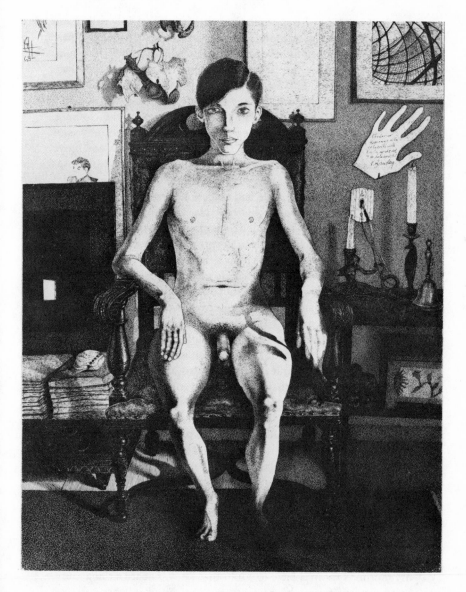

Drawing in Chinese ink (1966) by Federico Undiano (Argentina)

REQUIEM FOR A FUGITIVE

IT WAS NOT that I was afraid. Just that he was terribly pale. Even without ever having looked into his face I knew that he was pale in the same way that I knew how cold he was without touching him. He had been there for a long long time; he was there, in fact, before I came along. When I was a very small child I used to see him there whenever my mother opened the closet, and I would always look for his long hands hanging down among the clothing. At first I was too young to speak and couldn't ask who he was or what he was doing there, and by the time I began to talk and move about there was no longer any need to ask because my curiosity was gone. I just knew that he was there among all the dresses and hats. I knew that he was there, pale and cold, almost as if he wasn't there. At times I felt moved by his solitude and his faithfulness. My mother never came to challenge him in any way, but, for that matter, she never acknowledged his presence either. He simply did not require attention. It was enough that he was there, tangible but remote like the back wall of the closet.

When I had grown a bit I was given a room of my own and that increased the distance between us. Even so I did not forget him. Partly because it would have been impossible to forget him, and partly because I didn't want to. The truth is that I loved him. Not with a carnal love that would have made me want to touch him, to find out all I could about him. No, it was a different sort of love, almost nothing more than the certainty of knowing that he was always there when my mother had to go out and leave me at home alone or when there was a storm. More or less the same feeling that people have for an old knickknack or a piece of antique furniture. The only difference was that I could not stand the thought that someone else might feel the way I did; to state it clearly and simply, I was jealous. I knew nothing really about his private life, but still at times I had a sneaky suspicion that there might be something going on between him and my mother. Today is the first time I've ever had the courage to admit that, and I only admit it now because something terrible has happened. Many nights I lay awake and tense in my bed, straining to hear sounds—*certain* sounds—from my mother's room. I have to admit that I never heard a thing. Sure, from time to time I heard a creaking in the woodwork, or a rat scurrying secretly by, or any number of those innocent sounds that one hears at night. Those are common things that happen in all houses, I suppose—I say *I suppose* because I've never lived in any other house but this one. But even so I would shrink up with hatred at times when I heard them. I would imagine them in bed making love, and the mere thought hurt me more—much more—than anything else I have had to endure, with the possible exception of what happened this morning.

My mother was always very proper and correct. It's true that she had been a widow from as early as I can remember, but it's also true that she never made me an accomplice in her widowhood. She had her problems, sure, but she never shared them with me. She always worked them out silently, discreetly, knowing well that I knew but without ever once looking to me for help or advice. The same for his presence in the closet—she never discussed it with me. At the same time she didn't try to hide it, and that attitude on her part left me reasonably convinced that there was really nothing going on between them. She would open the closet door in front of me and I could peep in freely without her trying to hinder or encourage me. But she never mentioned him. She never mentioned him or any other man, either inside the closet or outside the closet. And I don't think it was because she didn't trust me. She never gave me any reason to think she didn't trust me, or, for that matter, any reason to think she did. Though we never talked to each other she was always polite and kind. I don't remember ever hearing her speak in a low voice or a tender voice or any other kind of voice, but that doesn't matter now. The essential point I want to make is that she never shouted. And if it's true that we never came to love each other, it's also true that we didn't hate each other. I really believe we stumbled upon the ideal form of communication and togetherness.

Our life was very hard. We never actually suffered from cold or hunger or any of those things. But life was hard because it had no color, no rhythm, no form. The days passed one after the other, on and on, on and on. Seven of them made a week, and then the week doubled to make a fortnight, and the fortnight doubled into a month. The months accumulated and formed years, and then the years piled up into decades—and nothing ever really happened. I had the feeling that I was living inside a bubble of gas, enormous and hollow, in constant rotation. Life only slowed down when I took advantage of my mother's absence and opened the door of the closet to look at him. I never dared to look up at his face because I thought a long period of training would be necessary before I could subject him to a direct encounter. It wasn't that I was ugly or disfigured, nothing like that. It was just that there was nothing unusual or interesting enough about my appearance to make me worthy of his gaze. What I mean is, his vision was made only for things that deserved it. So I was content to stare at his feet and his legs, moving up only a little above the knees to that point where his long hands hung idly at his side. That in itself was wondrous and dreadful—his feet, his legs, his knees, his hands. It was so overwhelming that I could not bear to look higher. The sight of him would have been too much for my eyes which, unlike his, were made for trivial things. He was barefoot and his feet were very slender. He had marvelous toes with a perfect bone structure and one small detail that distinguished them from all others—his second toe was bigger than the first and it had an indescribable perfection about it, with its tip slightly squared off and the nail slightly bluish, much as if he were anemic or very cold. It was with this second hypothesis in mind that one day with my head carefully bowed I switched some of the clothing around and left my mother's fur coat closer to him. That didn't seem to improve things at all because the following day the nail on his second toe was still blue. The only difference I could find was that the half-moon at the base of the nail was a little thinner. I couldn't see his legs now; my view was blocked by a white dress so long that it even hid his ankles. But even through the cloth I could intuitively sense the delicacy of his bone structure—a delicacy confirmed by his hands, those marvelous hands. They were worthy of a poem, a painting, a symphony. I know it sounds a little ridiculous for me to speak of them in such terms but I have no choice. Whenever we try to explain the unexplainable we sound a little trite. For that reason I exempt myself from any attempt to describe them. I will say simply that they were there, that even the splendor of his feet paled beside them. Those hands invaded my dreams. My dreams overflowed with those hands. At times they pointed out the path I should take, at times caressed my hair, at times danced as if possessed of a life all their own. I would wake up frightened by my own boldness—so frightened that I came to wish that in one of those dreams they would do something harsh and unfriendly so that I could hate them or fear them. But they never did.

Then last night my mother died. I was in bed in my room when I heard her die. The sound was unmistakable. None of her little music boxes, none of the casual happenings of the night, none of the lovers she might have had could ever produce such a sound. It was somber and hoarse like things that have no afterwards. I held still for a moment and listened without being affected in any way because I had always known she would one day die like everyone else. It neither scared me nor surprised me to think that that day could be yesterday, today, or tomorrow. After listening for five minutes or so I put aside the paper flowers I have the habit of making and went to her room. When I went in the intensity of the sound had already diminished, and when I touched her it ceased completely. I took it for granted that she was dead. I phoned the doctor, who confirmed my suspicion, and then I phoned the funeral home. They put her in a box and took her away. During the rest of the night I was more sleepless than usual. Now only he and I were left, and I had no idea how I should behave toward him, how I should let him know what had happened. My feeling was that people like him were somewhat difficult, too touchy maybe, and he was so much paler than the beings that I saw through the window that I was really at a loss as to what I should do.

This morning I summoned up all my courage and opened the closet door. He was there in the same place as always. It was only then that I had my suspicion confirmed, for up until then it had been merely a suspicion. My doubts dissolved and a certainty came over me. Yes, he really *was* an angel. I don't know if he was an archangel or a cherub because I don't understand anything about hierarchies, but I do know—indubitably, irreversibly, unmistakably—that he was an angel. I looked up at him. Something told me the time had come and I looked up at him. I must confess that I had expected a smile or some other show of affection, but there was nothing of the sort. I couldn't even tell if his hair was dark or blond, chestnut or russet. All I could see was an intense brilliance and all I heard was an almost deafening sound—no, how should I say it?— rustle?—yes, that's it—an almost deafening rustle of wings. He quickly flew out the open window, hovered over the uppermost branches of the plantains and then disappeared. I thought I heard his voice saying he'd return but he didn't say when. I don't really know if he said that out of kindness, just to console me, or if he'll really come back some day.

What I would never have imagined before is that a house could feel so empty without an angel. There is something inside me that waits for him to return, expecting him at any moment. Maybe he'll fly back through the window or maybe he'll just reappear where he was before. To keep him from taking me by surprise I've left all the windows and all the closet doors open. While he's away I'm preparing two wreaths of flowers, one for my mother's tomb and one for the closet where he used to live.

PORTRAITS

SATURDAY

I had never noticed him before. To tell the truth, there's nothing to distinguish him from all the others. The same bright-colored clothes, the same long hair, the same dirty drugged appearance. I had never seen them from up close until today. From the window of the apartment they all seemed to form one single mass, colorful but drab. The whole affair failed to interest me. Or, for that matter, to bother me. Even so I did sign the petition that the tenants in the building circulated asking for their removal. But nothing came of it. In the elevator I heard somebody say that someone very important must be protecting them. That struck me as amusing because they look so forsaken. I think it was that thought that moved me to go down to the square this afternoon. Yes, it must have been that. I didn't find anything strange about them, nothing such as the petition had claimed. They were simply there, in a way that didn't offend me. One of them smiled and made a sketch of me. He was like the others, exactly like the others, except for a string of beads with a little skull on it. All of them had necklaces but only he had a skull. The portrait was a good one. I know nothing about portraits really, but it strikes me as a good one. I think I'll have a frame made for it and hang it in the hallway by the door.

SUNDAY

I went out for a paper and ran into him. He asked me if I'd like another portrait. *I already have one,* I said. *Why would I want another?* He gave me a bright-toothed smile. *Have one done each day and you'll see what your face is like throughout the week.* I found that amusing. *You'll do seven of me then,* I said. *Seven is a magic number,* he said. *I'll do seven.* He asked me to sit on the cement bench and he began to sketch. I watched him as he worked. The truth was that he didn't resemble the others; he's always by himself and he always has a look of concentration. From time to time he raised his eyes and smiled at me. I felt weird because nobody had ever smiled at me— I mean, nobody had ever smiled at me as he did. His hands are finely made, almost blueish in color. When he sketches his hand moves rapidly. When he isn't sketching it holds completely still. Sometimes it even stops still in mid-air. There's something strange about that. I never saw anyone hold his hand perfectly still in the air for so long a time. While he was drawing me I felt ashamed— ashamed of wearing a suit, the old suit I use on Sundays, and a tie. I hadn't even shaved. The bottle of milk I had in my hand grew heavy, and ink in the newspaper began to stain my trousers. For a moment I had an urge to sit on the ground like they did. They would probably think me a little ridiculous. I restrained myself until he finished. When he handed me the sheet of paper I couldn't restrain myself any longer and I told him I had enjoyed today's session more than yesterday's. He laughed. *A sign that your face is better on Saturday than on Sunday,* he said. I paid him and left. I've put to-day's portrait beside the one he did yesterday. I look older, more worried, though the features are the same. Tomorrow I'll ask him his name.

MONDAY
Forgot about him until time to head home. There was a lot of work to do today. I came home tired, ready to take a bath and go to sleep. He met me at the door of the building. *What about our agreement?* he said. I said *Ah yes* and went with him to the square. His walk was slow, though he doesn't appear to be lazy like the others. I don't know exactly what it is but there's something about him very different from them. Sometimes I think he may have a sudden dizzy spell and fall. That's when he closes his eyes with one hand pressed against his head. Maybe he's hungry. I thought of inviting him to eat with me but decided against it. The neighbors wouldn't approve of it. Nor would the doorman. Aside from that, the apart-ment is very small and it's always a mess because the maid comes in only once a week. He's always barefoot, and his feet are finely made like his hands. It always seems that he's walking on leaves. I don't know how to explain it because there are no leaves on the square, not now. Only in autumn. His fingernails and toenails are transparent. When he was finishing up today's drawing I asked him his name. *My name is not made of letters or sounds,* he said. *My name is the whole of what I am.* I tried to ask what that name was but there was no time. He was already handing me the sheet of paper. I paid for it without looking at it. It was not until I got up here that I looked. It disturbed me. I am not a young man like yesterday and the day before. The face he drew today is the same one I see in the mirror by the entrance and that mirror always gives back a distorted image. I put the sketch on the table beside the others. The I felt it

was better to pin it on the wall of the room, just in front of my bed. I glanced out the window but couldn't spot him down there among the others.

TUESDAY

When I went out this morning I looked for him. I wanted to invite him to have a *café au lait* with me in the bar down on the corner. But I didn't see him. Last night it was cold. I've heard that they sleep on the square. At dawn I woke up thinking of him stretched out on the sand on that frayed military jacket he wears. I felt really sorry for him and couldn't go back to sleep. I found it hard to work today. I realized that the secretary has hairy legs and the boss is really quite fat. I know such things have no importance but I couldn't get them off my mind. This afternoon he was waiting for me on the corner. *Today's is the fourth,* he said. *Three left to go,* I answered. And I felt something tighten inside me. He has dark eyes that stare fixedly, holding still on one point in the same way his hands hold still. His trousers are ripped at the knees. I've never seen him talking with anyone. The others stay huddled together in a group, talking low among themselves and looking scornfully at people like me in suits and ties. He's always alone. Today he finished the drawing and handed me a daisy along with it. I had never even noticed that there were daisies growing in the square. To tell the truth, I don't think I had ever looked at a daisy up close before. They are round. Not perfectly round—what I mean is, the center is round and the petals are long. The center is yellow and grainy. The petals are white. I have placed it in a glass of water in which I dissolved an aspirin. They say that makes a flower last longer. Today's portrait is very unsightly. Not that it's poorly done, but that I look terribly old, gray, with a sad expression. I was surprised. It even made me afraid to look at myself in the mirror. Then I looked. I saw that it was my face he had drawn. Maybe he smoothed things over a little in the first drawing because he didn't know me then, and now that I'm one of his customers he can draw me as I really am. I noticed that the women in the other apartments were watching while I talked with him today.

WEDNESDAY

I thought the day would never end. Everybody at the office is so dull that time seems to take longer in passing. As soon as the hands of the clock reached six I grabbed my coat and ran down the stairs.

I bumped into the boss on the way. I noticed that he was hopping because his feet were swollen. There I stood gazing at his feet. He didn't seem as if he were walking on leaves. In the street I spotted a shop window full of necklaces and beads. He would be pleased, I thought. But what nonsense it would be, what with the month ending now and me short on money. Still I couldn't help myself. I returned to the store and went in. The salesgirl looked at me with a strange expression. *It's for my daughter,* I said. I left with a little package feeling heavy in my pocket, afraid he wouldn't be on the corner. He was. I saw him from a distance, very lean and tall. I lowered my head as if lost in thought. I started to walk on by him but he took hold of my arm. He took hold of it slowly. But even so I felt the pressure of his fingers. It was cold. I asked him if he wasn't chilly. *I don't feel the same cold that you feel,* he said. I didn't understand. The drawing turned out really ugly. I put it on the wall beside the others. Each day I look older. Maybe it's because I haven't been sleeping well. I have dark bags under my eyes; my skin is yellowish; there are thin spots in my hair. I shook his hand. It feels cold. Only two portraits are left to go. Today I discovered that his eyes aren't completely dark. They have tiny golden dots in the pupils like green eyes often do. The neighbors were watching me from their windows again, commenting softly among themselves. For the first time I didn't bother to greet them.

THURSDAY

Insomnia again. I stayed awake looking at the portraits on the white wall. It's horrible, the difference between them. In them I grow steadily older. It frightened me to think of the seventh drawing. And I closed my eyes. When I closed my eyes I thought I felt inside my head the same cold contact that I felt yesterday afternoon when his hand clasped mine. A touch that was cold and yet hot at the same time, firm and at the same time slight. Suddenly I remembered what he had said that day when he gave me the daisy. Was it *A flower is an abyss* or *A flower and an abyss?* I can't remember which but I know it was something like that. How could I have forgotten? I got up to look at the daisy. It was still yellow and white, still round and long. My day in the office was awful. Several times I made mistakes with my figures and I was rude to the secretary when she called my attention to them. She was offended and went to complain to the boss. I was afraid he'd call me into his office but he didn't. I pretended I had a headache and left early. In the bar I sat down and had two beers. When I stuck my hand in my pocket I felt the weight of the little package I had not had the courage to give him. The whole city was grayish even though the sun was shining. I saw fear in the faces of the people around me. At ten of six I got up. It was really a very pretty day and everybody was happy. I didn't look at him. I don't want him to think I feel envy or anything like that. I carried the portrait rolled up. For the first time the elevator operator didn't say hello to me or even open the door. In the portrait I look like a corpse. No, that's exaggerating a bit. I just look very downcast and beaten. The cold weather hasn't let up. Tomorrow I'll buy a bed. I want to invite him to spend these cold nights here. I'll say the bed belongs to my sister who's away on a long trip. I didn't have the nerve to give him the necklace, not knowing what he might think. Tomorrow I won't buy any cigarettes so I'll have the money for the last portrait.

FRIDAY

I only worked the morning today. By noon I couldn't stand the place anymore, couldn't stand those dull heavy people crushing the carpet like elephants. Couldn't stand those machines. I told the boss I felt ill. He was very understanding. He said he'd noticed that I look a little spiritless lately. I asked for an advance on the excuse that I needed to buy some medicine. Then I went into a movie theatre and sat through two runs killing time until six. In the film there was a young motorcyclist who resembled him. Resembled but no more, for I realized that there is no one else like him. I remembered my childhood, I don't know why, and cried. It had been a long long time since I had cried. At six I went to the square. But he wasn't there. I came up to the apartment and took a bath. In a few minutes I'll go back down. I don't know why but I'm crying again.

A terrible thing has happened. It's very late and he didn't show up. I can't understand it. Maybe he's sick or maybe he's had an accident, something like that. I can't bear the thought that he may be alone, hurt, maybe even dead. I have cried so much looking at the daisy he gave me. And it was today that he was going to do the last portrait, that I was going to give him the necklace and invite him to sleep here, to eat with me. I've just taken three sleeping pills and I feel a bit funny. Maybe he'll come tomorrow.

SATURDAY

Woke up early and went to the square. But I couldn't find him. I gathered up my nerve, approached the others and asked them where he was. Some of them didn't even acknowledge my question. Others among them looked annoyed. *But what's his name?* they asked. *You mean you don't even know his name?* I was ashamed to repeat what he had told me. It doesn't seem appropriate for a man of my age to say things like that. Nobody knew anything about him. I described his way of moving, his face, his blue trousers torn at the knees, his hands. Soon I lost my shame and told them how he seemed to walk on a cushion of fallen leaves, how his hands hovered motionless in the air, how his dark eyes fastened onto things. No one knew anything about him. I went to ask my neighbors. Three of them slammed their doors in my face and muttered things I couldn't understand. Two others told me they had rooms for rent, and I couldn't understand that either. I left and wandered about the city, spent the rest of my money on beer, couldn't find him. I phoned all the police stations and hospitals. I went to the morgue. He wasn't there. I went back home soaked in the rain, coughing and sneezing. I collapsed on the bed and fell asleep.

SUNDAY

I spent the day on the square. He never came. I took the portraits with me. I looked at them closely. There are six in all. The last looks like a corpse. They stared at me with scorn. I took the daisy with me. It was hot all day. I sweated a lot. I forgot to shave. This afternoon the secretary strolled by with her fiancé and saw me lying there on the grass. She didn't say hello but whispered something to her boyfriend. When it was already quite late I realized that he will never come again. I slowly walked back home but the doorman wouldn't let me in the building. He showed me a petition signed by the neighbors saying things I didn't bother to read. Then I came to this bar where I'm writing. It's raining outside. Maybe he's gone away, maybe he'll return, maybe he's dead, I don't know. My head is exploding. I can't stand it anymore. I spread the portraits out on the table before me. For a long time I looked at them. Slowly I pulled the petals off the daisy, one by one until only the grainy pith was left. The sixth portrait is a corpse. Maybe that's why he didn't come back. The sound of the rain is the same as the sound of his footsteps on non-existent leaves. *A flower is an abyss,* I repeated. *A flower and an abyss.* And suddenly it dawned on me that I am dead.

Aguinaldo Silva

AGUINALDO SILVA was born in Carpina (Pernambuco), Brazil, in 1944. He moved to Rio de Janeiro at the age of twenty and has lived there ever since, very active as a journalist and as a writer of short stories and novels. In 1978 he became editorial coordinator of the new gay cultural newspaper *Lampião*.

Aguinaldo Silva's first novel, *Redenção para Job* (Redemption for Job) appeared in 1961, when he was only seventeen years old. There followed, in 1965, his second novel, *Cristo Partido ao Meio* (Christ Divided in Half). Other novels include *Canção de Sangue* (Song of Blood), 1966, and *Geografia do Ventre* (Geography of the Body), 1968. His collection of short stories, *Dez Historiás Imorais* (Ten Immoral Tales) appeared in 1967 and was reprinted two years later. Silva's latest novels are *Primeira Carta aos Andróginos* (First Letter to the Androgynes), 1975, and *A República dos Assassinos* (The Republic of the Assassins), 1976. The former novel is a poetic celebration of homosexuality.

His story "O Amor Grego" (Greek Love), printed here for the first time in English, originally appeared in a Brazilian mini-anthology of three writers, titled *Vida Cachorra* (Dog's Life), in 1977. His Cinema Iris story first appeared in the fourth issue of *Extra*, a Brazilian literary journal suppressed by the government in 1977.

ELOINA'S LETTER AND TESTIMONY

[*A República dos Assassinos* (The Republic of the Assassins) grew out of Aguinaldo Silva's involvement with journalism, a profession to which he has dedicated much of his energy since 1962. His special interest, throughout all this time, has been the Brazilian subculture of organized crime and its complex interrelationship—not always hostile—with the organized forces of the law.

The Republic of the Assassins focuses on a particularly turbulent period in the police history of Rio de Janeiro—the years between 1968 and 1972, when the crimes of the infamous Death Squad reached their peak. It is a novelized account of the career and subsequent trial of Mateus Romeiro, a police official whose reputation as a man of the law has been abruptly eclipsed by the disclosure of his activities as a man of crime. The story of Mateus Romeiro (and thus of the vast network of corruption to which he belonged) is revealed, piece by piece, in the form of interviews, court testimonies, monologues, letters, and memoirs, by the people who knew him and were involved with him in some way or another.

The following two chapters from the novel explore Romeiro's relationship with a drag queen named Eloína, and dramatically reveal the aura of fear and violence that still hangs over the lives of the people who were touched by him.]

Eloina's letter

... you must certainly be wondering who is this queen who's writing to you from some unknown corner of the world, who refuses to address you in the tone you're accustomed to—that of your fan letters—but brings news of terrible things. Marlene Graça, you're doomed, marked forever like I am but you don't know it, stuck with the child of Mateus Romeiro and all the scars he left you. Because of that I'm writing to you now, now that he's abandoned you and fled. Just to let you know what kind of man you gave two years of life to, and at such a risk that now it will be hard for you to be what you were before, now that he's gone. Who am I? No, you don't know me, you've never even heard my name unless your ex-lover might have casually mentioned it in front of you, which is doubtful; he never talks about the people he kills, and he killed me, in a certain manner of speaking, one night in 1970, in a hotel room in Catete. It was there that he took my man, Carlinhos, and left him in the gutter. (Do you know what I mean when I talk about the gutter, Marlene? Did you ever realize that many nights when he came home to your arms Mateus Romeiro had left a man dead somewhere in the gutter?)

My name is Eloina. My whereabouts are unknown because I'm hiding from Mateus, though by now he doesn't even remember that I exist. I gave this letter to a truck driver, along with a little money, and got a promise from him that he'd mail it when he got to Rio. That way you will not know where I am (even though you're separated from Mateus Romeiro, you're still a threat because tomorrow you might go back to him. After all, you had a child by him.) but at the same time you'll hear what I have to say. During these past two years I've collected all the newspaper clippings that have to do with him and have followed step by step the news of his downfall, knowing it would have to happen because that lover of yours is cursed and he ruins everything he touches. During these two years I've prayed that you would manage to get away from him before he ruined you, and now I see that my prayers have been answered. It was with joy that I heard the news that finally he— that terrible man—had been unmasked, and that the death of Carlinhos, my lover, appeared in the list of his crimes. And yesterday when I saw in the paper that he had fled to Paraguay I decided to write to you and tell you everything, pouring out onto paper the terrible story that is choking me.

I worked for Mateus Romeiro. Do you remember the deal with the travelers checks? We, the whores and drag-queens, stole from the tourists in the dirty rooms of cheap hotels and then handed their documents and checks over to Mateus for someone to forge the signatures. That gives you some idea of the kind of things he was mixed up in, but that's not what I want to talk about (I committed my crimes, too, for sure, but for me the only way to make a place for myself in a world that rejected me was to steal something from someone). What I want to talk about is the death of Carlinhos.

It was through me that he met Mateus Romeiro. In those days we had a room on Taylor Street in Lapa. I had met him two years before and we moved in together because we were both very lonely. In just two years we became more than lovers: we were brothers. One was the column that supported the other, you know how it is—such things sound ridiculous when you try to say them, but for two people like us, so much alone, they were essential truths (you must be surprised by the disparity between my story and the language I use to tell it, but don't be: when I left home I was about to start my second year of Classical studies—I left because my family discovered that I was queer. Anyway, bit by bit, I began to do a drag number in a cabaret called Casanova, and Carlinhos dedicated himself to robbing rich old queens. It was in the cabaret that a woman asked me to take part in that racket with the travelers checks. I couldn't make up my mind about it until she told me that the leader of the gang was Mateus Romeiro, a police officer whom I knew by name and of whom I was very much afraid. If he could do such a thing, I thought, then why couldn't I? We made a date then, and I was introduced to the bastard (you may not believe it, but that same night he fucked me).

A queen in need, you know, is capable of anything. So it wasn't long until I was one of the most active members of the gang, and because of that I acquired a certain prestige in the eyes of Mateus Romeiro (who had me many other times, honey, rest assured of that). And so one day I told him that I had a friend who was worse off than I was and that he needed any kind of job he could get. He said that men were no good for the routine with the travelers checks but that he had something better. And he said for Carlinhos to look for him, several days later, in a bar on Rúa Prado Junior—that's where he operated from, remember? That's how it all began, how we got mixed up with him without ever thinking of the tragic end that was waiting for us.

The work he had for Carlinhos was risky—and I begged him not to take it but he didn't want to look like a coward. This was the job: running stolen cars from Rio to Mato Grosso and then coming back with a load of cocaine. Two days after their first meeting Carlinhos was already on his way with the first car, and there began the long chain of events that could only lead to an unhappy ending. I begged him to quit, but how could he? Mateus Romeiro paid well and was the kind of person you couldn't get away from; he gave all of his workers the feeling that he cared for them and was protecting them—that soft, warm voice of his, remember? And his silk-smooth hands, his cold gray eyes (even today I'm torn between pleasure and repulsion when I think of him, and if you no longer love him, you must feel the same way.

. . . yes, I'll put your mind at ease: he was almost always drunk when he made love to me. And because of that I learned to associate the smell of liquor with sex, with dirty things in general, because of the way he hunched violently over me and spilled his rotten, stinking breath into my face. It was awful, awful and at the same time sweetly morbid to feel him on top of me, knowing that pleasure was only a moment away, regardless of what I had to endure to have it. During those nights he gave me the impression of being mortally dangerous; when he held me in his arms I felt as if I were on the brink of death—I always imagined the moment when he would finally kill me, when he'd enfold me in a last embrace and leave me lying there. I always thought he'd do it in one of his harsh, impulsive moments, him about to pass out, with me balanced precariously on the fine high-wire of my fear. I remember once, in a half-empty apartment where he took me, how he made love to me on top of a carved chest. I sat down on the edge of the chest and wrapped my legs around his hips, and he bit one of my arms until he tasted blood, while I moaned—yes, I moaned and whined with pain because the carved relief on the chest dug into the skin on my back as he entered me. Mateus Romeiro always seemed to me to get too involved in each sexual act, giving all of himself as if that were the last, and yet all of them left him unsatisfied. Once he told me that it happened that way because I was queer, that with women it was different; he said that while I was staring at his cock, so desolate-looking after so much effort. He said it and I kept quiet, and I closed my eyes and breathed deeply: I knew it was a lie, but who would dare to contradict a murder machine? No, Marlene Graça, don't think out of pride that he was better with you, that he fucked you with less desperate deliberation, for I know that Mateus Romeiro's only real delight was death.

. . . soon I became aware of something that troubled me even more: Mateus Romeiro, contrary to what the women had said, was not the leader of the organization. There was someone else above him, or some thing, probably too complex for us to understand it, and that was what frightened me. I heard conversations, stored whole sentences away in my memory, and, at times, thought I was piecing together the riddle and that the whole secret would soon be revealed to me, but before long I always realized that I was mistaken and I'd have to go back to the beginning and start again. One thing, though, I knew for sure: it was not only we, the whores and drag-queens, who were entangled in that sorry affair, but also policemen, journalists, lawyers, businessmen, all sorts of people whom the newspapers considered worthy of great respect, and who, in the street, would undoubtedly step aside to avoid coming face to face with the likes of us. Our criminality, one might think, would make us equals, but that was not the case. We were still the outlaws, the persecuted ones, and I knew that one day, if necessary, we would be the ones on whom the weight of the law would descend (the fact that Mateus' crimes have suddenly been discovered doesn't mean that he's going to be punished. Somehow or other, the others will find a way to save him. Furthermore, I suspect that only some unexpected defect in the gears of the system led to his being discovered at all—a defect that will be very quickly mended).

Yes, we moved to another apartment—why not? We no longer lived where we had lived before, we spent more money than we'd ever dreamed of, but always with the ominous feeling that we had been born into the world to be punished. And in the meantime, the others, those who pocketed most of the proceeds from those rackets—they were clean and respectable, and almost any day you could see their names in the newspapers, with Mateus' name alongside theirs. I could see the situation clearly and tried to explain it to Carlinhos, who refused to pay attention to what I said. In a way he felt proud of being a part of the organization; the whole thing, to him, was just a kind of adventure, and as for the danger all around him, he couldn't see it or didn't want to see it.

It was about that time when the first men were killed. I remember that two of them, Jonas and Oldair, were friends of ours and had made many runs with Carlinhos. But he passed off their deaths as two coincidences. Even when Jonas' wife told me that it was Mateus who had killed him, and I passed the word to Carlinhos, he refused to believe it (Jonas' wife, only days later, threw herself from the fifth floor of a hotel on Tiradentes Square). And, at the same time, we were caught up in the passage of time; we had to work, to survive, and if I was eager to convince him that it was time for us to pull out and run away, I nevertheless postponed from day to day any mention of the matter, and soon Carlinhos would be off again, on another run to Mato Grosso in a stolen car, and when he would come back with the load of cocaine or vials of Anorexil and Pervitin there'd be another car waiting for him. Mateus Romeiro, with his voice always warm and soft, drew us deeper and deeper into the net, his gaze promising me things that I tried in vain to reject. Suddenly one night he appeared in the Casanova cabaret where I sang *El día en qué me quieras* dressed in a fishtail gown. That night he winked at me.

Promises, promises. He, at least, promised something—I must give him credit for that (see Marlene, how I began this letter on a note of hatred, and now I can't avoid a certain tone of nostalgia). He promised each of us a violent death, and if we were not aware of that, it was because we didn't want to be—to tell the truth, we were caught between the organization and the world, and the whole affair, I realized later, was a terribly complex closed circle in which the organization and the world were a single unit, the world being merely the base upon which the other rested.

It was about that time that Mateus Romeiro's deeds turned him into a national figure. His name was in all the newspapers; his gray eyes stared disdainfully at the world from all the magazines. And he went to live with you, remember? You were a talented entertainer and all the publicity was good for you, as it was for him. And in the meantime we were left to suffer the consequences of his crimes.

One day Carlinhos came home frightened and said he couldn't live with me anymore because the São Paulo police were after him. Some mixed-up story, never completed, about drugs, something about a quick escape from a hotel one morning at daybreak, in which he jumped from one window to another down to the ground to keep from being caught. That, I knew, was the beginning of the end (an investigation of the travelers check racket was already under say, and through it the hand of justice would at last reach out for Mateus Romeiro and he would be included among the guilty). He would move to a hotel in Catete and stay there whenever he was in Rio, he said, and I could do no more than visit him. Almost at the same time the "spawning season," as the newspapers called it, began: corpses, always with the same tell-tale signs, appeared floating in the Guandu River. Handcuff marks on their wrists, a thread of tough nylon around their necks, and enough .45 calibre bullets in their bodies to make them look like seedbeds.

During the last days that Carlinhos was alive I could only communicate with him by letter. By then, our past was over, buried once and for all. I was no longer the queen who lived by whoring and he was no longer the boy who assaulted rich old fairies: without knowing it, we were fenced in, and for that reason the organization would soon get rid of us just like it had gotten rid of all the poor devils found floating in the "spawning ground." (Remember, Marlene? The newspapers said the killers were policemen, but they never printed a line about the motive for the killings. And with that they left the conclusion up to the readers: that if the police kill

criminals, it's really for the good of us all). In my letters to Carlinhos I pleaded with him and begged him to get out while he
could, for the two of us to flee while there was still time. I was
aware of certain things, I overheard conversations in the cabaret,
and I could see the despair on the faces of the women whose men
worked for Mateus Romeiro; it was easy to see that something evil
was going on, something beyond our comprehension, but in which
we were hopelessly entangled.

And all in vain. One morning Mateus Romeiro came into the
cabaret and didn't even glance at me—that was the first sign. Then
Carlinhos had to take a car to São Paulo and he stayed there for
some time. It was then that we exchanged our last letters, all full of
promises and oaths which, as with so many others, we would never
fulfill. Have you, Marlene Graça, ever foreseen the death of someone you loved, knowing that there was absolutely nothing you
could do to prevent it? Well, I could foresee the day and the exact
hour when Carlinhos died. I sensed it; something inside me told
me that he was dead, that everything had ended. When I looked for
him that day, I knew already that he was dead, and I knew that it
was Mateus Romeiro himself who had killed him because we were
his responsibility and he would not trust anyone else with the job.

And I knew that I'd be dead too if I didn't get out and if I didn't
do it so quickly that no trace would be left of me. I hurried to put
between myself and certain death a distance that can only be measured by the many sleepless nights I went through, by the many
times I've had to pack my bags at dawn and suddenly change hotels
or take the first bus leaving town, by the constant uneasiness and
dread, by the fear and loneliness I've had to endure (and still, even
today, any person who comes toward me can be death in disguise,
hidden beneath the false look of a friend). So many miles and so
many cities I've put between myself and that certain death, and
here I am now where I can see how it was tentatively postponed—
and Mateus Romeiro is on the run too, just like me.

But you, Marlene Graça, are the one who must be warned: he
touched you, for two years he marked you with his silky hands, and
there certainly were nights when those hands, as they caressed you,
still bore traces of blood. How can you remain indifferent to all
that? How can you turn away from all the evidence, all the signs,
the whispers, the hasty visits he had at dawn, his sudden trips out of
town? How can you fail to link the name of your lover to all those
deaths that affected him so greatly?

... it seems that it all became too obvious (the gears suddenly jammed, as I've said before) and Mateus Romeiro was arrested. By that time you were no longer living with him, but you already had the son that he left you. And you were no longer a respected entertainer because no one would give you a booking. You must feel terribly alone. To your memories of Mateus Romeiro I would like to add these few of my own. Imagine, if you will, a man being killed in a gutter. Imagine him pleading for his life. Imagine the terrible look in his eyes. And now, listen to the shots—one, two, three—and watch the force of the bullets hurl his body backward. Look now: blood is spurting from the wounds, but he no longer feels it—it all happens so quickly, death lasts only an instant, and then it's all over. Keep in mind, Marlene Graça, that this is the scene I see every night in my dreams, acted out by Mateus Romeiro and Carlinhos.

He was caught and he escaped, right? His henchmen helped him to escape. A simple jamming of the gears, a flaw soon corrected, and then just a note in the newspapers. Mateus Romeiro is in Paraguay, Marlene Graça, and I'm here. As for you, I hope you've learned your lesson: all those crimes, you purposely ignored them; afraid of them, you chose to know nothing of them, all to keep your peace of mind. For two years I've waited for the right moment to write this letter. And now it's in your hands. You will certainly be called to testify, and you'll say what they expect you to say: that you knew nothing of all this, that you heard nothing. But that, I promise you, will not be enough to protect you from remorse.

Eloina's testimony

Yes, your honor. I knew Carlos Alberto dos Santos. He was my friend. What does that mean? It means that we lived together, that we fought together, that we pooled our misfortunes and set out together to confront life with the only arms we had—that is, our countenance and our courage. Yes, illegal acts, as you say; you are a judge and you are familiar with such things. We had our work on the side, if that's what you mean. Because, as you know, it isn't always possible to live according to the law. Not because you don't want to—on the contrary, it must be nice to live honestly, much easier and more comfortable that way—but if you have no money to start out with, and not even a place to live, and—

You knew Carlos Alberto dos Santos?

I have to answer yes or no and cut out the commentary, right? But if your honor wanted to hear so little from me, why did you send for me in the first place? After all, I was just living my own life, and far away from here, far away from your jurisdiction. If my presence was—how did you put it?—harmful and undesirable, then it would be better for you and for society if I were as far away as possible. No, I didn't run, I just didn't feel like hanging around here anymore, and I needed to make more money (By crime at night? What crime?). No, I'm not playing dumb. It's just that so many crimes take place—a dozen come out every day in the newspapers—and I don't understand why you attach so much importance to this one. Sure I liked Carlos Alberto dos Santos, but not enough to keep him from getting killed (it must be nice, being dead). I know what a trial docket is, but I've never been involved in such a thing, and I want to make one thing clear: I'm not here of my own free will.

A lawyer? What do I want with a lawyer? I haven't committed any crime, or at least not one of those that people have to defend themselves for. Just frivolous misdoings, that's all. But, okay then, back to the night of the crime. I knew that two men had taken Carlinhos away. The doorman of the hotel told me about it. He didn't say anything else about it—he was a disgusting little man who kept staring at my breasts (excuse me, your honor) and he drank a lot too. I think he was drunk that night when . . . that night when Carlinhos died (okay, that night when they killed him). We had made a date to meet in the hotel. He was very tired and wanted to sleep. Why was he tired? He had just come in from a trip—he went to São Paulo very often, you see, but he never told me what he did there. There are things you don't tell even your best friends. And what if it was something too horrible to tell? No, really, I think it was just a personal matter, a woman maybe, who knows? But if I had known it was, sure I'd have beat the hell out of him—you see, I loved him. You're not here, you say, to listen to trashy stories? But look at me, your honor, I'm cheap and trashy, and if you don't want to see me why did you summon me to your court?

Anyway, the doorman told me they'd taken Carlinhos away handcuffed. I think he said handcuffed, but I'm not sure. Why should I remember such things? You order me to remember? What do you mean, order me to remember? That's all a matter of memory, your honor, and I've forgotten—that was a long time ago and everything was very confusing. But I think he said it was two men that took him away. And right there I began to feel scared, I mean, after all, I didn't know what it was all about or what Carlinhos had been mixed up in, with all those trips and the weeks when he'd suddenly disappear. Maybe it was something serious, who knows? I remember that in those days the newspapers were full of stories about how the Death Squadron had just executed somebody, or sometimes two or three people, or even five at a time. And since I was very close to Carlinhos the people who killed him would certainly think I knew too much. Yes, as soon as the doorman told me they'd taken him away I had no more doubts: I knew they were going to kill him. People like us, your honor, get killed for the slightest reason and nobody gives any importance to the matter (I know, Mr. Prosecutor, but what you are interested in is proving that a certain person killed Carlinhos, and for that reason you attach a lot of importance to his death. If that were not the case, neither of us would be here.)

I ran away that same night. I threw my things into a bag as quickly as I could and headed for Avenida Brasil, and in a gas station there I caught a ride with a truckdriver on his way to Belo Horizonte. He thought I was a woman, but what a shock he had on the road—it left him speechless. He dumped me in the middle of nowhere and there I stood with my bag in my hand waiting for another ride. From Belo Horizonte I went to Governador Valadares because I knew a woman who worked in the red-light district there and she got me a job in a club.

We are not interested in your artistic career. What did Carlinhos tell you the last time you talked with him?

It was by phone. He told me, honey, I'm awfully tired and I need some sleep. Yes, as I've already said, he'd just come in from São Paulo, I think. Why was he not living with me? Well, it seems that he had some problem in São Paulo, some nonsense he was involved in, but he never really explained it to me. I think it had something to do with the woman I mentioned.

No, I'm not trying to be ironic, nor do I think of my manner of speaking as improper. This is the way I speak, and all my friends speak this way too, and this is the language of my milieu—I mean, among us there's no one who spends his life in and out of court. Carlinhos must have been tired because he usually called for me to come over as soon as he got in from a trip. That day, however, he asked me to wait a few hours. No, nothing about what he said hinted that he might have been afraid—he sounded like that always, tender, like an overgrown child, your honor. I'm not going to cry, no, because crying is a difficult thing for me. It makes people forget that they have other ways of defending themselves. Crying is for people who have a home and food and someone to protect them. It's a luxury that one can get along without.

Stop talking in circles.

As I said, he was no different from usual. There was no fear in his voice. He didn't say that anyone was after him. Mateus Romeiro? How could anyone hang around Lapa or the Prado Júnior and not know him? I knew him, sure, and I was afraid of him. He was a police official, right?—And I'm a drag-queen. You see, your honor, the police had already stolen thirty-seven wigs from me—imagine what an expense for me! But Mateus Romeiro, no, he was not interested in such things—imagine a serious policeman chasing a transvestite! And that's what I think he was, a serious policeman, because the newspapers said so every day. And why would I not believe the papers, your honor, if they only print the truth? Me, for example, I believe what I read.

No, your honor, I don't know anything about travelers checks. I confess that I lived by prostitution (like I said, a person has to make a living), but I've never stolen anything—I've never needed to because my customers always paid me well. And Carlinhos, steal? Well, he was not completely honest—I can say that now that he's dead—but he never stole, and he never assaulted anyone or did anyone any harm.

So you deny that you knew Mateus Romeiro then?

No, I've already said that I knew him. I even talked with him a few times, but always in the most formal way. He was a very serious man, he seemed to me, with a very strong character, generally kind and considerate. He never harassed us. I didn't come here to defend him, but at the same time I'm not here to attack anyone either. What I want most is to live my own life. All of my actions are part of a process with a single objective: my own survival. What you can't imagine, your honor, is how difficult that can be, just to survive, how one ends up with a permanent feeling that everything is too transitory, that turning a corner, any corner, is an irreversible act—and we get slapped with a stick from all sides, often without even understanding who hit us or why.

Mateus Romeiro, for all I know, was a good, honest man. If he stole, if he was a gangster, I don't know anything about it. If he lured in prostitutes and queens to steal travelers checks from tourists like you say, I don't know anything about that either. He never asked me to take part in it, and none of my friends ever mentioned such a thing. And if he was the one who killed Carlinhos—well, in all sincerity, your honor, I find that very unlikely. Why would he kill him? They didn't even know each other and I doubt that their paths ever crossed. They simply had nothing to do with each other.

Yes, he died. That's a fact that can't be denied. But, your honor, how many others died as he did? Wouldn't it be best maybe to try to understand why people die in such a horrible way, naked, with handcuffs on their wrists, in a deserted street? You have your title, your honor, and a secure life (excuse my boldness) and you cannot even imagine the terror that we feel when we read in the newspaper that someone has died that way—Carlinhos or whoever. You just get into the habit of thinking you may be next.

You deny that you were sometimes seen in public in the company of Mateus Romeiro?

No, I've never been to the places you mention, or at least not with him. I'm going to be frank, your honor, and maybe a little unfair to myself, but do you really think that anyone—except somebody poor and forsaken, like Carlinhos—would have the nerve to go out with me, to be seen with me in any place where decent people go?—I say decent people and I mean men like yourself (and don't think I'm cringing and fawning, your honor) and men like Mateus Romeiro, the man that you're hunting and trying in vain to somehow link up with me.

I'm not here to attack anyone, but to defend myself—

You're here because we summoned you to court.

—okay, because you forced me to come, because you tore me away from the place I had chosen to live in, without any explanation. You didn't even give me time to grab more suitable clothing because you had to humiliate me too, to shame me—all those halls full of people, all of them staring at me. I wouldn't go so far as to say that I'm a citizen, because the truth is that after all these years of confusion and pretense even I don't have a clear idea of what I am anymore. But I wish you would not treat me like a person you want to throw into prison on any excuse whatever, especially since all of you talk so much about justice. Your honor, if I've committed no crime, if nothing has been proved against me, if it's now perfectly clear that I have nothing to do with Mateus Romeiro—and, most important of all, if it's equally true that there's nothing I can do to bring Carlinhos back to life, and he was a person whom I loved, for whom I'd do anything in my power, then I ask that you let me go.

Then you mean that the witness has nothing more to declare?

MATINEE AT THE CINEMA IRIS

IT WAS IN Irene's Place in Lapa* that I first heard of the Iris Theatre. I had been taken there to meet Deborah the flying queen, and when we were all assembled around her someone quoted a phrase that was written in gigantic letters on the wall of the john in the theatre: THE IRIS TOO IS BRAZIL.

Irene's Place was on the Rua dos Arcos, and it had been given that name because of an Italian song that was very popular at the time. There in its three floors, in endless rows of rooms set off from each other by thin wooden partitions, lived dozens of people who could never go out in the street in broad daylight without being pelted with stones: ghastly queens, street criminals at the end of their career, vitiated prostitutes and their not very demanding pimps. My visit took place toward the end of 1966. In 1967 the building got special coverage in the newspapers: during the heavy January rains one of the staircases collapsed and the tenants had to crawl to their rooms on all fours up two planks that connected the second and third floors high above the gaping hole where the stairs had been.

In the midst of all the squalor Deborah pontificated like genuine royalty. That day we found her lying on a sofa that looked more like a very old and battered coffin; there she received us in spite of her being somewhat indisposed. We gathered around her, eager for a look—eager to touch her and examine her, I should say, considering our unwillingness to believe the stories told about her. A lawyer, a journalist, a banker, and an Army sergeant, we looked like some kind of special reconnaissance committee sent by the outside world. Sighing profusely and drooping with languor, Deborah explained the cause of her indisposition: she had swallowed the key to the wardrobe where she kept her little boxes filled with a medicine for epilepsy. She was not actually epileptic, but she liked to shoot the medicine anyway. It was the fuel, she said, that made her fly. She had swallowed the key on purpose because she was in need of a rest, and that day while we waited for her to go to the bathroom, from which she would return with the key and open the wardrobe, she was being treated by the other queens who flitted

___
*In Rio de Janeiro. —*Ed.*

constantly around her administering antitoxic dosages of apples and milk.

As that year drew to its close, Deborah's flight was the most talked about event in the bars and cafés of Lapa. Even the police of the Fifth Precinct spoke of her in admiring tones: after all, they had been privileged to witness her first performance, and one of them had even fired a shot at her with his .45 when he saw her fly out the window and glide gracefully over the crown of an aged tree of the species *Ficus Benjamin.* It all took place in an old building on Rua Frei Caneca where five queens and seven prostitutes worked under Deborah's adept direction. There they subjected their clients to a professional shakedown which they carried out with such efficiency that one day the gentlemen of the Fifth Precinct, after hearing dozens of complaints, decided to intervene. At dawn they raided the building, and on the fourth floor, having already taken into custody the queens, whores, and some of their unhappy clients, they closed in on Deborah as she stood with her back to a window. It was then that the miracle occurred. She climbed onto the window-sill with the right corner of her mouth twitching frantically—a nervous side-effect of her too frequent injections—and there she announced to the incredulous policemen her intention to jump. "Go on, faggot, jump!" they answered mockingly—"Jump and save us the trouble of filing a report. Go on and splatter yourself all over the pavement!"

It sounds impossible but it happened: Deborah leaped, and her body, as if it were equipped with springs, landed feet-first on the pavement some thirty meters below after tracing a smooth curve over the top of the tree. It was over before the police realized what had happened—one of them did squeeze the trigger of his pistol, true, but most likely he acted from sudden fear. Without looking back, Deborah strolled serenely to the nearest corner and disappeared.

From that moment on she knew no peace. That same night the policemen spread the story all over Lapa, and then it jumped the boundaries of that section of the city and reached the headquarters of the Military Police, as well as numerous other precincts. From then on the racket on Rua Frei Caneca was raided at least once a week by MPs or other groups of policemen who always followed the same ritualistic routine: they arrested all the queens and prostitutes, along with their clients, and then they cornered Deborah by the fourth-floor window and observed with a mixture of awe and disbelief as the flitted away. The queens and whores, already lined up by the door of the paddy wagon, put the finishing touch on the show with a clamorous round of applause which Deborah would pause to acknowledge before turning the corner. On her better days she sometimes added an extra goodbye wave for the stunned policemen still leaning out the window and gaping in disbelief.

I was twenty-three years old at the time, had just discovered Jean Genet and had just moved to an apartment at 46 Rua Visconde de Maranguape in Lapa, where, as I used to say somewhat vainly and foolishly, I could observe the neighborhood in its final days. (The building I lived in was actually demolished in 1970 to make way for an avenue.) It did not take me long to realize that I was Lapa's most insignificant resident. To reach that conclusion all I had to do was glance off my balcony at all the dethroned royalty that night brought to the corner beneath my apartment. There in the dim light I could watch them parade back and forth, exhibiting their tattered clothing and their scars.

Deborah was one of those royal figures. Lounging on her coffin-sofa with a ragged shawl drawn around her shoulders and a broken fan hanging from one of her limp hands, she too had her scars to exhibit—her incredibly abused veins, red and studded with little bulbous swellings, deformed by countless pricks and jabs from hypodermic needles. It was Alex what's-his-name, the banker, who recalled the phrase written on the wall of the john that night when Deborah mentioned that she intended to go cruise the Iris if the apples and milk revived her sufficiently. Then I resolved to check out the place too.

Nowadays the intellectuals of Ipanema love to stage nostalgia sessions in the Iris Theatre. They all show up dressed in the styles of past decades—the Twenties, Thirties, Forties, whatever—and take their seats in the old projection room with its once-impeccable art nouveau decoration. Meanwhile, the real drama takes place in the auditorium outside, acted out by queens, firemen, soldiers from two nearby barracks, construction workers, and a few prostitutes, none of whom are ever invited to join the party in the projection room. Of all the people in the theatre, only a few old women have actually come to watch the film.

The theatre is on Rua da Carioca, a rather shabby thoroughfare that runs into Tiradentes Square. The street, always badly pock-

marked and always under repair, is lined with decaying old buildings that date from the turn of the century, the same epoch when
the Iris was inaugurated. Anyone observing the theatre on a day of
consecutive runs could well think of it as a vast beehive. In the
lobby, along stairs with art nouveau friezes leading up to the two
balconies, multiplied to infinity by what remains of the great bronze-
framed mirrors, the spectators come and go, constantly on the
move. The signs and friendly words they exchange in passing suggest that most of them already know each other, and probably it
was there in the theatre that they first met. An employee stands by
the entrance, oblivious to the people entering and exiting. At the
refreshment counter a woman dozes while a cat lolls on the glass-
topped display case, its one open eye monitoring the movement to
and from the auditorium. The theatre's decline into irreversible
decadence long ago took its toll on the entrance and lobby too,
once so elegant with friezes and elaborate handrails, with the great
mirrors which time left smoky and blurred. Now, by the door, a
sign announces the double feature of the day, *Kung Fu Battles the
Sons of Karate* and *I Give Her What She Likes*.

In the auditorium the movement is the same as in the lobby and
on the stairs. Many people are seated but the majority remain
standing, continually wandering about. When I pause to let my eyes
grow accustomed to the darkness, feeling my way along the curtain
that covers the back wall, I stumble upon my first surprise: a sudden movement beneath my groping fingertips betrays the presence
of two, three, four, five, maybe even a dozen people hidden there
between the curtain and the wall, all piled and huddled against each
other. A few more steps along the dark aisle toward a dim reddish
light that says GENTLEMEN and I am just in time to see a fireman in
uniform press a moaning bulk against the wall, just in time to hear
unprintable words, the type of language that we never use in front
of our families—

I headed toward the bathroom to look for my first prize—that
phrase quoted by Alex the banker. To reach the john I had to make
my way to the end of a long aisle between the wall and the rows of
seats. Another red light at the far end indicated that that door too
was for GENTLEMEN. I stuck my hand out to open it but someone
on the inside opened it for me with perfect timing, as if he had
known I was coming. "I'm the doorwoman, dear," a tall black queen
announced. I slipped on by her, climbed two flights of stairs that

seemed to be the gates to hell itself, and then at the top of the last one, straining my eyes to see through a dense fog of cigarette smoke illumined by the yellow glare of a forty-watt bulb, I caught my first glimpse of the men's bathroom at the Iris Theatre.

It was nothing more than a hallway into which some thirty people had squeezed. Each of the three urinals was simultaneously in use by six, eight, ten people who groped each other coldly. They were fingering each other, inspecting and examining each other, with a calm nonchalance and a curiosity that struck me as almost scientific. The doors to two of the three stalls were closed, and strange noises came from behind them—sighs, wailings, lullabies, grunts, howls, screams, curses. The third stall, open but occupied like the other two, was the stage for a scene that attracted numerous onlookers who crowded against each other at the door and gazed. The smoke, the sounds, the yellowish light, the impassive faces of the people— the whole scene made my blood run cold with fear and I was about to turn and flee when I noticed that the doorwoman, who had ob- served me step by step, was now positioned squarely against the door at the top of the stairs. "Go on, honey," she said in a hissing voice as I turned back. "Go on, there's nothing to be afraid of."

Stunned, cold with fear, I took two steps forward while the people leaning against the walls quietly smoking their cigarettes transfixed me with cold, indifferent stares. It was then that I caught for the first time the odor of the bathroom at the Iris Theatre. I had experienced such a smell only once before, and then it was in a morgue in Recife. It was the stench of death, of corpses. Midway down the hall I stopped again, weak at the knees, and looked back toward the entrance. The doorwoman, still in position, rose up to block my retreat, her eyes flashing with sudden hatred. "Okay, come on now," she said in a harsh, aggressive tone. "Don't you think it's time you made up your mind?"

I inched forward again, passed the smoky, fetid barrier of the first two doors, and joined the circle of curious spectators who squeezed together before the third door to observe the action inside. I worked my way in among them and looked: there inside, their pants down around their ankles, two men were rubbing and bumping against each other, and they were going about it in a furious way, almost with rage, moaning and crying out, cursing, muttering obscene words. Three men from the circle of spectators were already masturbating silently, their eyes fixed on the scene. A feeling of malaise and nausea started to swell up inside me, and I tried to keep my eyes turned away from that incredible spectacle before me. (Later the nausea would worsen, to the despair of the doorwoman who helped me to vomit and tenderly called me a débutante.) My vision roamed about aimlessly, skimmed over a commode with a broken brim and then drifted up the walls. To my left, high up in a corner, I spotted the inscription I had come to look for. In big black letters written by a firm and decided hand, letters bigger and grander than those used to scribble the tormented literature that adorned the lower walls, it proclaimed its message for all to see: THE IRIS TOO IS BRAZIL.

Drawing by Arlindo Daibert (born 1952, Brazil), from the series *Fragments of an Amorous Discourse*.

GREEK LOVE

I

IT WAS GOOD FRIDAY when I saw Cristo Xantopoulos for the
first time. The bars in Recife's Zone* were closed, all except the
Greek's bar—a ship from Piraeus had just docked and the sailors,
disappointed because all the whores were observing the holiday,
had taken refuge there for lack of anything better to do. There was
no music in the bar, and the bouzoukis on the makeshift stage
looked more useless and abandoned than usual. It was rare, even
on nights of great carousing, for the Greek to play them. And the
Wurlitzer jukebox was unplugged, with even its red lights turned
off—a good enough warning for anyone who might have wanted to
slip a coin into it. Music on days such as that one was a sacrilege
even in the Zone.

We respected the holy days in the Zone, but not without a certain sorrow in the heart. The purpose and intent of our lives, to tell
the truth, was nocturnal, and whenever night fell and the lights
failed to come on, when the women failed to come out and the men
did not take their usual positions on the corners—even worse,
when silence replaced the fine threads of music that the wind usually wafted over toward the docks, blending all the different rhythms
into one disordered din—then we could not help but associate the
quiet night with sadness and death.

On Holy Thursday that terrible mood had already begun to take
hold of me. By midnight, without being told to do so, the waiters
set about closing the doors of the bars and the women began to
exchange half-despairing glances and the taxi-drivers hurried to get
away, driving their last customers—all men—back home. That was
not my first Good Friday in the Zone, but each year I hoped that
something new would happen, that the observances would have
been modernized and we could spend that sanctified night on the
sidewalks as usual without relinquishing once and for all our slim
chance for forgiveness at the end of our days.

Since Holy Thursday was over early, at midnight, that night I was

---

*Recife (1970 population 1,060,752) is a port city on the Atlantic ocean, capital
of the state of Pernambuco in northeastern Brazil. —Ed.

not permitted to take my usual after-midnight place on the center of the stage at a cabaret called Chantecler, where, sporting a very tight, gold-colored gown beneath the silvery glare of the floodlights, I sang *The day when at last you love me*. Instead, at that, my daily hour of glory, I was wandering about in the dark streets trying to avoid my usual companions who, on such occasions of sadness, usually succumbed to attacks of babbling, spewing out meaningless words at the rate of a million a minute. Between my lips I held a cigarette that one of the women at Optima's boarding house had given me. I had left in safekeeping my gown, my wig, and all the other adornments with which I nightly transformed myself into the most beautiful and deadly of women—those dark streets were never safe. Always one courted danger by being out late at night, and, if nothing else, one could be overcome by the deadly, foul-smelling gas that rose from the piss that year after year thousands of drunkards had spilled there.

Suddenly the Zone struck me as absurdly unfamiliar—the shutters all closed up, the red lights turned off, no sign of the men anywhere, and few women left in the streets. And I, sleepless (I never went to bed before dawn), would continue strolling until six in the morning, and then at last I would climb the flights of stairs leading up to my room. There, before falling into bed, I would water the fern that spilled out my window (after all, I am still a country boy, exiled and disinherited) and would glance out at the tower of the Church of the Good Jesus, visible from my room. Further beyond, I knew by scent more than by sight, lay the sea. Those were the steps I always followed before going to bed, and I would follow them on the dawning of that special day too—that terrible day with its petty-paced minutes and hours, designed, it seemed, to remind us that our cursed lives did not always have a place in the order of things: on Good Friday all the whores and drag queens, like vampires, took refuge in the coffins of their conscience.

But back to Cristo Xantopoulos. I woke up at four in the afternoon, still entrenched in my usual routine. As I brushed my teeth I glanced out the window and felt a shudder inside me—the stores were all closed, there were no trucks unloading sugar in the streets, and the beggars were dozing peacefully by the closed doors of the banks where, for once at least, the guards would not hassle them. I closed the shutters in fright—God, what a day, I thought, and the night would be worse—and went to Optima's boarding house for a bite to eat.

"Did you hear about the Greeks?" he asked me, his face literally dirty with rouge, powder, and lipstick, while he served me a meal of black beans with coconut, gooey rice, and two slices of an enormous grouper that a longshoreman had given him. "Well, they came in this morning, the poor things, and now they won't even have any women. The Greek is going to open his bar, though, and so at least they can find a cold beer."

I paid scant attention to what Optima was saying—the meal was awful and I still had to pay three cruzeiros for it. In fact, no one ever paid much attention to Optima. She claimed to be eighty-nine years old but the truth is that she was a least a hundred and twenty, without any doubt the oldest queen in the Zone. During her last drunken binge she told us how the buildings of old Recife had been constructed one by one; most of the people who gathered around listening had been born after the quarter reached its present form, and to them it seemed that it had been there forever with its dirty *sobrados*, those rambling, many-windowed dwellings from another century, and its multiple levels connected by incredibly high flights of stairs. At any rate, I ate my fish and went back to my room thinking that the Greeks, for all I cared, could well have sunk to the bottom of the sea, ship and all.

But it was written that one day I would wait for that ship, the *Achya Marina*, standing on the quay with despair and fear in my heart, that many nights I would pray for its safety, asking the saints to spread a carpet of calm along the length of its course. All of that was written in letters as subtle as the coat of powder I patted onto my face that holy night, with a light trace of lipstick and a few splotches of rouge to highlight the bone structure of my face. I wore my long black hair in a pony-tail, tied up with a rubber band, and beneath a black blouse my breasts itched, hungry for fingers and tongues. With the face of a madonna I made my appearance at the Greek's Bar that night, and that was how Cristo Xantopoulos first saw me. But, in a sense, I can't say that he actually saw me, for he never even looked my way. In those silent surroundings he could see nothing beyond his own overwhelming presence.

His jet-black hair spilled chaotically over his green eyes. From time to time he moistened his lips, and that made them glisten like the fires of hell. Around his neck a carelessly knotted purple handkerchief hung like a sign—that was a day of mourning, it seemed to say, and the man who wore it was named Cristo. He kept his arms on the table and the reddish light made them look even more tanned. The legs inside his tight trousers were the pedestal from which arose the baroque statue, sinuously sculpted, of a god. All around him a light flickered intermittently, intensely blue and perhaps dangerous if translated into words, for then its message would be, "Careful, I am impossible to tame."

I fainted twice at the sight of him. The first time I slumped over a table and breathed deeply, my eyes nearly closed. The second time I fell across the Wurlitzer jukebox with its lights all dead, and I swear that in that brief instant I heard all of its records playing at the same time. I recovered quickly when I heard a voice calling him by name, and I turned in time to see that he was not alone. There was another Greek with him and they had two women, two of those incredibly smelly cunts that exist only in the Zone and whose speech is an amalgam of unutterable words culled from a variety of languages. *Felicemen, s'agapo,* one of them said to him in Greek, repeating his name with obvious pleasure.

But he hardly saw her. He paid no attention to the little cunt in the same way that he paid no attention to me or to anyone else. Even if I had danced the most frenetic of mambos or dropped my pants and exhibited my golden-brown buns, I knew that he would not take notice of me. All the tricks and cunning of a devil would be required to make him finally attentive to something beyond himself. I was so certain of that fact that after leaning against the balcony and asking him one all-important question (How long would the ship be in port? —Five days he said) I left the bar and went home.

That night I dreamed. First about a purple cloth that clung about my neck and made me cry out for the son of God, and then about the body of Cristo curiously crucified in my bed. I woke up drenched with sweat, weak with desire, and for a long while I listened to the twang of imaginary bouzoukis—that melancholy sound that would haunt me in the days to come, marking my sleepless nights with its disordered tempo.

2

THE ORDER OF THINGS, even in the Zone at Recife, is immutable. Good Friday is always followed by Saturday, and Saturday for us is a day for making money. Aside from the Greeks of the *Achya Marina,* there were Japanese, Norwegian, and Lebanese sailors in port and their presence was a guarantee that business would be good. That night I would return triumphantly to the stage of the Chantecler and from there I would anxiously scan the tables, straining my eyes to catch a glimpse of Cristo—his eyes, his tanned arms, the purple handkerchief around his neck. If I saw him enveloped in that incredible aura of his I knew that my voice would splinter into a thousand scintillating slivers of crystal before him.

For someone with less experience, singing at the Chantecler would have been a difficult assignment, for there was always someone to find my presence irritating. If it happened to be a woman I could grind her to dust with a simple gaze, but if it were a man, a Norwegian for example, one of those unbelievable blond drinkers, strong enough to tear a human being apart in a few seconds with his big bare hands, then I had to behave exactly like a whore, wiggling my hips and fluttering my eyelids, savoring the unpardonable (and incomprehensible) insults that he showered upon me. The Japanese from the *Toshio Maru* were a dangerous lot too. When I failed to impress or amuse them I could feel their disapproving silence in the air, could feel it grow thick and heavy, transforming itself into a block of black stone which at any moment they could throw at me as I stood there on the stage quivering with fear.

But those discomforting nights could just as easily be nights of glory, and I somehow sensed that that particular Saturday would be one of the latter. It was a night when, as if by some strange design, each of the sailors would remember some pale and far-off figure for whom, in some place and in some time, he had sung *The day when at last you love me* without results. And so, with tears and cheers, they would give me a round of standing applause and I would have to sing the song again, and still again, until at last I would duck behind the bead curtain of my dressing room with one of my false eyelashes coming unglued from all the sweat, threatening to fall off.

Skinny, his nose delicate from sniffing cocaine, Manolo the Spaniard announced *la cantante de fama internacional,* the internationally famous songstress, and when the golden cascade of light poured down on me I had already spotted him. Cristo Xantopoulos was at the first table to the left with the same man and the same two women as the night before. The purple kerchief, his special mark, was still knotted around his neck. In his eyes, for the first time, I saw a reflection of myself, a small figure about to drown in their jade-green sea.

For me that night he was the only person in the audience at the Chantecler. My voice flowed out to him, loaded with such sentiment and emotion that everyone—Norwegian, Japanese, Lebanese —was at some time or another moved to the brink of tears. I sang *The night when at last you love me* in purring, caressing tones, aiming the song's message directly at him, letting it slip unobtrusively into his impenetrable heart. At one point in the song the pianist fingered the keys more or less at random while I spoke the words, and I don't have to say for whom I spoke them. I moved so close to him as I spoke, so shamelessly close to him, that the woman whose arm he absent-mindedly held whispered to me, "You like my Greek, don't you, Lina?" (Oh yes, I should have mentioned earlier that I am Antônio de Barros Cavalcanti by birth, but my stage name is Lina Lee.) Then she turned to him, just as I had wanted her to do, and sealed her own fate: in her gutter Greek she told him that I loved him.

Cristo turned his flaming eyes in my direction and I felt as if my silver-sequined gown had turned to dust. Stripped bare by his burning gaze, I picked up the lost thread of my song and continued in a trembling voice. His eyes appraised me from my platinum blond wig to my high-heeled shoes, but to my dismay they did not even pause at the spot where my breasts, swollen with a daily injection of fifty milligrams of Lindiol, panted for attention. I did not hear the applause or the hysterical shouts of the drunken Norwegians or the whistling of the Japanese. I barely smiled at the Lebanese sailor who threw me a red but half-wilted rose. Ignoring the calls for an encore, I left the stage and ducked into my dressing room, eager to rid myself of the adornments I had used in that mournful ceremony. My faith in my own power to conquer had been shaken.

A half hour later, in a thin blouse and pants that easily could have been used by a man, still wearing the false eyelashes that I would not take off until I went to bed, with my makeup more discreet but still covering my full face, I took from Manolo the twenty cruzeiros that were the price of my song and made my way quickly down the back stairway into the dark street.

And there he was. My God, he was there, waiting. With a cigarette in the corner of his mouth, his half-closed eyes glimmering
like fine green daggers, there stood Cristo waiting for me. I tried to
walk on by him but a hot hand blocked my way. I shuddered when
I felt his hand on my arm. His touch burned, and I almost cried out
in pain. I tried to shake myself loose but couldn't. Then he spoke,
and his voice was just as I imagined it would be. It was the voice
I had looked for in vain in all the men I had slept with until then.

"Go make a lot of money with the Norwegians and the Japanese,"
he said, "and give it to me. Then I'll go to bed with you."

His words rushed at me like dirty water, and I turned my face
quickly away to keep from being splattered by them. Immediately
I flashed an imaginary fan in the air; its slats made a strange perfumed sound as I closed it vigorously. He watched the gesture
closely and understood that he was dealing with a lady. To leave
him even more certain of that fact I finished by slapping him
squarely in the face.

I didn't wait to see the expression in his eyes. Instead I hurried
off into the dark street, stepping up my pace but stopping short of a
run because, if I ran, I knew that he would catch me quickly and
strangle me. I had gone barely a block when the street turned
darker and I felt him behind me. He pushed me into a sort of niche
between two large shoeshine stands set against a wall, and there,
backed against the wall, gasping, I beheld the face of Cristo Xantopoulos. He would be my executioner; I had chosen him, and then I
understood clearly that if there are turning points in the life of a
queen, that moment was one such occasion for me. If he killed me,
I reasoned calmly, never before would a life have been so deli-
ciously wasted. Beautiful and huge, that man closed in voraciously
upon me. I shut my eyes but opened them a moment later when
I felt his hot mouth against mine, his lips crushing and biting mine
until I tasted blood. Our mouths and bodies were stuck fast together, and I will never be able to say how many endless seconds
we stayed that way. I only know that when the silence finally woke
me up I was alone, still leaning against the wall. My lips ached and
my legs quavered as I fastened the sprained clasp on my blouse.
I brushed the back of my hand lightly across my lips, staining it with
blood. There I stayed until the sounds off in the distance drew
nearer and brought me back to life. Only then did I dare to take a
few cautious steps out into the moonlight, looking up at the *sobrados*
with their death-pale towers. Within me now that fatal feeling was

clear and well-defined: I loved him, and he knew he would be mine.

3

OPTIMA SHELTERED ME and cared for me that night. When I had stepped out into the moonlight and looked up at the death-pale towers of the *sobrados* I had understood that my life from then on would be different. A part of my old life, which I had arranged like an indecipherable riddle, had splintered into pieces and exposed some especially sensitive piece of what I had tried most to hide. Everything seemed empty of meaning then, whether it was singing *The day when at last you love me,* wandering from bar to bar in the Zone, or displaying the timid hesitancy that made my manner so appealing. The change meant that Cristo's power was operating upon me and that it would finally engulf me. As I stumbled along the dark street that night, one hand still holding my broken lip, I thought of the time three or four years earlier when I had first come to the Zone, full of dreams of the future. Yes, there was actually a time when I was new to the place, when everything looked fresh and terrible—the overly painted women, the drunken men, the sailors and their unfamiliar languages. And there was even a time when I could have left if I had chosen to, when I could have gone back to the home I had had to leave because of my scandalous behavior. They would have had their doubts and misgivings, sure, but still they would have welcomed me back like a prodigal son who had already suffered enough (and at this point in my remembering the taste of the terribly sugary candies my aunts used to give me always came to my mouth, and the memory of a rainy morning, and a sad melody playing—yes, I was a boy once, but then one day I suddenly discovered that I no longer knew what I was, and then I had to run away). The house would have been confining, yes, but there I would have been safe. There I could have grown fat and old if only those terrible attacks—that's what my mother called them— had not forced me out into the streets again, me, the possessed, in search of men and unspeakable pleasures, me, the fallen angel so beloved by my aunts and looked upon with pity and scorn by the neighbors. No, that was all behind me. Now I was in the Zone, among those *sobrados* whose death-pale towers pointed upward like the fingers of the God whose son I still loved. Nothing else made sense to me anymore.

I turned into the better-lit street where the bars were. The taxi drivers waved at me cheerfully and I returned their greetings mechanically. And mechanically I crossed to the other side, me, suddenly an outcast, making my way through what was left of the music coming all at once from all the bars. My eyelashes felt heavy; my movements were terribly awkward. For the time being at least, while I ducked between the cars, blinded by their headlights, I had nothing of the grace of Lina Lee, the internationally known songstress. I turned into another dark street crowded with men who stood gazing up at the windows with the red lights where sometimes they could catch sight of the women. Like a stranded fish I looked for the sea, and there it was in the distance, a green band glimmering with light. I leaned against the bulwark and it was as if I had dived into the water: I swam, swam, swam, letting the long tentacles of the seaweed touch and enfold me. With eyes closed I felt the sleekness of the fishes, felt the peace and tranquillity of that other world that parallels ours. Strengthened and renewed, I came back to the surface in time to notice that someone nearby on the bulwark was watching me.

It was a man. Probably he had heard me sing and was hoping I would accept his proposition. A Lebanese, maybe the one who had thrown me the rose. His eyes were jet-black, and the light that fell across his face left them hidden in two dark caverns of shadows. In the straight line of his lips I read a single word—desire. With horror I thought how before that night I had always accepted such invitations (and again the taste of candies, the image of my aunts) and how my body must have been changed by the touch of so many men in all those years. Surely it had undergone modifications, had been molded anew.

And then I discovered what had splintered inside me, what nerve had been exposed: never again, because of Cristo, would I be able to give myself with the same naturalness as before. I could do it, yes, submitting to those men who wanted me and paid for me, but always with the knowledge that they were defiling me, and that knowledge would make me suffer.

The man took two steps toward me. His eyes were like two knives already beginning to cut me to pieces. I drew back in horror —I want you, he said, and I'll pay—and then I saw myself standing between the present and the future, entangled in the many years that would follow my fatal meeting with Cristo Xantopoulos, and all the times I would need a man like that one there by the seawall—after all, I lived in the Zone. Yes, Cristo, I could never renounce the hands that had already touched me. And then, like a stalled machine suddenly running again, I smiled. He would embrace me, yes, and his touch would be like cuts from a razor, and my flesh would bleed, and to him, as to each of those to whom I would surrender myself after that night, I would give a little of myself. I would give until at last I would be consumed. But still I would go with him, for that was my destiny.

The stairway seemed incredibly high (some strange purpose had made the old builders of Recife's Zone design those stairways, so tall that they held a challenge for the lovers who squandered their energies in climbing them). At the top of the fourth flight of stairs I knew that Optima would be waiting, her eyes framed by the little window through which she kept watch on everything. Her face, I knew, would be excessively painted, made especially dramatic by the red light of her room, and in her hands I knew she would be holding the cowrie shells she threw from time to time on our behalf, whispering to us their messages, which we did not even stop to hear. Though I still had two flights of stairs to climb, the certainty that I would find him there was already a comfort to me. My visit with the old man would be gentle and friendly, a much-needed change of pace. But it would also be more than that because he was waiting especially for me.

When I reached the top of the stairs his reddish face appeared in the little window. "The cowries say there's a man in your life," he proclaimed.

I crumpled up there at the top of the stairs, my face against the dirty, worm-eaten wood of the railing. "There are many men in my life, Optima, and all of them are disgusting," I said. "There's a whole long line of them. Which from among them all have you chosen for me tonight?"

"The man I've chosen is an especially bad one," Optima answered, "one who will destroy you. No, destroy is a meaningless word. It would be better for me to say that he'll bring you unbearable revelations."

By that time I was already crying. Optima got up, closed the little window and opened the door. "Come in," he said in a soft voice that reminded me of my mother. "Get up from there before the rats start gnawing on you. Didn't you know this whole floor is crawling with them? I watch them come and go all night long—it's funny, you know, but rats work harder than women."

As he reached out his finely shaped arms to help me I noticed he was wearing a ridiculous white nightgown and that his thin hair fell in carefully arranged commas over his forehead. I got up and he escorted me in, and I knew that I could trust myself to him. Sometime in the remote past he had earned the name of Optima by acting as a kind of mother to the forsaken, all long before time marked him so deeply that even they had trouble seeing him as a human being. Yes, I knew I could trust myself to him, and I did.

"Yes," I explained, "there is a man, Optima, and his name is Cristo Xantopoulos, and I've barely seen him. But I've seen enough to know that he will change my life."

"Your life has always been open to change," he said. "It's something you carry inside you, and whenever I see you going down those stairs I always think that you were not made for the life you've chosen. For you have the gift of seeing how things change, how they shift about and rearrange themselves, though the changes take place only in the future. That's what you're doing now, seeing how that man will change your way of thinking. He hasn't begun to change you yet but you already know that he will."

"But why, Optima, why do I know?"

"Because you are still a man. A man, you know, is the most priceless of jewels. It's hard to break him, to shatter him into so many little meaningless and useless colored stones. And that's what the people here in the Zone are—just brightly colored stones with little trace of value. From time to time one of them gets divided even further, becomes even more of a trifle, and every night some of them are ground to dust. But you are still a whole stone, difficult to break. One day you will leave here without my having to tell you to get out, that this isn't the place for you. You can stay too, if you choose, but you'll never be like the others, and death is the price that you'll have to pay."

His arms nudged me gently toward the window and we leaned out together. There below, as if in a spell of dizziness, we watched the cars and the people, listened to the echoes of their voices.

"Night after night I've leaned out this window," Optima continued, "looking for some explanation for all this. The Zone exists, we both know, and like the rest of the city it's little more than a system with a single objective: to humiliate people, to crush them. On the other side of the river live the workers, the respectable people, those with fine habits and manners, but they are crushed and beaten in the same way that we are, except that their lot is worse. Here at least you can feel the wind against your face, and after the third drink or so that gives you a feeling of absolute freedom. Down there they can't. They go home early and spend hours in bed mulling over their misfortunes before they finally drop off to sleep. But the river that separates our two worlds is just an illusion. All of us, for better or for worse, live on the same mistaken shore."

Yes, I did have a gift of seeing, and I used it when I gazed at men, when I stood before them singing my song. It enabled me to play the right games with them, to lead them about as I willed. It enabled me to attract Cristo to me. I understood it all as Optima described it, though to be sure I had never been aware of it before. My aunts and the candies they gave me, the neighbors and their looks of pity and scorn when at the age of fifteen I did an imitation of Carmen Miranda on the sidewalk in front of the house. The women in the Zone, the sailors, those red lights and the surrounding darkness. I saw them all.

"He will pass over you like a flame," Optima said, "and the wounds will never heal. Nevertheless, you have no choice but to be burned, no choice but to burn him because that's what he is waiting for. That Greek, that man you love—he crossed all the oceans so he could be touched here by you."

How, I wondered, could that hundred-and-twenty-year-old queen talk that way? What made her so wise and seeing? She still held me by the arm as if I were a tiny child, and I saw her face almost against mine. Her breath was like that of a child, smelling of milk.

"How," I asked her, "can you know about everything? If you just live here and never go out, how can you know?"

Her eyes glimmered like two beads—no, more like two precious stones, two rare crystals never touched by impure hands. Then, without waiting for her to answer, I understood. She was there, whole in the way I was whole the first time I realized I was a man. She was a stone that nothing had ever managed to break.

Optima still rocked me and lulled me, humming a lullaby I had not heard since childhood, and I went to sleep in her arms. That sleep was the deepest I have ever experienced—I plunged into it like an arrow shot into darkness.

4

SUNDAY NIGHT I would not see Cristo even though I looked for him in all the places where seamen habitually go. In the Greek's Bar I paused for some time to listen to one of the crewmen of the *Achya Marina* sing an endless lament, hoping that Cristo might appear in the meantime. Then, much later in the night, someone told me the terrible truth: the cunt who had tagged along beside him all of those days—and to whom he showed such indifference—had finally lured him into bed, and there he was while I, worried and distressed, wandered the streets of the Zone in search of him.

That night I would not go to the Chantecler, and much less would I sing *The day when at last you love me.* The lubricious stares of the Lebanese would be too much to bear, along with the impatient behavior of the Japanese and the cool disdain of the Norwegians. No, all of that would be more than I could take. It would be terrible to look for his form there in the first row of smoky tables and not find it, unbearable to think of his golden body intertwined with that woman. Instead I walked, wandered about, seeking out as always the darkest corners, hiding from some acquaintance or another who would have spotted the signs of anguish in my eyes—anguish, because Cristo, the man I loved, was in the dirty arms of another woman.

I came at last to a recessed corner in the seawall and stopped there, leaning over to gaze at my pale reflection in the water. For a long time I stayed there pondering the changes that had taken place in me during the last few days. One memory came back to me again and again—the memory of those afternoons when I had dared to cross the bridge and make my way into the business district on the other side, into the downtown area where our presence was not permitted without the risk of severe punishment. For me it was like a dangerous expedition, an incursion into enemy territory. How weird it felt just to walk among all those people, me with my strange body and my ambiguous air, to hear their insults and see the lightning-like gazes they cast in my direction. It was something like a bet made with myself, a bet to see how far my courage would hold out as I felt their hatred swelling up all around me like a gigantic wave. The shopkeepers would hurry outside to insult me and the children screamed at me as I walked by. I answered their hostility with silent contempt, for the greatest insult I could throw back at them was simply that of my existence. I was a being who by the mere fact of being gave the lie to that neat world of security and love which they had built for themselves; I was a danger to them because, alive and like them, I was at the same time so different from them.

Often those incursions had unfortunate endings—once a man hit me in the back with a stick, and sometimes I had to run to keep from being pelted with stones. Almost always I ended up fleeing, but I always fled with a fierce, disordered sort of joy because I had proved that their balance was fragile and unstable, so easily tipped, that they were weak and not even bright enough to know it.

But I knew that our strength was a passing thing too—there we lived, a marginal people as they say, sequestered in old Recife, squeezed into the squalor of its decaying buildings, where we could feed our paranoia with plumes and brocades. I was not like the others, Optima said, because I could see things, could decipher their meaning after an ordeal of suffering, and that transfigured me. At the same time it kept me from thinking of turning back—I no longer felt any desire to walk the streets free of worry, with no fear of reprisals, for that desire too had come to an end.

Cristo. His golden form on a certain Good Friday of Passion. A sign: the subtle way that God had of telling me I was forgiven. And now to think of him in that woman's arms. It was too painful to bear. It meant that I was still not worthy of him, that I still had to fulfill a solemn act in that mysterious ritual before I could possess him.

With some difficulty I moved away from the seawall and continued. I needed to keep walking, to exhaust my body until it would no longer be bothered by my thoughts, and then I could plunge into the deep healing sleep that would give me all the strength necessary for the following day, which would be a Monday. I had only two days left before the *Achya Marina* would sail away from Recife, two days left to fulfill my destiny and then abandon myself to the depths.

Before going to sleep I had to go by the Greek's Bar again—maybe that cunt had not managed to get hold of him after all, I thought, and he might be there. At that hour on the Rua do Bom Jesus, where the bar was located, only the elderly whores were left, those whose only hope was that the man, after a night of drinking, might sense something maternal in them and then, acting out the dream of centuries, would go to bed with them and close their eyes imagining that they were making love to their own mother. I walked by them and thought how they looked almost dignified in their blue dresses with frills. I gave a slight smile to the one who pronounced my name—"Lina," she said almost in a whisper, "what about a sniff of coke?" I shook my head no and hurried into the reddish darkness of the bar.

The same shadowy forms as always. Behind the counter the Greek was caught up in a lengthy consultation with two men. At one of the tables the crew of the *Achya Marina* were chatting all at the same time, accompanied by three women who drank warm beer and interrupted them constantly. In a corner the Wurlitzer sat in silence. I recognized the man leaning against it—he was the Greek I had seen with Cristo during the last few days. I moved over toward the machine as if to examine it, pretending to read the names of all the songs it would play for me at the drop of a coin. I took my time about it, lingering there until I was sure that the Greek had noticed me. I sensed that he was inspecting me, but with no great curiosity. Then I turned and asked him if he was Greek. With a nod of the head he said he was, still with no sign of curiosity. It was not until I asked him if he was a friend of Cristo that he began to show interest in me.

He turned toward me then and in his eyes I could read a secret message: he would be faithful to Cristo's beauty until the end of his days; he loved him in his own fashion, but since they were both what is commonly called men, they could never touch each other. The object of his love was something supremely beautiful and intangible which he found in his friend. From something I had read long ago, some book whose author I don't even remember, the precise name for that extraordinary feeling came to me: Greek Love.

"Cristo," he said, repeating the name like a magical formula, "yes, Cristo is my friend." And then, just as the Wurlitzer would do if I slipped a coin into it, he began to talk freely.

He and Cristo, he said, had sailed on many ships, had visited many ports. He told me about the seas they had crossed, the storms they had weathered, the women they had known, and all the times they had been in jail together or had narrowly escaped death. Always together, he and Cristo, friends. Once in Jamaica, he said, he had sheltered Cristo with his own body—Look, he said, opening his shirt to show me a pinkish scar—from a jealous black man who had wanted to disfigure him because he was too beautiful and all the women were fighting over him. He said that Cristo was like his own brother, that they understood each other without any need for exchanging words. Neither he nor Cristo had a family, he said, but they were a family to each other, and each time he pronounced the name of his friend he said it as if it were a magic password that would guarantee him a privileged place in the scheme of things.

"And where is Cristo now?" I asked.

"With a woman," he said, his smile tinged with resentment. "They're all crazy about him."

Suddenly then he realized that I was a stranger, just a queen with an extravagantly painted face, someone with no right to the god whom he had set on a pedestal. He asked me abruptly where I had met Cristo. I nervously fingered the buttons on the Wurlitzer, closed my eyes for a moment and then opened them to gaze into the reddish half-light of the bar. From the bathroom came the pungent odor of the legions of men who had relieved themselves there. And then I spilled out my answer to his question and left the bar hurriedly, as elusive as a shadow.

"I know your Cristo," I told him, "and I've always known him. He is the man to whom I will give my love. In Jamaica you protected him with your own body, but only so he could come here whole, so I could have him whole, unscarred by other adventures. If there is one person in the world who can leave a mark on Cristo Xantopoulos, I am that person. And when I have touched him he will never be the same again. Even you will not recognize him then."

I did not need to look at him because I knew what the expression on his face would be. As I walked my last blocks that night I held the image of the man before me, clear in my mind, and in his eyes I could see terror and fear.

5

AFTER THE LULL at the end of Holy Week, Monday would certainly be a bustling day in the old quarter of Recife, but as always we would be excluded from all that movement. We had nothing to do with the busy coming and going of the trucks loaded with sugar or wheat or with the strong-armed black men who unloaded them, nothing to do with the people who filed in and out of the banks and the stores (though the money we paid for rent finally, after passing through many hands, ended up in the banks and stores). The most we could do was peep at them through our windows, and even that we did discreetly, knowing that we, for the ladies we saw come and go, were an insult and an outrage. Many times I paused to observe all that movement, and in spite of all I had been told to the contrary, I felt that I was a part of it. Through dark corridors and complicated reckonings I could discern a common thread running through the labyrinth of our lives, linking us all together like puppets, for the truth is that they, though seemingly determined to lead clean, upstanding lives, had their weaknesses no less than we. They too had sold themselves into some form or another of slavery. That knowledge helped me to be largely indifferent to punishments and misfortunes—just knowing that they, though they did not partake of our disgrace, were not really different from us after all, that behind all the disguises and beneath the cloak of calm with which they sheltered their lives, they too were helpless against their own destinies.

During lunch Optima asked me no questions—he was the same old man as always, a mummy silently observing as we ate, his eyes wide open but focused on an epoch not necessarily our own. What scenes those eyes had beheld, I thought, and what terrible odors his nose must have smelled, and his mouth, how many times it had been forced to hold its silence, and his face, what strange rites and contractions it must have undergone before it finally molded itself into the changeless mask it was now, where there was no longer any place for violent things such as hatred or joy.

When we finished eating—two or three other people had been eating along with us—he summoned me with a silent gesture and a movement of the lips that meant "Come." I followed him down the dark corridor and at the end of it he pulled a batch of keys from inside his blouse. It suddenly dawned on me that something extraordinary was happening—his behavior told me that he had something special to show me. One of the keys opened the door in front of us and he slipped through it as silently as if he were a shadow. I followed him and plunged into the darkness; my eyes adjusted to it in time to see that Optima, like a blind man in familiar surroundings, was moving toward a shuttered window. Seconds later I could make out vague shapes, and then I felt something brush my face like cool silk and I noticed a perfume in the air. He opened the shutters and I closed my eyes to keep from being blinded by the sudden light. When I opened them again I drew back in surprise.

The room was a bridal chamber. It was really silk that had touched my face, silk from an immaculately white curtain that the wind now wafted back and forth across us. The mirrors were all brand new, as were the white sheets on the ancient wrought-iron bed, and the walls were covered with a pink and blue paper that somehow had survived the many years it had been there. A smell of old things pervaded the air, things in permanent conflict with age itself. I could almost have guessed how many times Optima had entered the room in the last few years, how many times he had opened the window and set about cleaning the place, always perfuming the air afterwards with fine incense brought from Hong Kong by the sailors, keeping the room always clean and fresh as if it were waiting for a bride who, though late, could arrive at any moment.

I turned back toward Optima and he was gazing at me with the same changeless mask of a face, his eyes glimmering like some kind of quick, inflammable matter. And then he told me that I would bring my Greek there and that there I would sleep with him. The room had been ready and waiting for years, he said, for so many years that finally he had had to change the curtains and the sheets. It had waited for a night of love that never occurred because not everyone, he said, lowering his voice, was gifted with luck such as mine.

"Finally I could not wait any longer," he told me. "The loves that I had were never worthy of this room, just as they were not worthy of my most intimate secrets, and so I kept it as it is now, fresh, palpitating, always ready. I did my best to keep it from looking like a museum, and with a lot of work I succeeded. Whenever I came here the room always gave me an illusion of hope. It was always a bridal chamber and I was the bride, always arriving too late for my own wedding. I made this room my most intimate shelter, and here I spent whole afternoons when everything around me was threatening to fall apart, and always I left strengthened and renewed—ah, Lina, you don't know how vain the things of this life are! And I can say that during all those years I fed upon it—fed upon the purity of its curtains and its blue and pink walls, on the breeze that came through the window and the wild winds that blew on the coldest nights of winter. When I threw the cowries the other night and then you passed by and I saw the shadows that accompanied you, I remembered that your room is nothing but an empty space up there and that true love always requires a place worthy of it. This is the room where you will love your Greek. You deserve it as much as I do because you are much like me. I have decided, and now all you have to do is bring him here."

It would not be true to say that there were tears in my eyes, for I had long ago learned not to cry, but something akin to weeping made them tremble and I had to recover my composure before asking Optima if I were really worthy of her secrets.

"Now the secret is ours," he said, "and so it hasn't been broken."

Cristo Xantopoulos was all I could think of as I left my bridal chamber, and on the way down the stairs I pronounced his name aloud with such an intensity of feeling that he had to hear it wherever he might have been. The force of my love was such that he could no longer fail to feel it. It drifted through the air like a great black cloud, and toward a definite goal: it was Monday, and that night I would summon forth the storm.

At dusk that day I passed silently in front of No. 206 Rua Vigario Tenorio—he had slept there the night before, and though that meant nothing (it was as if his body were still untouched, waiting for my touch), I could not keep my eyes away from the second-floor window where I knew his whore would be. She, in the meantime, had been watching me since I rounded the corner, waiting to call down to me until I glanced up at her.

"Lina!" she shouted, "wait a minute! I want to talk to you."

There was no way to avoid it. She would tell me everything, the whole story of how the Greek had made love to her, down to the most trifling and sordid details. I would listen with the interest that she had expected to awaken in me, and I would make a few malicious comments while jealousy ate me inwardly like an acid.

"Guess who I fucked with last night? With the Greek!"

"With what Greek?" I asked, pretending to be indifferent to the whole matter.

"Oh, come on," she said, "the one with the purple kerchief, remember? The one you kept staring at in the club."

"Me? Staring at a Greek?" I answered in a harsh tone. "No, honey, not me. They all have smelly feet."

She blinked for a moment, confused, but only for a moment.

"Well, *his* feet don't stink," she said. "His name is Cristo and he looks like the son of God in the flesh. And God how he fucks—he spent the whole night on top of me."

From that point on I knew she would lapse into lies, for no man could work himself up so much over a whore, and especially not

Cristo Xantopoulos, such a master of himself. But I pretended to listen anyway and let my own thoughts run their course while she talked. Soon the ominous night was falling around us, darkening the buildings and leaving only a thin strand of light to struggle against the darkness back over the docks.

When the darkness had finally won out and the street lights had come on, the little whore finished her story with a detail about how the Greek had kissed her as he left her room that morning. None of it had really wounded or affected me, for now I felt certain of myself. She had come into the picture merely to add her bit to my union with Cristo—in the days to come she would be a witness to the fact that he had come our way and that I had possessed him. That night in the cabaret I would take the necessary measures for letting everyone know. It made no difference what seas he had sailed or what beds he had slept in. It was written that no one would ever touch him as I would touch him.

6

ALL MY PLANS would have to be faithfully carried out that night for there was no more time. It was the urgency of the matter, I knew, that impelled me. The following day the *Achya Marina* would leave for I knew not what ports, and if that happened without my finally coming face to face with Cristo it would be like deferring a part of my life and being left suspended amid floating hopes, struggling against despair until the ship, at some unknown date, without altering its intricate course, would return to Recife. Even so, in some far-off port he might meet his destiny in the form of a glimmering dagger or a woman—who knows?—and so an endless series of contingencies would determine whether Cristo, the man to whom I had offered myself, would return with his ship.

The urgency of the whole affair spoiled and inhibited my first steps that night. In the makeshift dressing-room at the Chantecler I had to do my makeup again and again, retouching the highlights and the shadows until I had found the exact tone for my face—and during the whole process I felt like a ghost. It took much more time than usual; I could count the minutes as they slipped by like sand carried away by the wind, and inside that atmosphere of urgency I behaved like a deep-water fish suddenly hauled up into the light. From outside in the club came the blare of the music, the more or less despairing shouts of the women and the cynical answers of the men, the incessant movement to and from the Wurlitzer jukebox as it grew heavy with coins, divulging its rhythms in exchange for more. Suddenly motionless, calm, I hovered on the edge of those noises, a brush held before my face, and probed the space that separated me from the big room outside in an effort to pick up some sign of Cristo's presence there, Cristo my beloved, while I applied a thin layer of eye shadow around my eyes. It was still the face of a ghost that stared back at me from the mirror, and if I failed that night to transform myself into the triumphal allegory I had so long nursed within me (me, the beloved son of dreams), I knew that my face would remain that way forever, ghostly, drained of hopes.

And he was not there. I glided through the poorly lit hallway toward the stage as Manolo announced *the internationally acclaimed songstress,* and while the floodlights were still off I stood there breathless, waiting for the light, vainly scanning the darkness for some glimpse of his face. The tables were all full, the same people as always—the Japanese and Norwegian sailors, the painted women trying to convince their men that they were somehow better— more womanly—than I was. And at the tables in the back near the johns, half-lost in smoke, I could make out the even more expressionless faces of those who saw the cabaret as a dream or a species of adventure: young boys, middle-aged men chewing unlit cigars, a few old ladies. It was in homage to them that I began my song, knowing that my public would dislike me for it. I tried to sing beyond them all—Cristo was somewhere in the streets, with his woman maybe, but where?—tried to project my voice toward a point so distant that the people gathered there before me would not even be able to hear it. The first reaction came with the fourth or fifth line. A Japanese whispered something to his companion and she answered with a strident burst of laughter. They had the right to laugh and I couldn't blame them. The light dazzled me and suddenly I felt weird, foreign to that environment. An unfamiliar and terrible sensation came over me: my clothes, my makeup, my false eyelashes—they all weighed upon me, felt uncomfortable and strange. My body seemed subject to unexpected reactions; it was not as definitive and concrete as I had imagined it up until that Good Friday when I met Cristo. In the middle of a line I thought of breaking off my song, of running away from that place and pulling off all my clothes and plunging into I don't know what kind of purifying liquid and then going to sleep—but no, I couldn't because that night was my night and I had to act fully my part in it.

During the first break I closed my eyes and tried to get things straight in my head. I hurriedly recounted all my past triumphs, skipping the failures, and began again with faith and renewed hope. The final minutes were less tense and strained; I felt that some contact had been established with the hostile crowd, and once I even thought I saw a smile.

Anyway, I was near the end of my act. I whirled about for the last time and finished off the song to a light round of applause. The floodlights winked and then went out. Manolo moved back to the center of the stage and I ducked out of view, walking to a corner table and taking with a wicked smile the glass that a woman there grasped like a flagstaff in her fist. This is my blood, I told her after a long draught, and she peered with alarm inside the glass when I handed it back to her. I did the same thing at the next table, and then at a third, before realizing that I would become weak if I con- tinued to drink—and God knows I needed all my strength for the night that lay before me. At the fourth table then I handed the glass back to its owner without drinking from it and hurried off to the bathroom. I needed to see my face again, to make sure that it was still in place, still the same sculpture that hours earlier I had fash- ioned from powders and creams.

The johns at the Chantecler were in the back of the establish- ment, very dimly lit, and the one for the men and the one for the women both opened onto the same large empty room with a giant mirror glimmering on the wall. It was there that I intended to inspect myself. The whores, strangely enough, always steered clear of that mirror because its full-length image seemed to offend them —which was not the case with me since whenever I looked in a mirror I saw only what I wanted to see.

But that time the reflections were different. During the first few seconds there in the half-light I could not understand what was happening (at first I saw only two ill-defined forms) but then I saw that one of the two people fighting there was Cristo and I recog- nized the other—in spite of her bloody, disfigured face—as the little whore who had been with him during the last few days. Frozen stiff, glancing out of the corner of my eye at my own haughty image in the mirror, so much like that of a dark, dignified lady, I watched that awful immolation: coldly and knowingly he beat the poor woman while she coldly and knowingly consented without a ges- ture of protest. He seemed about to destroy her, to transform her into a puddle of blood, and she wanted him to do it—or so it appeared, for he punched her in the stomach and chest without her raising her voice against him. If it had not been for the dry sound of his blows the scene would have been a silent one. The only other sounds came from the club outside.

The episode could have lasted for five seconds or for an hour, with me motionless beside them, doubled by my image in the mirror. It was one figure against the other until the woman began to yield and fall, sliding slowly down the wall toward the floor, though still with a certain resistance that made me think she wanted to take advantage of his blows until the last—Cristo's hands were without doubt a punishment she felt she deserved and so she desired it. Her mouth, eyes, and nose were covered with blood and her face was a red formless mass when at last she slumped into a sitting position, her back against the tiles of the wall, her soft hands palms-down on the cold floor, one of her shoes missing. There she fell, and then she simply sat there and breathed deeply—yes, her posture seemed to say, after so many years of whoring she had at last reaped her just reward.

Then he spoke, clearly to me but without turning around. "I hate whores," he said, "I hate the whole lot of them." And then, looking into my face, he said it was time for us to go. I took his hand. We made our way along the darkest side of the club and then hurried down the stairs. We were well on our way out when we heard the screams of someone who had found the battered body of the woman on the floor in the room between the johns.

That night many people witnessed our triumphal passage. Cristo never at any moment let go of my hand along the length of the three streets we took, and he coldly ignored the stares of those who stopped to watch us pass. (Could he have felt, as I did, that we were bound together forever, that our hands would never separate again, that our shadows were about to merge into one strange and impossible shape?) Finally we reached the foot of the stairway. High up there at the top I knew that Optima would be waiting for us, still steadfast after her long century of patient waiting.

We stumbled hurriedly up the stairs, and when our bodies touched on the steps they emitted dangerous sparks that dazzled the small crowd of people who had gathered below to watch us climb. (Those who had the privilege of seeing us go by must surely have known that we were lovers.) We could not pause to look back because the night was slipping inexorably away and still there was so much to do—we hurried into the little hallway where Optima was waiting with open arms, splendidly attired and painted like a grand lady from another century, a fan clutched in one of her hands. With her upper lips drawn back in a triumphant pucker she welcomed us like the vivacious lady she could have been if only the die of fate had fallen differently. She embraced the two of us and ushered us in, closing the door silently behind us. Then we heard her voice echo between the ancient walls as if it were delivering a weighty sentence, and Cristo's hand grasped mine more firmly and I repeated in a low voice the words that Optima had just said, words that she had undoubtedly kept stored away for all those years—

"At last, here at last."

7

IN THE BRIDAL CHAMBER only one small detail had been altered: the shutters were now padlocked with two heavy chains. Even so, the wind that came through the gaps between them made the curtains tremble like gossamer webs. Before the mirror on the dresser I began to take off my eyelashes, and it was then that I realized that everything had taken on a strangely unreal feeling, somehow beyond the initial reality into which I had thrown myself —the long walk through the streets holding Cristo's hand, dressed in the adornments I always used in the cabaret: the gown, the plumes, the ghostly face. As I removed my eyelashes I felt his overwhelming presence behind me. He began to undress and I turned in time to appreciate the process—I wanted to drink in all his gestures, all his movements. His chest, smooth and hard, emerged from his half-opened shirt, and then he freed his feet from his shoes (he never used socks). His pants fell, revealing the thighs I had so long dreamed of, and beneath his white drawers I could guess the volume of his sex just below a reddish line of hairs. He stood naked then, just as I had always wanted him, just as I had imagined him for so many years. I had lived for him, just to know that he was mine, to have him waiting for me. That, beyond any doubt, was love, that overwhelming presence, that enactment of a rite that would bring about in us an impossible transformation—at last we would be one. Thinking of that I pulled off my dress and all my other clothing and stood naked in the half-darkness. Now it was he, Cristo, that incredible Greek, who gazed at me. I whispered his name and immediately realized that only his name mattered, that he would never know mine because what I stood for was nameless.

I took a step forward and his body flashed like blue lightning. His sex began to arch up fiercely beneath his underwear and my sudden awareness of it made me tremble because the same thing was happening beneath the strap that concealed what was for me that least esteemed part of my body. Is that the way we would meet, I wondered, in trickery and deceit? No, I decided firmly, and with a quick gesture I pulled off the strap, letting him see me completely naked. He took a step toward me and stopped to remove the underwear which had now become uncomfortable for him. Free now, his sex frisked about, reared up and then stretched itself like an arrow in my direction. I had breasts and he had a strong hard chest. But even so we knew that we were alike. After that conclusion, which we reached together with no recourse to words, we at last could touch each other. Cristo's arms were hard, and they had that incredible smell of man which I had learned to recognize and savor in the darkness. But now I was seeing him in the light that came through the gaps in the shutters, framed by the silence of the *sobrado*, while outside, always attentive, Optima kept watch. He reached for me, and for the last time in my life I felt fragile; he carried me toward the bed and placed me upon it like an offering, and then he stretched his body out beside mine, and he kissed my eyelids, and he closed my mouth while his hands descended the length of my body, and he groped for my breasts and fingered my navel, and his lips explored all the recesses of that hellish paradise, and I screamed his name, and again I screamed his name and then he broke into an incredible manly groan and his legs intertwined with mine, and my body lunged forward unexpectedly, and at last he imprisoned me with his tongue again inside my mouth, and then I neighed: we were riding each other like horses. Then we set off on the long ride, his body against mine, the muscles of our arms stiffened in a grieved embrace. Yes, he was mine, there was no more doubt about it. We were sailing toward the same port. His hands kneaded my body while my mouth crawled down his back in one prolonged caress. And then it was he who began again. He hunted out again the most hidden recesses of my body and kissed them, took possession of them, and in that virgin bed our limbs tangled like an indecipherable puzzle—he sucked me and I sucked him—always closing closer one upon the other, and again he broke into that groan, which was the groan of the first man, the ancestral male, and I groaned as he groaned.

The night urged us on. It was our night. After it, what else could life offer us? We were nearing the end. Our bodies thrust one against the other, and I could feel the sweat from his forehead on my lower stomach. After a while we went back to the first position, and in the darkness our eyes met in a mute question: would I fuck him or would he fuck me? For a moment we wavered with doubt, and then we plunged. He slipped a pillow under my hips and I raised my body, opening my legs toward him. With a shout he entered me. His arms were heavy around my neck and his determined mouth bit my shoulders. At last he exploded and I could feel him spilling inside me, and I came too while he was still panting. Several minutes passed before he dared to breathe, and even then he breathed with great caution: we could not bear to shatter that incredible order which our bodies had created.

I don't know how many times we took that same path that night, and if someone were to ask me now, I would not be able to say what we talked about. Time fenced us in from all sides, for we knew that dawn would come soon and then the *Achya Marina* would leave, taking him with it. I remember that Cristo talked about his country, that one image came up constantly: a dry plain, some white houses far off, and, after a long hard walk beneath the midday sun, the violet sea disappearing into the distance. That was a memory that he had carried since childhood, a memory that had followed him everywhere—perhaps his vision of his country was limited to that single remembered image.

All night while he talked I explored his body, trying to coax from it the mystery that had first attracted me to it, that certainty that he was beautiful and proud, that nothing could really degrade him— I kissed him and absorbed his scent for I too needed to store up memories to sustain me after his ship had sailed. But, as I said, time slipped by like sand blown by the wind. Again we threw ourselves into that struggle from which both of us always came out conquered. For long minutes we seemed to soar above time, but finally we had to return to earth—and then it was later than before, and soon dawn would be coming. He said something about how I must have known, the first time I saw him, that it would come to that. And I smiled. Yes, I knew even then. The constant tension of life had made me into a seer, one who could read the future and ferret out the meaning of the slightest gestures, one who could see storms coming from afar. There I was, a well of wisdom because I had learned to see things before others saw them. That, for me, was the only way to survive.

"Yes, Cristo," I said. "When I saw you in the Greek's Bar I knew that you would be mine, and in all the days that followed I dedicated myself to letting you know that. A moment of carelessness and you would never have known and the ship would have sailed away and our failure to meet would have been irremediable for the two of us, even though you would never have been aware of it."

"Will everything be different from now on?" he asked.

"Yes," I said, "our lives have been changed forever because finally we are one. And we will be one forever, even when the *Achya Marina* is far away on unknown seas."

I turned back toward him and was about to kiss him when I noticed the threatening smell of smoke. I sniffed the air and he did the same until he smelled it too. Something was burning, and our skins bristled at the thought—we were drowsy animals in the woods, asleep but at the same time alert in a state to which our new-born sensitivity had brought us. He raised himself up and looked toward the door. Almost at the same time we saw it: in a corner of the room and all along the ceiling the smoke was seeping in like some deadly gas.

We jumped from the bed together and rushed to the door. It was locked from the outside. I screamed for Optima, repeating the old man's name again and again, and Cristo began to hammer at the door with his iron-like fists.

"Optima! Optima!" I screamed. "What's happening? Please, Optima, what's going on?" And as I screamed I watched the smoke, much heavier now, creep down the wall and slowly fill the room. The curtains, I noticed in spite of my panic, were strangely inert. Not a breeze was blowing. And then, as I screamed Optima's name again, I heard her voice on the other side of the door.

"Yes, the door's locked," she said calmly and unhurriedly. "I myself have locked it."

"But why? Why?" I shouted as the smoke filled my eyes and Cristo, still naked beside me, tried in vain to force the door open.

"Because this is the way things should end," Optima answered. "The house is burning down and I set it afire."

"He's mad, completely mad," Cristo muttered.

"Optima, was this why you loaned me your room?"

"Yes, dear, and I know what I'm doing. Listen to me, Lina. Are you really sure you want to leave that room? After what has happened to you there do you really want to go out into the world again?"

"Yes, let me out!"

"But why? Why?" he said, speaking now in longer and softer tones. "Remember what your life was like before this little interval, before this night. And think what it will be afterwards. Do you want to live for five hundred years like me, always waiting, sniffing the air for things you have no right to? Do you want to end up like me? Is that what you really want? No, I can't believe you would be that way. You are different somehow. Even now you can understand how important it is to stay there inside, to burn until the end, for then you will be left with only that night and nothing will come after it to defile it."

Madness, madness, I thought while Cristo ran in a desperate rage to the closed window (ah, so this is why the window was chained— the whole thing was carefully planned). He dashed back to me and stared at me coldly, trying to detect some sign of complicity in me.

"No! No!" I told him. "I want to live too."

But then my thoughts took a strange new turn when the flames broke out with a deafening noise along the cracks where until then there had been only smoke and I noticed that the heat in the room had increased alarmingly. In spite of everything, that night was what I had yearned for during the whole of my life. Why prolong it, knowing that it would waste away and come undone, that soon it would be nothing but a pallid memory? Why wait for my body to wither and fade until I would be nothing but a shadow, a poor creature to be pitied? Why struggle to keep alive a memory when the years would slip on by and nothing else would be left to me?

"If we die now we will be eternal," I muttered to Cristo, knowing that he would fail to understand.

On the other side of the door Optima tapped softly. "I am here," he whispered, "don't be afraid. I will stay with you until the end because this is what I want too. Don't be afraid. There's only the three of us, with all of the rest of the world outside. The stairway is all in flames now, and the people gathered together down there in the street must be commenting that Optima is up there in the flames. But not one of them will bother to come after me. So, you see, there is only the three of us."

The flames ate their way down the wall toward the bed. One of the curtains suddenly burst into flame and seconds later it fell, and then the first tongues of fire sprouted from the floor. Cristo screamed and drew back from the window that until then he had tried to force open. He looked at me, his eyes full of fire and fear, and in an effort to calm him I told him that we were going to die. Outside we could hear the flames destroying everything, closing in around our room as if they had reserved it for the last. I called to Optima but she no longer answered, and then her image flashed quickly before my eyes—Optima, dressed in a long white gown like a lady from another century. This is the way he always wanted it, I thought as the ceiling and one of the walls turned to live coals—so this is the way she wanted it all to end. Cristo stationed himself then in front of me, both of us still naked, and his eyes locked with mine. Letter by letter I wrote inside my head the words that would be my last testament. The heat had become unbearable. We had only a few more minutes of agony to endure, and still I feared that he had not understood, that he would die in despair and we would go by separate ways then to that place where all things have their end. I moved toward him. He was still staring at me, his eyes like deep dark wells, and for the last time I spoke his name, Cristo, and for a brief fleeting moment his forehead wrinkled in a sign that he had understood. Then his eyes grew suddenly clear, jade as they had been the first night I saw him, but at the same time filled with hope. We had been two, but now we were one, or at least he was what I had always dreamed of being. The fire suddenly swallowed us up and I lost sight of him. When I caught a glimpse of him again—my last glimpse—he was writhing in the flames.

The last thing I saw before dying was my own body floating above the flames and smoke, hovering high above them. In the street below a stormy multitude closed in around what was left of the burning building while a siren wailed helplessly. Then my vision broadened, taking in the surrounding streets and the dark calm sea, the docks and all the ships motionless there with their red lights blinking. I gazed down, floating in a region of coolness and peace. The sad twanging of a bouzouki came from the Greek's Bar. I hovered above it all, floating higher and higher, leaving the Zone far below and behind. It was then that I closed my eyes, ready for death.

Edilberto Coutinho

EDILBERTO COUTINHO is a journalist-author born in 1933 in the state of Paraiba, Brazil's Northeast. He holds a law degree and has already published ten books. Three of those books are collections of short fiction, which is his favorite genre. Other works include essays, critical anthologies, and biographical studies—such as *Rondon, o Civilizador da Ultima Fronteira* (Rondon, the Civilizer of the Last Frontier) and *O Romance do Acúcar—José Lins do Rego Vida e Obra,* dealing with the famous Brazilian novelist of the thirties.

Coutinho began working as a journalist for *Jornal do Brasil,* the leading newspaper in Rio de Janeiro. He has been a correspondent in Europe, for three years, for *Jornal do Brasil* and *Manchete,* a Brazilian weekly magazine. While in Madrid, Spain, he edited a special issue of the magazine *Mundo Hispánico,* dedicated to various aspects of Brazilian culture.

Coutinho was only twenty years old when he published his *Onda Boiadeira e Outros Contos,* his first collection of short stories. Two years later appeared his *Contos-II.* The literary critic Sergio Milliet said of this early work: "He renews the Brazilian short story, giving it a lyrical quality of the highest caliber."

Um Negro vai à Forra (A Black Man Gets Even), Coutinho's third book of short fiction, was published in 1977 and was well received by critics. Critic Armando Correia Pacheco wrote: "In his short stories Coutinho reveals complete control of the technique of this difficult literary genre, knowing how to raise day-to-day banality to a superior dimension—that of the psychological level in which reality is deeper and more authentic." Novelist Jorge Amado affirmed: *"A Black Man Gets Even* is one of the best creations of Brazilian fiction in recent years."

Presença Poética do Recife (Poetic Presence of Recife), noted as one of the most important of Coutinho's books, had its second edition in 1977. Novelist José Candido de Carvalho wrote of the book: "With ingenuity and supreme art Coutinho has given us the biography of Recife in verse." (Recife is the major city of Brazil's Northeast.)

Edilberto Coutinho currently lives in Rio de Janeiro.

LOST IN RECIFE

Why not surrender myself to the immense sea
If I'm in the need of sun and my dreams convince me
I'll never feel at home here?
What is missing? A companion perhaps?
The whole day long I wait for an answer,
Lost in Recife, where by chance I've come to be.

—Edson Régis

I

PHONE CALLS one after another, each person calling out of frustrated Christmas expectations.

Cornered by their anxieties, my friends call from their homes, and I reflect on the fact that my family, in spite of all the difficulties, has never been a bore. Luciana is already in tears, Marcos says, because we're not doing anything tonight. So I suggest (that readiness is what gets you into trouble, my mother will say) that we all get together here at my place.

I remember well enough the conversation I had yesterday with Marcos. Maybe my reaction to what he was trying to tell me disappointed him. That's why I tried to be more friendly with him than with the others who had called earlier, with whom I barely managed to exchange the standard greetings which they offered to me. (My family has never been a bore: one consolation. I should make a note of that for when Mother and Helena start pestering me by bickering constantly among themselves).

2

IS EVERYBODY COMING? For a moment I'm afraid that unexpectedly through some stroke of absurdity all the workers from the Industrial Department of SUDENE* will come through the door... all the technicians and their wives, followed by a contingent of administrative workers. Of course, it's not going to happen. Most of my fellow workers don't have any idea where I live.

---

*SUDENE (Superintendência do Desenvolvimiento do Nordeste)—a Brazilian agency for the development of the northeastern area of the country.

Marcos will invite three or four people.

Back on the phone, he starts to fantasize. What if we all show up in tuxedos and evening gowns? Wouldn't that be a gas?

Which would you wear, I ask him, a tuxedo or an evening gown?

Everything's ready. I'm waiting for them all to show up at any moment.

3

AREN'T WE GOING to do anything tonight? Helena comes up and asks me as soon as I hang up the phone, suspecting that something may be brewing. A big lively party with lots of Christmas spirit.

I wasn't expecting anything to happen tonight, and so I don't feel the frustration that my wife seems to.

We opened the children's gifts. (Let's open the children's gifts, I said when she asked me if we weren't going to do something today) beside a Christmas tree as phony and unconvincing as Marcos' communism. Incredibly phony with those little wads of cotton pretending to be snow, and I think of Marcos (What has he done with his talents?) while I look at the tree with a kind of pity. He told me that he had gotten the jump on history and written a poem about a peasant who'll be killed in the class struggle in a sugar mill in Pernambuco. He mentioned that as he sipped his whiskey, squinting at me with his little short-sighted eyes. Isn't it a great theme? he said.

I'm not a literary critic, I told him, but it seems to me that you can take any theme you want and make a good poem, or a bad poem. It all depends on the poet.

4

THOUGH SHE CAN'T AVOID a certain degree of exhibitionism when she refers (in a code language she thinks has been deciphered) to her American lover, today Helena is playing the role of a good wife, good daughter-in-law, good mother, good housekeeper. What a foolishness! She's going about indulging in affable chit-chat with my mother, both of them seeming awfully insincere as they peck each other on the cheek beside that ridiculous cellophane tree.

It's Christmas. Rejoice, Christians, rejoice!

Angels Are Singing in the Highest. Stille Nacht. Alleluia! Helena puts these on the stereo, but what good are Bach, Carl Adam, Franz

Gruber and Villa-Lobos if nothing can fill me with true peace and gladness tonight?

My wife looks at me inquisitively, maybe thinking that I'm plotting some way to get even with her. Maybe she's waiting for me to act like a man is supposed to, like a real he-man in the rough-and-ready days of the Old Northeast.

And why don't I feel inclined to do anything? Cowardice, fatigue, lack of nerve? I don't know; maybe it's resignation. I admit it: inertia is the climate I thrive in. Mario de Andrade, I admire your Macunaíma. Oh, Saint Mario of the Brazilian low-life. *Ai que preguiça* (I feel so lazy). And Christmas makes me feel empty. Like Andrade's hero, no desire to take the stand people expect me to. Without even that side of my personality (the bad side) which my wife hopes to see flare up in me in a crisis of machismo that would justify her behavior.

5

AT LEAST IT SEEMS the kids liked their presents. Little Sergio put his ring on his finger right away and then went to his room pushing his toy truck, while Rodolfo, still tiny, understood nothing of the ritual of the Gift of the Magi. He cried through it all, with Helena or my mother holding him in their arms. In an effort to distract him, his granny took him too close to the tree and he put out his finger for one of the lights and got burned. I grabbed him and Mother ran for the kitchen saying that butter is best for burns; she came back to cure her grandson, anointing his finger with the butter and talking to him in a babyish voice as if she were mentally retarded, oh-poor-poor-little-fingeringer-granny-gonna-fix-baby-finger-yes.

I took my son from her and soon he tried to smile, but then he remembered the pain and started whimpering again. Then our Serginho came back to the living room and said he'd lost his ring. We had seen him playing with his ring, taking it off his finger and putting it back on, showing it to everybody, rolling it on the floor. And so he ended up losing it, but he didn't seem to be upset. It was as if the ring had simply acquired another characteristic: it was pretty, it was made of gold, it was lost.

The kids departed the scene. They had already done their bit. They kissed their parents and their grandmother hurried them off to bed (Gotta-go-sleepyweepy-now) and as they were leaving the room I imagined a ridiculous scene: Mother, certain that Helena was being unfaithful to me, would ask why we didn't get a divorce (and, since *she* was the guilty party, *we* could keep the kids) and I, very serious, would point to the kids and say no, we have to stick together for their sake, because they need a mother.

6

MARCOS, LIKE HELENA, seems to fear (hope) that I'll react violently in either a personal or a judgmental way.

For that reason he's worried about me.

We should talk it over, Marcos said, when he took me to the bar where we drank whiskey and munched on our *cáscaras de siri*: some really delicious stuffed crab shells. He was serious but I was bored by the whole thing, as uninterested as I could be without appearing rude, as attentive as I would be to the reading of another of his poems.

Helena had asked him to get a few friends together and come over to our house to spend Christmas Eve. But it was supposed to be a surprise to me.

And she wanted that guy Bob to come along. Do you know him? Yes, I told Marcos, I know who he is. The American supervisor of some projects being planned by the Alliance for Progress, all very active now that it's been announced that President Kennedy is going to visit Brazil.

Was that all?

It wouldn't have been very appropriate for me to add: My wife's lover.

Then it occurred to me that Helena wanted to get all of those people together so that she could show them (especially the men, including her Marlon Brando) how I neglected her. And the worst part of all (she'd find a way to make her point, she's very good at that) would be that I didn't neglect her *for another woman*. I just simply neglected her, and she would play one of the roles she's best at: that of the tragic victim. (I imagine her in the arms of her big burly American, the two of them kissing like in those old movies; in one of those incredible positions that make you wonder how the actors manage not to dislocate their spinal columns).

Let Marcos call anybody he wants to, I don't care.

Okay, I told him, as long as it's not more than four or five people. Marcos knows I don't like crowds, especially in my own house. When he called just now he seemed uncertain as to whether I wanted to have them over, and especially the American. *Especially the American!* Let them come. Let everybody come, heaven help me.

7

AFTER MY MOTHER took the kids to bed Helena and I were left in the living room with nothing to say, bored and silent. Then I got up and asked her if there was any coffee in the thermos. She said there was some and offered to get it for me. No, don't bother, I said, thanks, all very politely, and went to the cupboard to get the coffee myself.

I drank it without sugar and went back to the living room. There's Helena with a book open, reading or pretending to read, in English, I suppose, and it won't be long before she'll be annoying everyone, deliberately, by using English phrases. I've begged her not to use English all the time, even in the most trivial little stories, but it's useless. Are you jealous? Why should I be, I said, caught by surprise. After all, she said, I speak English better than you do. No, my dear, it has nothing to do with that; it just seems pointless and stupid to me for you to give yourself over to the enemy that way, almost without meaning to. To me it's something absurd, something I can't quite understand.

To the enemy. At times Helena seems quite candid; it strikes her as strange for me to refer, with no trace of remorse, to anyone in our close social circle as an enemy. For her they are our unconditional friends.

And she's about to open the door to a terribly uncertain future, ready to wipe away a past that at least was familiar, intimate, spent with me (and Mother will be surprised if it's she and not I who finally suggests the divorce, as I believe Helena will do). That past of ours, so full of romantic love in spite of everything. And I could overlook her infidelity (Is it possible she knows that?) but can I forgive her foolhardiness too? I don't know why but it irritates me to see her behaving so irresponsibly, and here she is seated in front of me with the book open before her unmoving eyes and we can find nothing to say to each other, as if we had decided that looking for a solution would get us nowhere, that whatever must happen will happen and that it's no use struggling against the scheme of things, that that's just the way life is.

8

I WAS EXPECTING nothing (I repeat, nothing) to happen to-night. But Marcos' wife is crying, and just now he asked me if we weren't going to do something. Aren't we going to do something tonight? he said.

Another Christmas crossed off the calendar, and Luciana is crying, I think, because time is passing too fast for her. I suppose it won't be too long before she'll get a facelift and then she'll come out ageless with all her wrinkles stretched away, just as her mother did not long ago, and she and her mother will look like sisters then. Careful when you laugh, avoid too much sunlight, go easy on the alcoholic beverages, crying must be bad for you too, Luciana; you'd better start now.

And Helena? Her eyes are fixed on a book she opened at random. Better to leave her alone. My wife must be looking through the book (she shifts her eyes now) for some striking phase that she can repeat during the Christmas Conversation. Nothing like *time is money* but something that will make it clear how hateful I am and how charming and attentive her American is.

For me it is a Christmas without angels. Oh, how I wish there were some equivalent in Portuguese for the Spanish expression *sin ángel,* which is so full of meaning. Without magic maybe? Without charm?

It wasn't my idea, tonight wasn't my idea, and now suddenly I feel vulnerable to the fear that my life will be one of frustration, just like Luciana and Marcos and maybe that foreigner man named Robert (Bob, Helena's Bob), just like Helena and Mother. And if Marcos were to show up in drag and the kids could see him they'd think he was being funny, Mother Christmas, or Madame Santa Claus, and frustration is an insidious thing, Helena, my dear, did you know that? No, you don't know that, and when you find it out it may be too late, we could all be dead.

9

IT MUST BE BOB, my wife says as the telephone rings again. Without asking who Bob is (*officially* I don't know) I pick up the receiver (Is that fear in Helena's eyes?) and am talking on the phone, yes, it's him, go on reading. On the other end someone starts to read me a telegram.

My face lights up. Helena puts her book aside, gets up from her chair, stands close to me and looks at me inquisitively. Eduardo is coming, I tell her.

I know she doesn't know who Eduardo is. I don't care. Now I can hear the music of Christmas ringing out loud and clear. *Angels Are Singing in the Highest! Alleluia!*

IO

EDUARDO IS COMING tonight, Christmas Eve, one year Christmas Eve later. *From the very first moment when we met, by chance, at a party, we were surprised at how close we felt, how intimate, how necessary to one another* . . . This is the translation, which I began to attempt, of a passage of Montaigne. It was in December of last year, in Rio (Helena hadn't insisted on going with me as she usually did, and I felt alone and free). I got around quite a bit. Got in touch with people I knew before I was married and made new friends, many new friends.

I think I was just trying to numb myself because I was not (and still am not) ambitious enough to seek a lasting solution. The problems would continue, I knew, when I got back to Recife. Rio was just a brief escapade, nothing more.

I went on some real binges, and I remember a certain night, I was returning to the apartment that I had rented for fifteen days through a realtor agency. A living room and a bedroom in Copacabana, just a block from the beach, with everything I needed right at hand. A business trip that was as good as a vacation. And that night I did a terribly crazy thing.

Yes, something really crazy, and I never told anyone what I did. Maybe I'll tell Eduardo now, depending on how our conversation goes. He dropped me off that night in Rio, and after he said goodnight at the door of the building and drove away in his noisy car I stepped into the elevator and then, with my key, I started to scratch a name into the wooden wall.

I turn to the right and reach out with my hand, gripping the hard key tight between my fingers so I can make a deep scratch, and there, exactly where I was going to write, someone had already scratched the name ED.

Had I done it in another moment of drunkenness? Or had someone other than myself written those letters? I never called him *Ed,* and maybe the whole thing was just one of those crazy coincidences, and anyway, what did it matter who had scratched the name there? The important thing is that seeing it made me feel a new richness in our friendship, I don't know why, and I came back to Recife, Eduardo, thinking that somewhere in Montaigne there's an explanation for the inexplicable character of our meeting and our feelings of closeness in Rio. *Because it was he, because it was I.*

And now, Eduardo, you're coming unexpectedly, on a Christmas Eve that had promised me nothing.

II

MARCOS AND LUCIANA arrive. He's wearing a very colorful shirt (Italian silk, I think) and she's in a long dress with a low neckline that reveals the pearl between her breasts. Helena extends her hands to Marcos, who acts as if he were going to kiss them (it's just a game between the two of them, both mad about the theatre) but holds them away from his face and proclaims in a comically grandiloquent manner:

> *Her long hands*
> *asked only for a kiss*
> *and for some return.*
> *Lamenting the forgotten Trojan mare . . .*

A big hit, laughter all around. His boss, I tell Marcos, keeps him on the job not because he's such a good economist but as a touristic attraction, since he's the first communist *doublé* as a surrealist poet born and bred in what our publicity releases refer to as the New Northeast.

In the meantime I keep wondering how they'll react to Eduardo, who at this very moment must be landing in Guararapes Airport and who'll be here in less than half an hour.

When I invited him, back in Rio, he said he'd come some day whenever the mood struck him but wouldn't let me know until he was on his way. A whole year has passed without our hearing from each other and now he's keeping his word.

Two other couples show up. We eat, laugh, drink, and babble incessantly, no one seeming to pay any attention to what anyone else is saying. For a moment Helena's voice rises above the others. Everybody's here and you didn't bring Bob? All the guests look at each other, shocked and amused. Marcos is Helena's target; she fixes her green cobra eyes on him. Yes, it's true, he says, trying to sound natural, everybody really should meet Bob.

I listen with no great interest as Marcos sings the praises of my wife's lover. He's been in Brazil only a short time but he already speaks good Portuguese, which is rare for a gringo, and he's very different from the usual stereotype of the American, very open, and for him South America isn't just the back yard of the United States. I think that's more or less the thought of Marcos' speech. I've heard it all before.

Other voices in the living room, I don't know what they're saying, then the sudden squealing of brakes in front of the gate. I'm sure of it and I announce for all to hear: That's a friend of mine coming in from Rio, someone none of you know. His name is Manoel Eduardo.

ONE FOOT OVER THE ABYSS

SEAS, VALLEYS.
On top of the world's tallest mountain. But the geography lesson shows no sign of sinking into his hard head.

In front of the open book, his head supported by hands beneath his chin. He daydreams, eyes closed. Mother comes and catches him by surprise as he sits there lost in his fantasies.

Who?
Is His Honor at home? the man at the door asks.

So that's where you were bitten? the boy said to the young man.
Domício smiled. It doesn't hurt, he said, but it can be fatal, you know, unless the poison is removed.

In his anxiety the boy violates the virgin words. They exert a strangely seductive force upon him.
Tolhar, steptrum, tostripute.
Words. He turns them inside out, shifts their letters and syllables about, trying to get deep inside them. In these acrobatic exercises they become other words, other sounds. But André, seduced by their newness, by their novelty, repeats them over and over until his inner voice summons up from memory the same old familiar images as always. End of the game. What we already know has no charm about it.

Time creeps by and André feels something boiling inside him. On top of the world's tallest mountain, one foot over the abyss. Casanova comes and brushes against his legs under the table. A hearty kick sends him away yelping. A few short, sharp, hoarse howls, settling down behind the chest in the corner of the room.
If he were a bitch: *tolhar, steptrum, tostripute.*
Dog:
You son of a bitch.
André hums a tune as he brushes an insistent fly away from his nose.
Hizunner, shizunner, shit.
Hizunner is a tostripute.

Friday afternoon at six, Domício had said. That's a good time. The others will all have gone away by then.

Sticky humidity in the air. A sultriness that you can almost reach out and touch.

In André's daydreams now, something that happened Monday, four days ago already. Four days since he last saw Domício.

Seated at the dinner table André pretends to be studying his geography lesson. He doesn't have a special work-space of his own, not like his father, that great big man who shuts himself up in his study and then the house rule is that nobody can intrude on him without permission.

How can he keep his mind on the lesson (ah valleys, mountains, seas . . .) when his thoughts are wandering far away, always farther and farther away from that room, those books, and that atlas? On the riverbank he learned from Domício that a snake can bite a man without leaving a mark.

Look here, Domício said. Look close and see if there's any sign. No trace of it, right?

So that's where you were bitten?

Domício, Dominus.

Lots of books in the house. André thumbs through the *Book of Proper Names.* There is it—*do . . . domi . . . dominus:* lord, master, owner.

Lord and master and a victim of snakebite. Now, four days later, André still can't keep it out of his mind. Because his thoughts toss about and carry him back to the riverbank, back to the water flickering like liquid flames late that Monday afternoon.

The poison, Domício had said, has to be sucked out of the body. If not, he added in tragic tones, the victim dies.

André asked Domício, standing beside him, what he meant by "sucked." With his legs spread wide apart Domício said, Suck was like this, see, like this, and he stuck his thumb in his mouth and moved it back and forth. André at first was a bit undecided. Afraid of anything new. Afraid of novelty (a word he'd just discovered recently). Sitting on a rock he gazed at that chest, that flat stomach, that iridescent fuzz glistening in front of his face.

Suck, sucking, sucked. To draw liquid from, by action of the mouth; to draw in or take up, by or as if by suction, absorption, or the like. That's what the dictionary said.

The happy plants sent down
their hungry roots,
searching the earth for sweet saps
with the greed and dark fury
of stout young cubs sucking
the lioness' breast at night.

With feverish excitement he read these lines from Guerra Junqueiro's *The Last Days of Our Heavenly Father,* chosen by the man who compiled the dictionary to demonstrate the use of the verb "suck."

Now, after sending Casanova away with a kick, André tries to focus his eyes on the atlas. It, at least, is more interesting than the other books scattered on the table. But all to no avail. And here comes Mother and she spots him with his elbows on the table, his hands cupped about his face.

Ah-hmmm, she grunts, a few inches from his ear.

The clock on the wall ticks off the seconds with deadly regularity.

So you think it's cute to mistreat a poor little animal? says Mother, still hovering beside him.

Here, here, come on, little baby, she calls tenderly, taking Casanova up in her arms.

Swimming in the river. The most pleasant distraction, for André, that the stunted little town could offer. How many times do you have to be told? How many times? You are *not* to go swimming in the river. Schistosomiasis, giardiasis (he liked that word particularly), amoebas—all the dangers that I've warned you about (Father speaking) and I want you to remember (Mother speaking now) that you're the Son of a Judge and you shouldn't be running around with those ruffians down there. They're just not good enough for you.

André envies his brother, free and far away from home in a religious boarding school. A kind of punishment maybe? Maybe. Or for sure. But at least he's better off there.

Mother leaves the room with Casanova cradled between her broad cushiony breasts.

Could I speak with His Honor?

The man wants to know if André's father is at home.

In his obsession with the dictionary looks up the word "whore," enthralled by the string of other words with the same meaning, all jotted down for use in his game, a parody of the word games in the Sunday paper. Whore, prostitute, harlot, strumpet, bitch, trollop, hussy. Fed up with dear ol' Dad. You can't do this. For once and for all I'm telling you that you can't do that. Do you heeeaar me? Yes, that's Hizunner's great function in life, to decree prohibitions, with Mother throwing in her irksome two bits, reminding him, You're the Son of a Judge and you can't get mixed up with just anyone, understaaand?

Hizunner? Yes sir, he's at home.

And he went to call his father.

Sullen and distracted, he failed to notice when his mother came back.

With Casanova still in her arms, she talks, her mouth glued to André's ear (Does she think I'm deaf or something?), her voice heavy with displeasure. Do you think you lesson's going to seep up through your elbows? I don't even like to think about what your father is capable of doing if you flunk again. The least he'll do is ship you off to the priests at the boarding school, like your no-good brother, so you can learn a few of the rules of life. But not before giving you a good thrashing. Do you know what I mean? A good one, a really good one.

A sharp strident sound.

Teeth clenched with hatred. *Tostripute, steptrum, tolhar.* He brought the knuckles of his right fist down sharply against the tabletop. And then he got up and walked away and the woman was left talking to herself. Oh, if only the Good Lord had seen fit to give me a daughter (she always thought about the little daughter who would have behaved like an angel)—anything except these two sons, these crosses I have to bear, oh these sons who bring me nothing but heartaches and troubles. She followed the boy to the door. On the street her shouts pursued him, sounding in his ears like the wailing cry of some wild animal.

Son, come back. Cooommmmme baaaccck.

At a furious pace André made his way through the town until, sweaty and afire with heat, he came to the road. Before taking the side road that leads down to the river he stopped. He shook his clenched fist in the direction of the house. Gasping. Panting for breath. With sweat trickling down his whole body. Free. He took the side road. Troubled. He passed by the flowering cashew tree with bushy vines growing insolently around its thick ancient trunk. Troubled but free.

He unbuttoned his shirt and lay down on the ground. Eyes closed, his face toward the sun, he rested his cheek on the palm of his hand and lost track of how long he waited. I, André, Son of a Judge by the Grace of the Omnipotent Lord of Heaven and Earth (unhappy plants, hungry roots), I should be at home studying, at home studying (sweet saps, greed and dark fury), a good boy, but what am I instead? A bad boy, a devilish brat, my mother says, me and my brother both (stout young cubs). Mother always knows best. A boy of class, yes, but not a good little boy (sucking the lioness' breast at night), no, not that. Forgive me, Lord of all Suffering. Amen.

A soft sound of steps. It's Domício coming. *Dominus.* He approaches, his footsteps crushing the grasses. Mother firmly maintains that it's best to keep company only with boys from good families, boys like Alberto, the mayor's son. He's the type you should associate with, understaaaand? André thinks for a moment of Alberto, the Alberto who always argues with his cousin about whose turn it is to play the role of father in a kind of family pantomime they often dream up. Father comes home from work, has dinner with the family. Out for a drive in the car (three chairs lined up) and then everybody off to bed. Mother, played by André, says it's time for bed, let's go now, and distributes affectionate goodnights to everyone.

Domício came up and touched him with his foot. André held still and opened his eyes slowly, already certain of who it was. Four days ago, four days already. Sitting on that rock over there he had removed the poison from Domício's body. Domício had showed him how. Don't stop, please, don't stop, his hands around André's neck, don't stop now. All of it, get all the poison, all of, aaaaallll of it, his fingers clutching André's hair—
Domício, back again. A common ruffian, Mother had said scornfully. A person without class, she pronounced him. That long-nosed ruffian.
You know what he is, Mother? He's a victim of snakebite.
He's *what?*
But André spoke and then ducked out of sight.

It was a Monday. And it was Domício. André knew him only by sight. Domício worked at the supermarket and he brought purchases home for his mother.

How old are you? she asked him that time as she took the groceries from him.

(That strange habit she had of staring severely at people as if they were constantly engaged in wrong doings and owed her an account of their sins.)

Sixteen.

(The same age as Big Brother, shut away now with the Marists in his boarding school.)

She looked at him from head to toe and continued her questioning.

Are you in school?

Annoyed, Domício wrinkled his nose.

Not now, ma'am.

(André noticed how the hairy nostrils in the boy's pointed nose broadened when he said no ma'am.)

No ma'am, Domício said, staring her coldly in the eye. That long-nosed ruffian. So sassy. She didn't give him a tip. André saw that his mother didn't like the way Domício stood up to her gaze. Because it was supposed to make him lower his eyes, because it was the kind of stare that says you're a nobody, a ruffian, a person without class, a sorry good-for-nothing. Yes, Mother allowed herself attitudes of that sort, just as if she had the right to command people and order them about, always itchy to know the why and wherefore of their business, with all the details spelled out clear so she could compare, judge, and pass sentence. André would never try to explain anything to her about the snakebite.

So that's where you were bitten?

You know what he is, Mother?

A victim of snakebite, he said, and she didn't have the slightest idea what he meant.

Monday, four days ago.

Just as it's about to get dark, Domício returns. He begins to pull off his clothes, his eyes fixed on André. His bare feet, strong and sturdy like the feet of a man, mark the fine sand. André watches him remove his shirt. He sticks his left hand in the pocket of his jeans. His fingers fumble about inside as if he were looking for something. The other kids must be back in town by now. Soft drowsiness after the swim. André lingers alone on the bank of the river, sitting on a rock. And Domício approaches, his pants undone, making a display of that patch of russet-colored fuzz that grows beneath his navel and just above a shifting bulge that swells up under his pants. As if he had some kind of coiled spring between his legs, it occurred to the boy.

Domício sticks his right hand in his other pocket. The two hands in his pockets hold up his unzipped jeans. He takes a crumpled cigarette from his right pocket and lights it. Without taking his eyes off André.

He points to the spot where the snake bit him.

A late ray of sunlight licks the thin brushwood growing along the river. It's him, André thinks, him again. Omnipotent Lord of Heaven and Earth, he thought as he stretched out flat, face-down. *Dominus vobiscum.* He clutched the ground beneath him and waited. Deliver us from evil, from all evil. Listening to the water flow softly through the tepid dusk.

Domício comes and lies down beside him. He feels the boy's hot breath on the back of his neck and his heart beats more fiercely. With a gentle gesture Domício stretches out a hand and touches him on the shoulder. André shudders, glued to the earth.

Darcy Penteado

DARCY PENTEADO was born in São Roque (São Paulo) in 1926. He received in artistic initiation in publicity in 1944; began illustrating books a year later; and has designed settings and costumes for the theater from 1947 on, including settings for television from 1955 to 1960. His paintings have been in more than twenty one-man exhibitions in São Paulo and in other Brazilian cities. He has also exhibited in the main artistic capitals of the world: New York, Lisbon, Buenos Aires, Hamburg, Paris, Rome, etc. His paintings are on permanent exhibit in many museums around the world, such as the Fogg Art Museum (Harvard), São Paulo Museum of Modern Art, and the Institut für Auslandsbeziehungen in Stuttgart.

Penteado began his career as a writer with *A Meta* (The Goal), a collection of short stories published in São Paulo in 1976. That book was a popular success and was followed in 1977 by a second collection, *Crescilda e os Espartanos* (Crescilda and the Spartans). Of his two stories printed here, "Snow White Revisited" is from *A Meta*, "Jarbas the Imaginative" from *Crescilda e os Espartanos*.

SNOW WHITE REVISITED

Some time later she bore a child whose skin was as white as snow, whose lips were red like blood and whose hair was as black as ebony. They named the girl Snow White. . . .

The dwarfs fashioned a casket of crystal so that she could be seen from all sides, and on the lid, in golden letters, they engraved her name and her royal lineage. They placed her inside the coffin and carried it to the center of the forest where it was left exposed, and they all took turns standing beside it to keep it safe from wild animals. But there was no need for that, for all the animals of the forests, even the vultures, the wolves, the bears, the owls, and the delicate doves, came to weep beside the innocent maiden.

—The Brothers Grimm, 1812

ONCE UPON A TIME there was a very pretty princess whose real name was Antonio Matoso Nunes de Alvarenga. She belonged to a grand old family in the state of São Paulo, the Nunes de Alvarenga, who were almost direct descendants of the Indian chieftain Tibiriçá through his daughter Bartira, whose Christian name was Dona Isabel Dias. She had been married to João Ramalho, an adventurer, who dedicated himself to the pursuit of runaway slaves. They were, in short, a family of the highest lineage in spite of João Ramalho's obscure past in Portugal.

From a very early age, Antonio, the youngest child, showed feminine tendencies, preferring play-houses and dolls to games of soccer with his brothers and classmates. His mother, unconsciously or otherwise, tended to reinforce his feminine bent since she already had three sons and had ardently hoped that her fourth child would be a girl. Antonio came close to fulfilling her desire . . .

His skin was white and as pure as snow, his cheeks and lips as red as blood, his hair as black as ebony—though I, as narrator, should perhaps give a more regional touch to my story by saying that his hair was as black as the wings of the *graúna,* a bird which I've never seen, but which, so I've heard, is so black that its feathers have a purplish sheen.

Antonio then was a lovely child, and his beauty, reinforced by those contrasts, grew more and more pure as the years went by. There was no one who failed to admire him. *He's a perfect little angel,* his great aunts from the backlands exclaimed, or *he's an absolute darling. What a living doll,* crooned the friends of his mother. *We're gonna have a faggot in the family,* his older brothers muttered.

The only threat to Antonio's beauty was the sun during their holidays on the beach at Santos, for it showed no mercy toward his pale, delicate skin. As for the rest, his beauty was pointed out and envied by all. When he was twelve years or so and in the full splendor of his beauty, his mother died. For two years he was cared for by the maids in the family house, but then the father, who spent part of each year in Europe, as was the custom among good *paulista* families of the time, returned with a new wife, a French ballerina who had been born in Warsaw and with whom he had fallen madly in love. Antonio and his brothers were then shipped off to a Marist boarding school from which Antonio was expelled a year later for "indecorous acts committed in the dormitory and in the rest-rooms." What the director didn't tell the family was that he had been caught in the act and that the priest charged with the sur-veillance of the dormitory was also dismissed from the school.

During his time at the boarding school, his real name, Antonio, was virtually forgotten and he came to be known as Snow White, the name which would stick with him from then on because it was more appropriate for his physical type and his radiant complexion.

The noble lineage of Antonio—of Snow White, that is—was not subject to doubt, but the first official title in his family was that of Baron, the Baron of Alfazema, which the Emperor Dom Pedro II bestowed upon his great-grandfather, a countrified plantation owner from the northwestern uplands of the state of São Paulo. Actually the Emperor had planned a long tour of his dominions, during which he would spend each night in a plantation house. Automati-cally then the following morning, while His Majesty washed his face or sat on a chamber-pot engaged in his morning necessities, his private secretary would endow his host with a title of nobility. In that way the great-grandparents of Snow White came to be the Baron and Baroness of Alfazema, after their immense plantation which bore that name.

The courtly title, like so many others bestowed in the same cir-cumstances, was ill-fitted to the simplicity of the rustic planter who received it, and to an even greater degree it clashed with the character of Miss Gertrude, his illiterate half-breed wife, who spent most of her time darting in and out among the slaves in the plantation kitchen, dragging her old heelless slippers (she could never get used to real shoes) and dressed in a long housecoat made from a cheap cotton print.

One can imagine Miss Gertrude's apprehension when she got the news that the Emperor would be her guest. She gave as much attention as she knew how to refinement, exaggerating somewhat in the reception and the meals, just as might be expected from a person of simple habits, untrained in the niceties of fine etiquette. She even tried to use the only pair of shoes she had, but she hobbled about so clumsily that her own husband suggested that she go back to her usual slippers, cautioning her to use a longer housecoat that would hide her feet.

But in spite of the exaggeration, which always made him uncomfortable, the Emperor took a great liking to the couple, so much so that in the letter conceding to them their noble titles he placed an appendix saying that of all the baronesses in the Empire upon whom he had bestowed the title, Miss Gertrude de Alvarenga was the one who made the best roast suckling pig with *tutu de feijão,* a side-dish of bacon and beans.

But the greater title of princess came to Snow White through her grandfather, the eldest son of the Baron of Alfazema, who came to the capital from the provinces to study law. Soon after heading back into the hinterlands with his diploma in his hand, this eldest son had to take over the management of the plantation upon the death of the old baron. He managed it so well, with such aplomb and good judgment, that he soon transformed himself into the first coffee king of the state of São Paulo.

He was the first coffee king in the state, though it is known that a certain Italian immigrant, through a confusion of dates, might also have laid claim to the title. The abolition of slavery* was a great blow to him financially but he managed to retain his own entourage, his economic title and the noble privileges attendant thereunto by selling a goodly portion of his lands. Those titles and privileges were handed down to the father of Snow White, but in a rather precarious condition, and he too pared down the family fortune by neglecting the plantation and selling the harvests prematurely so that he could spend the money in Europe. This state of affairs continued until he finally lost the plantation to the Italian immigrants who had come to take over the work once done by the slaves.

---

*Isabel, Princess Imperial of Brazil, acting as regent during the absence of her father Dom Pedro II, abolished slavery in 1888. —*Ed.*

And so it was that when Snow White reached the age of eighteen, the financial situation of her family was like this: her two older brothers were well-off because they had married—one to the descendant of some Lebanese immigrants, the other to an Italian girl—and both were involved in the lucrative enterprises of their wives' families, much to their own betterment. The third brother had been in the United States for years pursuing some kind of technical career and had become so alienated from the family that they no longer heard from him. The father, in the meantime, had died, leaving most of what he had to his French bride, including the family mansion in the aristocratic section of the city and the paintings and other objets d'art that he had acquired at European auctions.

And Snow White's situation, lamentably, was this: expelled from two schools for indecorous acts, she had barely managed to get through high school. Marvelously beautiful but poor and rejected by her family for her effeminacy, she lived in a tiny house on Rua Helvetia, her only income being from the rental of a second matching house beside hers. The two houses were the only goods allotted to her by her father's will. No one could say that she was insensitive to art and beauty, since most queens have those tendencies anyway, but she nevertheless had no strong cultural background. Even so she was a devoted reader of Proust and she adored Paris, or what she knew of it vicariously, since her lack of means made it impossible for her to take a trip to Europe. She still had a good family name to live up to, but no profession to provide her with the means. The poor little creature, what a miserable life she must have led!

During the days of Snow White's youth, homosexuality was not the amusing, permissible, sportively wanton, well understood, flattered, deified, encouraged, apotheosized, and widely practiced thing that it is today. Far from it. Women were women then and men were men, real he-men, with no middle ground. There was no room for transvestites and androgynes. Queens were not even queens: when the ladies were obliged to mention them, they blushed behind their fans and called them *mariquinhas,* "little Marias." Their husbands referred to them as effeminates or inverts; and for the vanguard youth, those ahead of their time, they were *frescos,* the fresh ones, or *veados,* queers. In actual fact they were pariahs, segregated and pushed aside like wandering bands of lepers who offended by making a public display of their putrefaction. The whole situation was tragic, truly tragic.

In that hostile climate, poor and orphaned, Snow White had to tread her stigmatized path, and she plodded on like Christ on his way to Calvary, bearing her own cross, though with more time at her disposal and with more discretion. More time, because Snow White died at a much riper age than our Savior, and with more discretion because her brothers would probably have killed her if they had seen her making a public spectacle of herself.

They almost killed her as it was when they learned that she had been seen hunting men along the Viaduto do Chá. The oldest brother, also the most intransigent because of his ardent Catholicism, had taken the title of Baron of Alfazema, without any real claim to it, and he intended to transmit the title—if you can imagine such a thing!—to the first son born from his marriage with his Lebanese bride. He was righteously indignant then at the shameless way in which Snow White had been seen—to use his words—"dragging the family's good name and tradition through the gutters." He threatened to exile her—that is, to put her away in an insane asylum—and to take legal steps for confiscating her two houses on Helvetia Street. Imagine what misery the poor thing had to endure!

Snow White left her brother's office stunned and terrified, trembling with fear.

In those days the Avenida Paulista was still a quiet place. Between the mansions which the grand old *paulistas* managed with some difficulty to maintain after the fall of the Stock Market and the Thousand and One Nights palaces which the *nouveaux riches* erected on the last available lots, there was still, as there still is today, a wooded park left in its natural state, with peaceful graveled walkways interspersed with beds of wildflowers. In that oasis, far from the heart of the city, Snow White took refuge from the moralistic fury of her family. Shielded by the groves, she strolled and cruised at will from late each afternoon until nightfall, safe from the denunciatory gaze of those who had taken it upon themselves to inform her brothers.

She was a pioneer or precursor for that section of the city, opening new territory for those who came after her. By the time the motto *São Paulo can't stop growing* was invented and proclaimed, Snow White had already spent a great deal of time on her battlefront, pushing back the horizons of the fastest-growing city in the world.

The wooded park soon became an intimate part of Snow White, and, as the years went by, she came to be considered a part of it. The two blended together, one into the other. Late each afternoon when she began to frequent the woods, the masons who were building the last mansions on the avenue always stopped by for her. Years later when the area underwent a building boom and the palaces began to be torn down to make way for high-rise apartments, new workers—the sons and grandsons of those of yesteryear—came to trespass in her woods, and Snow White was still there on duty, patiently waiting for them.

But certainly everything was not the same as before. The years had passed through her, by her, and over her. In the face of one who was once a queen, as fresh and sprightly as a rosebud, wrinkles appeared, and her eyes took on a swollen look, losing much of their former radiance. But her skin remained impeccably white—she avoided the sun at all costs—and her hair, with a little help from Black Mystery by L'Oréal, continued to glisten like the blueblack wings of a *graúna*.

Her real life began at four o'clock when she took the tram marked "Avenida" on the corner of Rua Helvetia and Avenida São João and headed for her park. She would arrive before sunset, just in time to see, enraptured and removed from the bitterness of the world, the children who played in the sandy open spaces between the groves and those who rode their bicycles along walkways under the watchful eye of their guardians. Then she would take her position on a stone bench near the pissoir, beside the path that the construction workmen were almost forced to take. She would go into the pissoir, wandering about and exiting as many times as necessary, but she never lingered long after nightfall because the climate of São Paulo, as everyone knows, is very unstable and the wooded areas of the city, though few, often become rather damp at night.

It was a splendid September afternoon when Snow White, seated on her private bench watching the beams of sunlight sink behind the vegetation, happened upon an epochal idea: to continue in the park forever, even after death. The idea took such possession of her that she couldn't sleep for four nights in a row. But her sleepless vigil was not in vain because she used it to work out her plan, detail by detail.

First, she dispatched an official letter to the mayor informing him of her intentions and requesting his authorization for perpetual use of a small space in the park. Next she began to save money, skimping wherever she could, in order to finance the manufacture of a casket with a bronze frame and sides and lid of three-ply, shock-proof glass in a clear-gray color slightly tinged with pink. She took such pains because she had no intention of being buried. If it were a question of being placed under the ground, then any cemetery would do. What she wanted was the certainty that her pale beauty would continue to be contemplated and admired in the open for centuries to come and that the woods would protect her, filtering down upon her just the amount of light needed to illuminate her without ever blemishing the whiteness of her skin. After all, if she had become a symbol of life, part of the patrimony of the park, then it was only right that she should continue to be so after her death.

The mayor found the proposal so absurd that for a moment he was on the verge of tearing it to pieces from anger, thinking it was a joke perpetrated by some political enemy; but then, out of a routine sense of duty, he had it filed away. The next mayor received an identical letter, and he too placed it in his files. Snow White's petitions continued to be filed away, one for each of the mayors of the city of São Paulo, and, by considering that the first was dispatched during the mayoralty of Dr. Prestes Maia, who came to office around 1940, one can easily calculate the number of years that Snow White waited for an answer.

But finally the answer came: a mayor who had just taken office received the customary petition, and since he had great hopes of transforming São Paulo into a touristic and cultural center, he decided that the poor queen's crystal casket might work to that end by becoming one of the attractions of the city. He presented the petition to the City Council and supported the idea with such vehemence that he obtained a majority of the votes.

Snow White then received an affirmative reply, coupled with the condition that she and the landscape artist charged with redoing the park make a careful study to determine the best site for her casket. She chose a small glade surrounded by stately cypresses, a spot that seemed to have been conceived as the setting for a little temple. The approach was through an unassuming gravel path, very lovely and worthy of her.

The old princess had been postponing her death, waiting for a mayor who would understand her. With the money that was left over from the construction of her casket she had some plastic surgery done on her face which left it smooth and unwrinkled, just as it had been in that far-off time when she was eighteen. Then she had a gown worthy of a princess fashioned from pink nylon netting with a high satin collar, bought a diamond tiara, false but very convincing, had a good manicure, retouched the roots of her hair with black dye, and perfumed herself with a generous splash of Mitsouko by Guerlain. Finally she was ready to die . . .

In a supermarket she bought a very pretty red apple into which she injected a powerful insecticide, and then, fully adorned and attired, she lay down on the cushiony bottom of her casket. Calmly, in the final enactment of a ceremony planned long before, she took a big bite of the apple and fastened from inside the inviolable lid of her tomb. Just to be safe she took a second bite from the apple and swallowed it. Then she concentrated all of her attention on her own beauty so that the stomach pains would in no way register in her face and annul the results of the plastic surgery.

For one last time she gazed up at the heads of the cypresses, with clefts of sunlight filtering down between them and a multitude of little birds flying back and forth through the glade in search of nests. It was dusk, neither cold nor warm, when she closed her eyes and died.

The mayor turned out to be a man of great foresight! Snow White's tomb became the greatest tourist attraction of the metropolis and then of the country itself. Neither Juliet's tomb in Verona nor that of Lenin in Moscow could draw such crowds. On certain days of fine weather, but especially on Saturdays and Sundays, the line wound around the pissoir and stretched as far as the sandy area where the children played.

But something which no one, not even the mayor, had expected began to happen later, magnifying to surprising proportions the myth that had formed around Snow White: several years had gone by since her death and her body seemed unchanged, her skin still fresh and white, her cheeks and lips flushed red, and her hair as black as ebony, or as black as the wings of the *graúna*. One opinion was that the rarefied air and the invulnerability of the casket had forestalled decay, but that explanation failed to hold water since the worms of putrefaction, instead of coming from the outside, inhabit our own bodies and innards, indifferent to whether they have air or not. When the time comes for us to rot, we will rot regardless of where we are or whatever condition we might be in.

Therefore, if Snow White continued and still continues to look as fresh as when she was alive, it must be because something strange, something heavenly is taking place.

That is what the people began to murmur among themselves, and as everyone knows, the voice of the people is the voice of God. The crowds no longer came simply to gaze, moved by a morbid curiosity; now they came to worship, to adore. Someone in a state of despair happened to take his troubles to her; he prayed for a favor and his prayers were answered. The news of the miracle spread with the speed of a television image. It was unquestionably an act of God.

At the present time the immense line of people that winds around the pissoir and stretches through the walkways of the park and out into the next block is no longer made up of curious tourists but of pilgrims, the great majority of them injured or crippled. They come from the far corners of the world to stand before her, hoping for a miracle.

And almost always it occurs! In view of that fact, a request for canonization has been sent to the Pope, signed by thousands and thousands who have been amply rewarded for their faith. If the investigation being carried out by the Vatican's Department of Beatification and Canonization turns out favorably, Brazil, in the course of this present century, will be blessed with the joy and enormous honor of having a saint of its own: Saint Snow White or the Saintly Faggot, to use the affectionate names by which the faithful call her.

May God and Holy Mother Church see fit to grant us that favor.

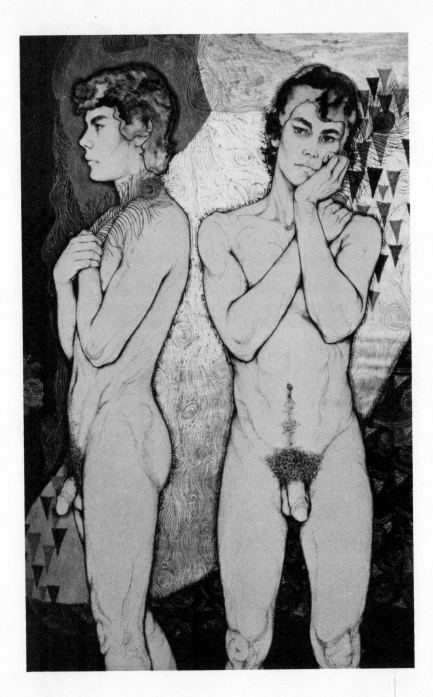

Painting by Darcy Penteado (Brazil)

JARBAS THE IMAGINATIVE

IT HAPPENED BY CHANCE: he was pursued, without great expectations, merely for a daily adventure, by Dr. Genozildo Garanhos, a lawyer, the assistant director of ICIC (the International Collective Insurance Company) and jurisconsultant for the Savings Bank of the Automotive Workers of the State of São Paulo. It happened by the door of a downtown movie house. Dr. Garanhos became his discoverer, responsible for what we might call the "golden age" in the brilliant and imaginative career of Jarbas.

But who was Jarbas after all? Apparently a nobody, or a somebody with nothing exceptional about him—nothing at least that one could readily see or presume. A husky street boy of twenty or twenty-one, just like all the others that hang out downtown, at the disposal of anyone who wants them. His height was normal; he was neither handsome nor ugly; and his overall appearance was healthy, like someone who plays soccer in an empty lot on Sunday afternoons. Jarbas was always an upstanding young man, honest and hard-working, never one of those idle types who live by exploiting queens. He had sex with *entendidos* because they appealed to him, not for monetary handouts, which he never accepted anyway, though he was not averse to dinner invitations, drinks, and eventual gifts. Everything about him was balanced, with nothing tending toward exaggeration. His real charm, therefore, did not reside in that anatomical feature which our libidos (yours too, dear reader— don't pretend otherwise) caused us to imagine a moment ago when I was listing his fine points and qualities.

And so his behavior was well suited to the image of a solid citizen, a business employee of moderate status—with the one exception of his prodigious imagination, and, a byproduct of it, his bizarre sexual behavior. In a man of great experience and sophistication that behavior would have been understandable and reasonably acceptable, but in him, a person whose milieu should have conditioned him to simple, routine tastes, it was remarkable to the point of seeming impossible.

"You are a shy little girl, virgin and helpless."

Dr. Garanhos had placed his glasses on the bedside table and unbuttoned his shirt, and as he unbuckled his belt and began to lower his pants he noticed that he was getting a bit potbellied.

Jarbas' statement caught him then with his pants just above the knees.

"What did you say?"

Still clutching his pants with his hands, he held still and looked at the boy who had already stripped and was in a half-reclining position on the bed.

"A shy little virgin, I said. You are a shy little virgin."

Garanhos could not believe his ears. Just a little kidding, no doubt. He felt like laughing but restrained himself because he had just met the boy and his great experience in such things told him that laughter can cause a new trick to become hopelessly inhibited, thereby spoiling his performance. Still holding up his pants, he took a couple of steps toward the bedside table, put his glasses back on and looked at Jarbas more closely. The boy gazed back at him with a look of enchantment, as if he were face to face with a princess from the Thousand and One Nights.

"Are you trying to make fun of me, kid?"

But the boy seemed distant, enveloped now in his fantasy.

"Oh, my little virgin," he purred. "Say that I've seduced you, say that I've brought you to this room against your will..."

The lawyer, half frightened by that time, decided that the best he could do was to play along with the boy, acting as if nothing out of the ordinary had happened.

"Yes," he said after he had taken a moment to study the situation, "yes, I'm a ... shy little virgin, completely helpless, and you have seduced me. But ... what's wrong with you, boy? Are you not feeling well?"

Jarbas jumped up from the bed and with an impulsive movement grasped the lawyer's hands, enfolding them in his and holding them tight against his chest. At that moment Dr. Garanhos' trousers fell to the floor.

"Of course I'm not feeling well, my little one. My conscience is hurting me because I've forced you to—"

"—but you haven't forced me to do anything!"

"Yes, I forced you! I've seduced you! I've kidnapped you from the home of your parents and forced you to come with me to this suspicious hotel where I intend to deflower you. Tell me I'm a scoundrel for acting that way with an innocent fifteen-year-old virgin like you. Tell me what a wretch I am!"

"Well, if you insist..."

In spite of his fear, Garanhos had a hard time restraining his urge to laugh, but the whole thing was so unexpected and original that he soon began to be excited by it, and then he played along.

"You're a wretch for acting this way with me," he said, and then, for emphasis, he added, "Tyrant!"

Jarbas enveloped him in an affectionate embrace, sinking his hands into the flaccid flesh of his midriff. "Don't think badly of me, my darling," the boy said. "My desire for you knows no bounds, and that's why I seduced you and brought you here."

"Oh, don't worry. Rest assured that I don't think any less of you for it. But don't you think it would be better to go to bed instead of standing up like this?"

"No, no, no!" Jarbas exclaimed. "You have to fight back! You can't just let me steal your virginity without first struggling to defend your innocence."

Garanhos searched the boy's gaze for some sign of insanity, or at least for some distant trace of an aggressiveness that might be cause for alarm. But all he could find was a pure expression like that of Botticelli's angels, and only then could he understand what was going on in the boy's mind. God, what a marvelous imagination, he thought to himself, and then, delighted by it all, he threw himself heart and soul into that fantasy world.

"Please, please," he begged, "I'm just a poor helpless little girl. Oh please don't harm me!" And pulling his pants back up hurriedly he withdrew into a corner of the room. Jarbas went after him, hugging him again.

"Don't be afraid, my little one," the boy said. "I'm mad with desire for you but I'll only touch you with your consent, and I'll only do what you command me to do—I promise, I promise!"

"Okay, then, just let me pull off the rest of my clothes."

"No, no! Not that way! You must not lay bare your delicate little body. Even if I force you, do everything possible to preserve your chastity."

"Oh, of course," the lawyer said as he modestly buttoned his shirt with his left hand (his right hand was still holding up his trousers so that they would not fall again). "And what should I do now?"

"You must defend yourself against your seducer. But no matter how much you struggle, my instincts are stronger and I'll try to tear off your clothes."

"But take it easy, okay? This is the first time I've used this shirt."

"I won't tear your dress, my darling, don't worry about that. I'll pull your clothes off gently, delicately. You can yield a little from time to time, *but keep up the struggle,* understand? A little virgin always struggles, even when she loves her seducer and desires him. Do you desire me?"

"Of course I do. Can I pull off my shirt now?"

"No, no, I've already told you that I'll pull it off for you," Jarbas answered as he closed in on Garanhos, drew his shirt back a little and touched his hairy chest. "Come on, react now. Say you don't want me to do this."

"No, I don't want you to!" the lawyer protested, trying to give his words a melodramatic tone as he lay his hand on that of his seducer.

"But now I can see that your resistance won't hold out for long, right? You're losing your resistance, letting yourself be seduced, letting yourself go. Come on and say you are, say you are . . ."

"You're right, my resistance is gone."

And so it had. The boy's hands had already removed the shirt and were gliding over the man's chest, shoulders, back, and arms. The lawyer was engrossed by it all. And then came the pants. Slowly Jarbas pried open the hand that held them at the waist and again they fell around the man's feet. Next, like an obedient maiden, the executive lifted first one leg and then the other so that the boy could remove them.

"Resist a little. You're giving in too quickly."

"But what can I do?—you're so much stronger than I am . . ."

"Run from me! Run around the room!"

With a leap he escaped and ran around to the other side of the room. Jarbas chased him but the lawyer tricked him and ran back to the other side of the room where he threw himself onto the bed, pretending to have fallen accidentally. The young man grabbed him then, bending over him, and kissed and caressed his back excitedly.

"Now you want to give up your virginity, don't you? Say that you do."

"I don't know if I'm ready for that . . ."

"You are!"

"Then go ahead!"

"But not in such a hurry, damn it! Don't you understand that you have to put up a fight and push me back and scratch at me first?"

"Yes, but I don't know if I can hold out much longer because you've got me excited with all of your horseplay . . ."

"But you can hold out a little while longer. After all, you're an innocent virgin. *You have to convince yourself of that!*"

"I'm an innocent virgin... I'm an innocent virgin... I'm an innocent virgin..."

"Now I'm going to try to pull off your panties. React! Defend yourself!"

Garanhos held on to his drawers as best he could, thinking that they would get torn in the scuffle. But Jarbas was a delicate seducer, and as before he little by little pried the man's hands apart and slowly stripped him naked. Maybe now, Garanhos thought, we can get on with the matter at hand.

But the boy continued. "Now I've stripped you naked," he said, "and now, my crazy little virgin, you're eager for me to deflower you, right? Come on, say you're eager."

"Yes, I am."

"But you shouldn't be! Cover your privates, little girl. Don't you see that I'm devouring you with my eyes?"

In doubt as to exactly what he should cover, Dr. Garanhos put one hand in front and one behind. Jarbas then climbed on top of him again with his hot body, his erect sex prodding the man.

"Don't be afraid, my little one. I'll be very gentle. My innocent little girl is now going to be transformed into a contented woman. Trust me, trust me..."

Afterwards, it took Dr. Garanhos some time to convince himself that such a thing had really happened.

Jarbas had no telephone in his house, only in the office where he worked, and even then he could only make or receive social calls after office hours. Eager to repeat the adventure, or perhaps to engage in some variation of it, Garanhos phoned him three days later.

"Really I don't think it would be worth the trouble," the boy answered. "We wouldn't have much to talk about now. But maybe later... who knows? In the meantime, maybe you can recommend me to your friends."

And that is what the lawyer did. A month later all the members of his circle of friends had already been cast in the title role of "The Farce of the Defenseless Virgin" and their collective impressions had been shared with everyone in the gay bar they frequented. By comparing the different stories, Garanhos realized that Jarbas varied his routine only slightly from one performance to another, and that led him to think that the boy was not as imaginative as he had originally assumed him to be.

But in spite of the fact that the topic grew quickly worn and stale from so much commentary in his circle of friends—or maybe due to that fact—Garanhos soon longed for a second session with the boy. If for no other reason, he liked his body. *But maybe later . . . who knows?* the boy had told him, and by now a month had already gone by. So Garanhos phoned again and this time the boy consented.

As in the first encounter, Garanhos took off part of his clothes, unbuttoned his shirt, placed his glasses (needed because of his shortsightedness) on the bedside table, and savored the fuzzy image of the naked boy lying on the bed. Then he spoke the phrase that he knew by heart from having said it so many times himself and having heard it repeated so often by his friends:

"I'm a poor little virgin, shy and defenseless."

He underscored his words by discreetly closing his shirt, hoping that his acting would meet with the approval of the boy.

"What do you mean, you debauchee? An old experienced whore like you trying to pass yourself off as a virgin? The mere idea . . ."

"But . . . but Jarbas . . . I don't understand . . ."

"So you don't understand, do you? Well let me explain. You're a prostitute, an old maid who never managed to hook a husband, and so you give yourself to the first man that comes along and wants to fuck you. You need a man, and the more men you can have, the better. Isn't that right, you whore? You're horny, right? Well, you've got your man for today!"

The boy struck him forcibly on the chest, and before the lawyer could recover from the shock he tore off his clothes and threw him on the bed. He kept up a running commentary on what was happening, mixing his comments with commands for the old man to do this or that, all in a manner quite different from their initial encounter, but still with a certain degree of aggressiveness.

When the scene was over and the lawyer had recovered from fright, he felt that this adventure, in spite of the way it had developed, was as exciting or perhaps more exciting than the first, largely as a result of the renewed imaginative capacity of the boy. He had hoped to re-enact a scene for the sake of nostalgia, and suddenly he had found himself participating in a wholly new drama, unpublished and unexpected.

"Uh, Jarbas, you may be bored by my asking . . . but that story of the virgin . . . are you not doing it anymore?"

"No, that was only up until the end of last month. We need variety, don't you think? Recommend me to your friends, okay?"

It goes without saying that the scene of the "Old Maid Who Gave Herself to Prostitution" was played, with slight variations, by all of Garanhos' friends, and that, as before, their comments were widely aired in their chats at the gay bar.

Around the first of the following month Garanhos phoned for another appointment, confident now in the boy's imaginative powers and in his monthly changes. In his room, as on the two previous occasions, Garanhos took off part of his clothing and waited for his orders, which were forthcoming:

"Take off the rest of your clothes and get on all fours on the bed. This is the zoo, and today you're going to be *my* camel . . ."

João Silvério Trevisan

JOÃO SILVÉRIO TREVISAN was born in Ribeirao, Bonito, Brazil, in 1944. He has written since his adolescence, when he received two national prizes for short fiction. After studying philosophy at the university he left to make films professionally. In 1970 Trevisan wrote and directed a full-length movie, *Orgy, or the Man Who Gave Birth,* which was soon banned by the Brazilian censors as "totally improper" and "pornographic." In 1971 his film *Maria de Tempestade* (Maria of the Storm) won a prize from the State Cinema Commission of São Paulo.

In 1972 he left Brazil for a long trip through Latin America. He then lived for a year in Berkeley, California, and for another year in Mexico.

Trevisan presently lives in the city of São Paulo, Brazil, working as a translator and writing scripts for movies. He is one of the editors of *Lampião,* a new Brazilian gay cultural paper. His book of short stories, *Testamento de Jônatas Deixado a David* (Jonathan's Bequest to David) was published by Editora Brasiliense, São Paulo, in 1976. (The title story from this volume is the one translated here. This story won a prize in 1975 in the Latin American Short Story Contest in Mexico City.) Trevisan has written a play, *Oh Beloved Fatherland!* and is working on his first novel, *Scanty News from Melinha Marchiotti.*

JONATHAN'S BEQUEST TO DAVID

Almost on tiptoes he entered the chapel, obedient to the bidding of what is generally called the heart. He sat down in one of the pews, muttering to himself. "I love," he said, "but who is it I love? I love but my love is formless. I am ready, Christ. Yes, I love Christ, but who, after all, is Christ?"

I made my way slowly into the chapel, pausing to savor those moments when the whole world seemed to invade my being and I opened wide to it, absorbing into myself the soft light and the indescribable climate of peace. As I entered my vision turned back upon myself, and though the stained-glass windows were too modest and unassuming, my entrance was like the entrance of a king. Perhaps it was the modesty of the chapel that made it so touching; the objects inside it, humble and ordinary in themselves, seemed to conceal something grandiose and mysterious. It was Holy Week and during Holy Week all things were somehow changed, altered. Limits of time and space were no longer clearly marked; the chapel, as the center of all our activities, functioned like an anti-time machine. It mattered but little where we happened to be or what we were doing because only our feelings had importance then. We were possessed by something that paid no regard to the difference between good and evil, however much we had been taught to distinguish between the two. A permanent miracle, lasting only a week, illumined the chapel and lent a special glow to our faces, not because we smiled more or slept better but simply because, without knowing it, we were touched by passion. In our passion, so strong that it seemed about to drown us, all of our senses mingled and became confused like those of newborn children. We no longer thought in terms of sorrow or gladness; we were conscious only of that Week, which for us was a week of passion.

In the sanctuary of the chapel stood a sensual Christ with an air of grandeur and mystery about it. At the time I did not know that Christ was really a feeling or that during Holy Week that feeling would grow keener, stronger. Because of that Christ coursing through our veins everything we saw was bathed in love. We felt love flowing between us all, from one to another and out toward all of our fellow men; we felt it in our liturgy and our chants, in the humble nightly act of brushing our teeth, in the voluptuous touch of our nightclothes against our bodies and our limbs. During that week our sensibilities reached such an intensity that love overflowed and took on a whole new dimension that led us to trespass on the mystery. Without our suspecting, the Christ of the Passion had lured us into unknown territory, and suddenly we were vulnerable to a virus that invaded our adolescence, taking possession of our seventeenth year.

Speech was not prohibited in the refectory but we took our meals in silence. From time to time an eruption of laughter would break the holy aura which, for reasons we could not explain, marked our meals and made them seem like a continuation of the hermetic climate of the chapel. It was there on a Holy Thursday that I, feeling suddenly lightheaded, broke into uncontrollable laughter. I laughed because one of my fellows, so sullen and cautious, spilled a whole bowl of zucchini into the lap of his cassock. We were already dressed for the evening ceremony, all in the black robes reserved for special occasions. I imagined how my colleague must have felt with the zucchini and its reddish broth running down his robe, staining the festive black that we wore only on such occasions of love. He glared at me resentfully, and then, in his peculiarly decisive manner, without a single word, he got up and walked away. My laughter dried up immediately and a sense of guilt descended upon me. I had acted rudely, grossly. After the meal I went to the playground, the only spot where we could lay aside our feeling of holiness and let life take its normal course—normal, at least, until time for the next ceremony. I looked for my colleague and asked him to forgive me. We both walked into the unfrequented woods out behind the buildings, the same woods where I often went alone to meditate on the Gospels and ponder the essence of the love of Christ. For a long time we said nothing. He was no longer angry. Unlike me, he was one of those people who react quickly to external annoyances, digest them quickly, and then once again see the world as before, calm and unperturbed. For that reason he did not hesitate to forgive me. Though we were in the same class we had never gotten to know each other well. Perhaps we had felt a secret respect one toward the other, but neither of us had ever shown it openly. In fact, we hardly ever spoke, much as if we had no concern for each other. Those were the things we discovered as we talked there in the woods.

At the ceremony of the Washing of the Feet I served as an

acolyte to the officiating priest. My friend, with his cassock still not dry, took the role of one of the Apostles there that evening. I helped the priest dry his feet; they were narrow and pointed, dark-skinned, and they smelled of talcum powder. I dried them slowly, watching the white towel soak up the water. Before straightening up I glanced at his face. He had been looking down at me. I almost smiled at him.

He dried the other's feet unhurriedly, and as the cloth grew moist he thought to himself: "What was it like, this love that Christ bore toward his apostles, and what was their love for him?"

After supper we saw each other again and smoked a cigarette together. "You had the face," he told me, "of Saint John the Evangelist, Christ's favorite."

"And you looked like Saint Peter," I said with a smile, "the most surly of them all—the surliest but also the most determined and headstrong."

That same night, before going to sleep, I went to his bed, drawn by something I could not resist, the sacred impulse of the Spirit. I told him good night, calling him by his name, Marcelo.

On Good Friday I was still helping with the ceremonies. I saw Marcelo again. On Holy Saturday I stood beside him singing in the choir. We looked at each other without knowing why, caught in the deep but tranquil sorrowfulness of our Gregorian chant, touched by the bareness of the altar and chapel, by the rich drowsy light that fell over us and humbled us. That night at the Ceremony of the Resurrection we all dedicated ourselves to the perfection of silence. We moved about without making a sound until that moment when the officiating priest intoned the tidings of the Resurrection in a voice which, it seemed would throw open all the tombs of the world. The chorus of hallelujahs sent shivers through our flesh. We marched out slowly, each with a lit candle, and on the way back to the refectory we all exchanged embraces. That was what the Resurrection meant for us—great hugs and embraces. I embraced Marcelo, still unaware that we two, in our own manner, had fathomed the mystery. The next day, Sunday, everything smelled of gladness and April sun. Marcelo and I went for a walk in the fields, up to the base of the mountains and along the river. White flowers were still blooming in the pasturelands and we strolled among them, a part of them. A strange sense of peace swelled up inside us—strange because it was accompanied by a disturbance of the spirit such as we had never known before. We acted out a parable from the New

Testament, the one about the wheat and the tare. We were at peace with ourselves, but still, throughout the afternoon, we felt the tumult and agitation of the tare, all without drawing a line between one emotion and the other.

We soon began to meet every night after supper, walking endlessly back and forth across the playground, trying to define a secret that only we would share. The members of the Community understood, for they all had their special secrets. We discussed everything imaginable, conversing with a tenderness that came swelling up from within us, greater and stronger than we, though still we did not bother to give it a name. It was not long until we were seeing each other again before bed; we said good night, exchanged long gazes, and then took our leave. Hardly a month had passed before we were together morning, noon, and night. We had become close friends. We worked and studied together in those times of constant ebullience. We experienced the world as if there were no limits to ourselves, hurrying to share our effervescent discoveries with each other. It was then that we decided to revive the community garden, so long neglected and abandoned. We planted lettuce, potatoes, wild chicory, and carrots. Each afternoon we went together to watch the new leaflets being born. For us they stretched, unfurled, and readied themselves. By the time the carrots were big enough for picking I had reached a confused and troubled understanding of it all.

I was passionately in love. While we pulled up the carrots I pondered the love that stirred and turned within me, bringing on fits of dizziness. Often I stopped my work and just gazed at Marcelo, who carefully designed all of his looks and gestures. He was the only Marcelo in the world, it seemed. His arms would reach down and his fingers would dig into the succulent earth; his legs would tense and stiffen as he pulled up each carrot. I followed his movements, noting how they quickened the exploding rhythms of my blood. Something was seething inside me, something unfamiliar and curiously painful, and it was all I could do to restrain my urge to cry out the impossible words of love that I had stored within me while the plants were growing. The harvest was slow, a week long. On the day when we finished some valve broke and those words sprayed out like water from a hose, like water from a broken dam, stronger than the river that flowed nearby, stronger, much stronger.

"I must tell you something," I said after supper. "I feel strange . . . something really strange . . ."

"Me too... I know that I love you too," he said quietly from some untapped depth of tenderness, speaking with the customary caution that was so strong in him and so lacking in me.

We went mad playing adolescent games that seemed more meaningful to us than all the rest of life. I gave him my favorite photograph of myself. I gave him the flowery shirt that had earned me so many admiring comments. I gave him a book called *Platero and I.* Whenever I came across a pretty pebble I picked it up and saved it for him. I gave him little images of saints with declarations of love, looking at him ten times in ten seconds. I gave him my diary so that he could read all about me. I gave him the candy my mother sent me, and the most beautiful crucifix I had. For him I wrote two poems and a great many prayers, and my friends and brothers became his friends and brothers. Then he suggested that we give all we had to each other—clothing, money, books, everything—so that our love would last until the end. We agreed, and there was no longer any question of his and mine because everything we owned was ours. He gave me money to buy the books I wanted—because his father was richer than mine, he said—and he insisted that I use his wristwatch and his Parker pen. We became the two best students in our class; in our study groups we were outstanding, and once we presented a joint paper on philosophy that rightfully won the praise of all. At one point I discovered that Marcelo intentionally gave wrong answers on his exams to avoid getting higher scores than I, and then I noticed that he was becoming more and more sociable, in imitation of me, and that he had begun to comb his hair like mine. One day he gave me his best pair of jockey shorts as a gift.

"Marcelo, what can I do?" I asked him, "my love has no end."

During the vacations I became troubled. We were together, but the doubts were mine alone. How, I wondered, was it that Christ loved his disciples?

Christ cradled John's head against his chest and slowly stroked his hair. And Christ told Peter that he loved him as himself. But above all he loved John, his little John.

Marcelo in the meantime rode about wildly on his horse, shouting as he chased young steers across the fields. I suffered alone because I did not understand the mystery that was challenging me. In the same measure that I loved, I suffered, and with the same intensity.

"Marcelo," I told him, "I love you even more than I had thought. Is that not a sin?"

I shut myself up and cried alone. I could not even bear to ride horseback beside him because I carried within me stubborn evidence of the weight of my love. A punishment of sorts, I could not deny that evidence which kept me from riding.

His loins ached with passion, restrained but rebellious. For days he could hardly walk. His testicles burned with an eagerness that collected there between his legs, heavy and smoldering. The pain was more than a witness to his passion; it was a silent complaint.

Things continued as before until the night when Marcelo called me to sleep beside him in his bed because of the chill. I leaped from my own bed into his, close to him under the covers. But I began to sob, and it was through my sobs that I asked him what we could do to become simply friends again.

He did not let me finish. By candlelight he reached for a Bible and opened it to a passage that he had already marked. "The soul of Jonathan," he read aloud, "was joined to the soul of David, and Jonathan loved David as he loved his own life. Then David and Jonathan were joined in friendship, for Jonathan loved him as himself. And Jonathan took off his tunic and gave it to David, along with his other clothing, even to his sword, his bow, and his belt." Marcelo closed the book and touched my face with his hand.

"You see," he said, speaking softly in a voice never touched by doubt, "you see—we have done as they did. We love as they loved, which is the way God wills it to be."

That was all I needed to hear. In one unbroken and unrestrainable movement we threw off all our clothes. We had nothing else to exchange. We caressed each other slowly, like one who clumsily and hesitantly opens a coffer of delights. I discovered the hairs on his chest, the muscles in his neck, the shape of his fingers. One of them had been partially cut off and I learned to love it above all the rest. I discovered the scent of his armpits and his hair, was fascinated by the perfume of his groins. For me they were the groins of the world. From that night on we went to bed early and got up when the sun was already high in the morning sky. We rode our horses through the fields, and during our rides, lost in the pure pleasure of feeling the wind on my face, I thought again and again how at last I had found the love I always searched for in the Gospels.

"Isn't it true," I shouted back at him laughingly, "that Christ loved the way we love?" Marcelo simply smiled, confident and certain, and answered with a nod of his head.

From that time on our only sorrow was in the fact that we were not one. We returned to the seminary from the holidays. We worked together, prayed together, meditated and studied and played together, but still we were two. At the same time, though, we came to be an important part of the Community. Marcelo was elected leader of our class and I organized the Literary Club and saw it through its liveliest days. Everyone saw us together. There was astonishment in some eyes and resentment in others but we did not distinguish between the two—not, at least, until after we discovered what we had needed all along. The uppermost floor of the building was an immense storage room for things no longer in use. The dirtiness of the place did not matter to us. We spread a blanket on the dusty cement floor, pushed back the spiderwebs, and made a new world for ourselves there, a world where our bodies, locked in a desperate embrace, could lessen somewhat the anguish of being two by groping toward oneness. There, surrounded by old chairs and tables, broken glasses, torn curtains, and discarded images of saints, we ruptured each other's skins and felt our blood mingle and transfuse. Above us bats shrieked feverishly, excited by the exploding redness of our blood. We made love until late in the night. After several weeks we both had become skinny and the rings under our eyes were only one of the details that everyone noticed. Very quickly we became the favorite topic of conversation among the hundred and twenty boys who, like us, were studying for the priesthood. They were intrigued by the secret we had stumbled upon and refused to share with them. We could not have cared less. Irresistibly, night after night, we found our way back to the blanket that held our world. There we lay at daybreak on a certain morning, naked as always. The youthful beauty of our bodies had made us delirious; moaning and groaning, we were engaged in acts that once we had considered obscene. That morning the darkness gazed down upon us while the dead eyes of the saints looked on as always and the bats flitted about excitedly. Suddenly a flaming point of light broke the darkness and the tremulous glow of a torch spilled over us. I jumped back in fear. Marcelo scrambled to his feet, his eyes wide open, and the bats shrieked all the more fiercely. Amid their shrieking we heard the voice of the rector.

"So it is true," he said.

Marcelo acted as if nothing had happened. With the same certainty as always, in his voice never touched by doubt, he gave an answer that I never heard him resort to again.

"Yes, Father," he said, "it's true. This is the love of Christ."

Many years later the lover gazed at him in the dim light.

"I can only understand how beautiful it is to love a man," he said, "when I am filled with passion for a man, as I am now."

And then he turned aside. In the dimness he saw the past and thought he glimpsed something beyond, perhaps the future. Christ no longer crossed his mind. He knew simply that death would come some day with no apologies and no fixed date. "Only he who loves wholly will have lived," he thought with great clarity, "only he who interprets the mystery without regard for the official rules. For him who dares, the prize of love. And after love, death."

How lucid his thoughts seemed to him then, and he imagined himself lying there forever, free of remembrances, naked, looking forward.

Valery Pereleshin

VALERY PERELESHIN (Valery Franzevich Salatko-Petryshche) was born in Irkutsk in 1913 into a family of old Polish gentry. In 1920 his mother brought him to Harbin, China, where he graduated from the YMCA High School and later studied law and theology. As an adolescent he had some of his poems published in a local newspaper, and in 1932 he joined the literary journal *Rubezh* (The Frontier).

From 1939 to 1943 he assiduously studied Chinese in Peking. Later he moved to Shanghai and then Tientsin, and in January 1953 arrived in Rio de Janeiro. While in China, he published several collections of verse—*En Route* (1937), *The Goodly Beehive, The Star above the Sea,* and *The Sacrifice*—and a translation of Coleridge's "Rime of the Ancient Mariner." All these are now out of print.

After years of hibernation in Brazil, he returned to literature in 1967, publishing in *La Renaissance, The New Review, Novoye Russkoye Slovo, La Pensée Russe, The Contemporary,* and elsewhere. He published *The Southern Home* (1968), *The Swing* (1971), *The Sanctuary* (1972), *From the Mount Nebo* (1975), *Ariel* (1976), an anthology of Chinese poetry (*Verses on a Fan*) and *Li Sao* by Chü Yuan (1975). His anthology of Brazilian poetry, *The Southern Cross,* was published in West Germany.

Ready for publication are his long (8,400 lines) autobiographical *Poem without Object;* a dramatic poem, *King Saul;* a second Chinese anthology, *A Shadow on the Curtain;* and translations of the *Tao Te Ching, A Spiritual Canticle* by St. John of the Cross, and thirty-five English sonnets by Fernando Pessoa.

Pereleshin writes in Russian and the poems published here are translated from that language. Simon Karlinsky, the translator, teaches in the Department of Slavic Languages at the University of California, Berkeley. He is the author of *Marina Cvetaeva (Tsvetaeva), Her Life and Art* (1966) and *The Sexual Labyrinth of Nikolai Gogol* (1976).

TO ONE WHO CONFESSED

To D. S. F.

The fertile Chinese hold a firm conviction
—I heard it often from their very mouths—
That those immoral creatures called jack rabbits
Can do without the females of their kind,

But manage still to propagate their species;
While in the village taverns in Brazil
Mustachioed *caboclos* will assure you
That deer's the animal that shuns its hinds.

They should at least consult a dictionary:
Stag starts with *ve,* a fellow starts with *vi,*
But they pronounce *veado* and *viado*
In dialects where it sounds the same to me.

Alumnus of religious seminaries
(Acaracu, then in Aracati),
You've been inscribed among those odious creatures
Whom any one may crucify at will.

Those very ones, who in a dormitory
Would clasp you passionately, one and all,
Tormented by desires they could not master
They'd plead with you: "Please let me, dear boy!"

Those very ones—but now they are the fathers
Of children no one dreamed of in those days,
Avoid you and are making you feel guilty
Because *their* lust was stronger than their shame.

"A deer, a deer!"—that's all you ever hear there.
They've branded you and everyone's been told.
But we are friends and I would like to give you
New freedom, which we'll share fraternally.

Just have a look: *Lefthanded Light,* a journal
With drawings, articles and interviews;
And here's *Orgasms of Light,* a book of poems:
I'll lend you both and you can take them home.
We're not alone. Believe me, there are millions
Who'll follow Leyland in the righteous fight
For our equality, for decent legislation
And for the right to live and be ourselves.

POET'S NOTE: In China, "jack rabbit" is a swearword, as in the expression "Ni chê-kè t'u-tzy, nan-nü fen pu ch'u-lai!" ("Why, you jack rabbit, you can't even tell a male from a female!") It is believed in China that jack rabbits are able to breed by means that are called "contrary to nature."

Caboclo is a Brazilian term for a person who is half white and half Indian. Acaracu and Aracati are small towns in the north of Brazil.

TRANSLATOR'S NOTE: This metrical version has omitted an important aspect of the poem: its playful and sparkling rhymes, the English equivalents of which would be somewhere halfway between the Byron of "Don Juan" and Cole Porter. Pereleshin's rendition of *Gay Sunshine* into Russian as "Lefthanded Light" (preserved in the translation) refers to his theory of spiritual lefthandedness, which consists of emancipating oneself from the imperatives of the species and family, and is a prerequisite for admitting one's gayness to oneself and others. The poem is addressed to a Brazilian friend of the poet's, whose biography and consciousness the poem reflects.

Veado (deer) is the Brazilian slang word for homosexual, comparable to the term "queer" in this country. *Orgasms of Light* is the anthology of poems and short stories published by Gay Sunshine Press in 1977.

SONNET FROM *ARIEL:*
A DECLARATION OF LOVE

That's quite a sweet confession that I got:
You write you love me for my verbal powers
Though I am not renowned among the poets
And other masters have a greater fame.

Well, why turn down the lesser good that comes our way?
I, too, love Sergio because on Sundays
He gives me rides in his three-seat sedan.
I love Antonio as a splendid house painter.

Among the barbers, I love the black barber Nilo.
Among the soaps, it's cocoa butter soap.
No salt but Morton's will for pickles do.

There's Dennis Weaver—I just love him as an actor.
Bald-domed Anselmo—him I love as tram conductor.
And you—I only love the translator in you.

November 6, 1974

TRANSLATOR'S NOTE: In the original, all the sonnets in *Ariel* are written in lines of precisely rhymed iambic pentameter. The rhyme scheme for "A Declaration of Love" is *a b b a, a b b a, c c d, e e d.*

STRAIGHT FROM THE SHOULDER

To Paulo Carlos Peixoto Cruz

If you were someone I invented in a dream
You would be soft as wax between my fingers
And would grow up a pampered adolescent,
A graft that fortunately took to me.

I would believe that in some distant land,
Having matured, you soar in flattened skies
Or are a horse-guard, prancing at parades
And spend your holidays upon the moon.

If you were . . . But in Rio de Janeiro
I met an ordinary *brasileiro*
And fell in love with him, straight from the shoulder.

After I woke, I fashioned from my dream
No fortune's darling and no wealthy heir,
No smartypants, not even a heartbreaker!

January 28, 1977

ADMIRATION

"You are so handsome! Why, with such a model
I could have sculpted a crown prince in marble
Disguised as a discobolus and found
Distinguished, wealthy patrons for my art.

And you'd be celebrated and admired,
Whole schools of art arising from your form
To dazzle—such are the vagaries of fate—
Rome, the infallible Eternal City.

At an exhibit under Roman pines
Art lovers would imbibe your lovely lines,
Their mouths atremble, gulping avidly . . ."

But as I think all this, the hostile punk
Feeling my steady gaze upon his body
Calls out: "Go to hell, you cocksucker!"

August 11, 1977

Cassiano Nunes

CASSIANO NUNES was born in Santos, Brazil, in 1921, the son of Portuguese immigrants. At the age of sixteen he began to publish articles in the literary supplement of the newspaper *A Tribuna* in his native Santos. Soon after that he studied American literature in the United States and German literature at the University of Heidelberg; in 1964 he received a degree in English and German Literatures from the University of São Paulo. From 1962 to 1965 he was a lecturer in Brazilian literature at New York University; in 1966 he returned to Brazil to join the faculty at the University of Brasilia, where he has remained until the present time.

Since his debut as a writer at the age of sixteen, Nunes has written extensively, with three volumes of poetry to date, numerous books of prose and literary criticism, and Portuguese translations from the work of Walt Whitman, Emily Dickinson, and Langston Hughes.

The poems translated here are from his *Madrugada* (Dawn), published in 1975.

Franklin Jorge

FRANKLIN JORGE lives in the city of Natal, Brazil. The poems printed here originally appeared in his book *Improprio para Menores de 18 Amores* (Unfit for People with Less than 18 Loves) (1977).

Cassiano Nunes

ALTA NOITE

Alta noite, leio Marianne Moore.
Passos no lajedo.
Olho através da grade.
De fora,
os dois gorjeiam cumprimentos
com a cordialidade aflita
do vício carecido.
Tão acessíveis suas carnes claras,
tão disponível
o frescor de sua juventude!

Partem desajeitados
com a recusa amável.
De novo, a solidão.
Há luz demais!
Procuro agora
versos pássaros.
Busco, também carente,
remota, salvadora canção.

IMPROVISO

Só no instante
em que te beijo a boca jovem,
é que percebo
a verdade sem remédio
da minha idade,
os séculos que nos separam,
tanta neve,
tanto desperdício,
montões de rosas murchas,
lixo,
em mil alamedas.

LATE NIGHT

Late night, reading Marianne Moore.
Footsteps on the pavement.
I glance through the grille.
Outside
the two of them warble greetings
with the pained cordiality
of their lustful need.
So accessible their clear flesh,
so available
the freshness of their youth!

They draw away clumsily
at my friendly refusal.
Loneliness again.
There is too much light!
Now I search for
bird-like verses.
Also in need, I hunt
some far-off saving song.

IMPROMPTU

Only when
I kiss your young mouth
am I aware of
the irremediable truth
of my age,
of the centuries that separate us—
so much snow,
so much waste,
piles of faded roses,
dust
in a thousand shaded groves.

LE DÎNER SUR L'HERBE

À noite, foram chegando pouco a pouco
ao parque umbroso
(a treva rumorejante).
Desconhecidos uns dos outros,
vinculava-os apenas
a opção profunda.
Com naturalidade
desnudaram as almas,
afrouxando roupas...
O sexo acendeu como um fósforo.
Uma intensa felicidade
(tão breve!)
no desafogo.
Findo o improvisado festival,
retiraram-se sem despedidas
para os seus subúrbios,
dispostos a roer
por mais uma semana
a côdea do quotidiano.

BREVE SERENATA

Como posso queixar-me
de solidão,
se possuo a noite
e a sua canção?

A noite é tão vasta
que me perco nela!
Amor! Acende a estrela
de tua janela!

LE DÎNER SUR L'HERBE

At night they made their way
little by little
to the shaded park
(the rustling darkness).
Strangers one to the other,
only their deep choice
bound them together.
With naturalness
they lay bare their souls,
loosening their clothing...
Sex flared up like a match.
Intense happiness
(so fleeting!)
in their disencumberment.
Their impromptu feast over,
they withdrew without a goodbye,
back to their suburbs,
ready to gnaw
for another week
on the crust of day-to-day life.

SHORT SERENADE

How can I complain
of loneliness
if the night
and its song are mine?

The night is so vast
that I am lost in it!
Love, light the star
in your window!

Franklin Jorge

POEMA DOS DESAPARECIDOS

Parem o trânsito!
Que a polícia,
sempre eficiente e benemérita,
intercepte o movimento
nos aero-portos,
estações rodo-ferroviárias,
e vamos todos,
homens e mulheres,
indecisos sexuais
versáteis, lésbicas,
como irmãos,
procurar os desaparecidos.
Os desaparecidos estão gemendo
como afogados dentro de um poço.

2 POEMAS PARA REINALDO ELIAS

1

Teu nome
mais parece
uma fruta
feita na medida
de minha fome.

2

Pronuncio
teu nome
e um gosto
de fruta
perdura
em minha boca.

POEMA

Meua olhos estão doentes
quando, ansiosos, cravam-se
no teu ventre—
que é como um irrequieto pássaro,
trêmulo sob as patas de uma aranha
ou ante o olhar de uma serpente.
Todo o meu corpo acha-se doente,
dos teus venenos tocado:
no meu delírio, demente,
perfuro-te com a minha língua
a lanço âncoras no teu ventre.

PEÇA FINAL

Este pedaço de hóstia
que resta em minha boca
é a perna
ou o sexo de Jesus?

POEM FOR THOSE
WHO ARE MISSING

Stop the traffic!
Let the police,
always efficient and meritorious,
halt the movement
in the airports
and the railroad stations,
and let us all go,
men and women,
the sexually undecided,
the versatile, Lesbians,
all like brothers
in search of those who are missing.
They are groaning
like drowned men down in a well.

2 POEMS FOR
REINALDO ELIAS

1
Your name
is like
a fruit made
to the measure
of my hunger.

2
I say
your name
and a taste
of fruit
lingers in
my mouth.

POEM

My eyes ache
when, eager, they stare at
your stomach,
which is like a restless bird
trembling under a spider's paws
or held in a serpent's gaze.
My whole body aches,
touched by your venoms:
mad, delirious,
I pierce you with my tongue
and drop anchors in your belly.

END PIECE

This bit of the host
left in my mouth—
is it Jesus' thigh
or his cock?

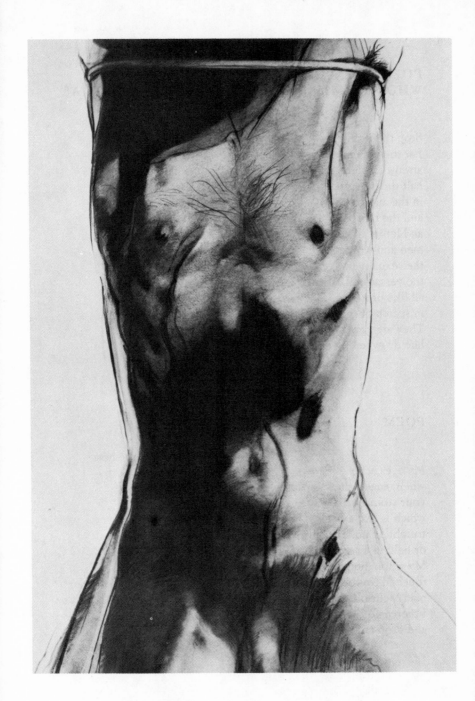

Pastel (1975) by Luís Caballero (Colombia)

Three Colombian Poets

PORFIRIO BARBA-JACOB (real name Miguel Angel Osorio) was born in Santa Rosa de Osos, Antioquía, Colombia, in 1883. He was self-educated and led a bohemian, wandering life, sometimes working as a journalist. He traveled and lived in Costa Rica, Jamaica, Cuba, Guatemala, Honduras, El Salvador, Mexico, and the United States. He died in Mexico City in 1942.

Barba-Jacob wrote of himself: "I am a child of Antioquía, of the Jewish race, which explains my penchant for melancholy, and I live like a Gentile with no hope for a coming Messiah, or like a pagan in the latter days of Rome."

JAIME JARAMILLO ESCOBAR was born in the southeast part of the province of Antioquía, Colombia, in 1932. He is an important member of the Colombian literary Nadaist movement (1958–1978). During this period he published his work under the pseudonym of X-504. In Colombia he is well known as a poet and writer. He was awarded the "Cassius Clay" Prize of Poetry for his book *Los Poemas de la Ofensa,* published in 1967 by Tercer Mundo, Bogotá. The greater part of his work remains unpublished or scattered among literary magazines and periodicals. He maintains that "in eternity there is time enough to wait for its publication." He currently lives in Bogotá and works in publicity.

The poems printed in the present anthology originally appeared in the book *Los Poemas de la Ofensa.*

JAIME MANRIQUE ARDILA was born in Barranquilla, Colombia, in 1949. By the time he was thirteen he had read all of Dostoyevsky, Tolstoy, Flaubert, the Brontës, a lot of Dickens, Balzac, etc. Around that time he began to write fiction and poetry. Later, under the influence of the "nadaistas," he wrote short stories.

Manrique moved to the States at the age of sixteen, and for almost six years studied at the University of South Florida. Through some friends he was introduced to the work of Roethke, Plath, Sexton, Hart Crane, Emily Dickinson, and Cavafy—"When I finished reading Cavafy's *Collected Poems* I destroyed all the poetry I had written for ten years, and decided to begin all over again."

He now lives in Bogotá with painter Bill Sullivan and Daisy the dog.

Porfirio Barba-Jacob

ELEGÍA DEL MARINO ILUSORIO
(FRAGMENTO DEL DELIRIO DE LA NOCHE
EN CULPAN)

Pensando estoy... Mi pensamiento tiene
ya el ritmo, ya el color, ya el ardimiento
de un mar que alumbran fuegos ponentinos.
A la borda del buque van saltando,
ebrios del mar, los jóvenes marinos.

Pensando estoy... Yo, có ceñiría
la cabeza encrespada y voluptuosa
de un joven, en la playa deleitosa,
cual besa el mar con sus lenguas el día.
Y cómo —de él cautivo—, temblando, suspirando,
contra la Muerte
su juventud indómita, tierno, protegería.
Contra la Muerte,
su silueta ilusoria vaga en mi poesía.

Morir... ¿Conque esta carne cerúlea, macerada
en los jugos del mar, suave y ardiente,
será por el dolor acongojada?
¿Y el ser bello en la tierra encantada,
y el soñar en la noche iluminada,
y la ilusión, de soles diademada,
y el vigor... y el amor... fué nada, nada?

¡Dame tu miel, oh niño de boca perfumada!

ELEGY FOR AN IMAGINARY SAILOR

Images come . . . and my thoughts take on
the rhythm and the burning colors of a sea lit
by sunset's fires.
Drunk with the sea, young sailors frolic
about the deck of their ship.

Images come . . . of how, on some delightful beach,
like the sea kissing the day with its tongues,
I would gird the voluptuous and ruffled head
of one of those men,
how I, his captive, trembling and sighing,
would protect his tender, untamed youth
from Death.
(Safe from Death,
his shadowy form wanders through my poetry.)

Death? Is it possible that this sky-blue flesh,
soaked in the juices of the sea, so smooth
and burning, will one day be twisted with pain?
Does being beautiful
on a magical planet mean nothing?
And the dreams we dream on starry nights,
our illusions crowned with suns,
and strength, and love itself . . . will all these
come to nothing?

Give me your honey, child of the perfumed mouth!

Jaime Jaramillo Escobar

ACTA DE LOS TESTIGOS

Yo, Nicanor, declaro que él era bello e inocente.
Yo, Diofanor, declaro que él era bello e inocente.
Yo, Agenor, declaro que él era bello e inocente.

Trescientos días atravesó en su bicicleta hasta que llegaron las grandes fiestas de la ciudad.
y bailó con su vestido de Pierrot delante de los invitados, quienes se
mordían la lengua y lo aplaudían con sus manos pálidas
Yo me subía a un árbol de la avenida para verlo pasar,
y después me iba galopando por las calles, desbocado de admiración

Yo, Diofanor, convulsionado por el verano que desleía mi sexo,
circulando por mis venas semen a cuarenta grados en las calles de la
ciudad,
encerrado en la brillantez del verano como una araña en un laberinto
de cristal,
andando de torre en torre perseguía su sombra
como un pez persiguiendo el agua de los arroyuelos que huyen por
el desierto,
como el pájaro que persigue la aurora que le da la vuelta a la tierra,
como el cristal de murano que persigue la lluvia que anda por los
montes para cogerle una gota.
Lo esperé en el cruce elevado, lo perdí en los ascensores y lo volví
a encontrar en la plaza del Obelisco:
fue interceptado sucesivamente por una columna de soldados, por
un tren ambulante y por un eclipse de girasoles:
y en un momento de ofuscación fue interrogado por las bailarinas
de ballet, por el cable de tensión del Arco Iris y por el árbol
del pan.
Ya para entonces yo mordía el calcinado limo de las calles
como una tenaza, come una serpiente, como un fuetazo en el polvo,
como el camello que viene todos los días a comer el vello que crece
en mis piernas.

WHAT THE WITNESSES SAID

I, Nicanor, declare that he was beautiful and innocent.
I, Diofanor, declare that he was beautiful and innocent.
I, Agenor, declare that he was beautiful and innocent.

He rode his bicycle for three hundred days until the city's great holi-
    days came around,
and he danced dressed like Pierrot in front of the guests, who bit
    their tongues and applauded him with pale hands.
I climbed up a tree on the avenue to watch him pass by,
and then I went galloping through the streets, stampeding with
    admiration.

I, Diofanor, convulsed by the summer that diluted my sex,
in the streets of the city with 104° semen coursing through my veins,
shut up in summer's brilliance like a spider in a crystal labyrinth,
pursued his shadow from tower to tower
like a fish pursuing the water of streams that flee into the desert,
like a bird in pursuit of the dawn that returns it to earth,
like Murano crystal in pursuit of rain in the hills, eager to catch a
    drop.
I lay in wait for him at the raised crossing, lost him in the elevators,
    and found him again on the Plaza del Obelisco;
he was intercepted successively by a column of soldiers, by a moving
    train, and by an eclipse of sunflowers;
and at the moment of obfuscation he was questioned by the bal-
    lerinas from the ballet, by the rainbow's high-tension cable,
    and by a breadfruit tree.
By that time I was biting the charred lime of the streets
like a pincer, like a serpent, like a whiplash in the dust,
like the camel that comes every day to eat the fuzz that grows on my
    legs.

Yo, Agenor, esperaba silenciosamente a la sombra de los bastiones
en las empenumbradas esquinas de la calle de las palmeras rosadas
con las manos en ángulo tocándome la punta de la nariz.

Tanscurrido un año me puse en camino hacia la cueva de los letreros
para consultar en las antiguas inscripciones el misterio que bullía
en el fondo de su corazón.

Una esfinge de diorita miraba impasible las manos pintadas con
polvo de oligisto.

Esto quería decir: Hoy en día está de moda saber mucho.

Así pues, volví y estuve otro año grabando una estela triunfal con las
varias manifestaciones del espíritu de la ciudad,

y luego me fuí a dar una vuelta en mi astronave de recreo para re-
cuperar los dos años anteriores y regresar al punto de partida

porque tenía varias cosas qué hacer con respecto a las preocupa-
ciones de mi amor.

Y así está escrito en al palimpsesto de Sodoma: "Se acordó de sus
amigos y honró su memoria por cuanto el fuego (había) con-
sumido su corazón."

Yo, Jaime, escucho a los testigos y callo.

Todo esto me parece muy confuso y sospechoso. Probablemente se
trata de ocultar algo.

¿Qué sucedió mientras tanto, mientras todos esperábamos qué
transformaciones se operaron, que los testigos soslayan tan
delicada como cruelmente?

Acaso el joven, habiendo descubierto los toneles en que sus mayores
guardaban la cerveza,

fue a parar, embriagado, a la orilla del río donde la noche lo marcó
con sus estrellas candentes,

después de lo cual, habiendo sido conducido por sus amigos a desconocidos lugares

fue sucesivamente introducido en las cámaras secretas de los viola-
dores

quienes...

¿Acaso el cadáver encontrado en al lago era el suyo?

Tenía las manos atadas, dice el Acta, pero los testigos se niegan a
reconocerlo.

I, Agenor, waited silently in the shade of the bastions
on the beshadowed corners of the street of the pink palms
with hands at an angle touching the tip of my nose.
After a year had passed I set out for the cave of the signs
to search its ancient inscriptions for some word about the mystery
that boiled in the depths of my heart.
A sphinx of diorite gazed impassively at hands stained with powdered oligist.
This was its message: Nowadays it's fashionable to know a lot.
And so I returned and spent another year carving the sundry mani-
 festations of the spirit of the city on a triumphant stela,
and then, in my plaything spaceship, I took a spin about to recover
 the past two years and return to my point of departure
because I had several things to take care of in regard to the worries
 of my love.
And so it is written in the Palimpsest of Sodom: "He remembered
 his friends and honored their memory, though the fire had consumed his heart."

I, Jaime, listen to the witnesses and keep my silence.
All of this sounds rather muddled and suspicious to me. Probably
 they're trying to cover up something.
What happened in the meantime? What transformations, delicately
 and cruelly looked at askance by the witnesses, took place while
 we all waited?
Perhaps the young man, having discovered the barrels in which his
 elders stored the beer,
ended up drunk on the banks of the river where night branded him
 with hot stars,
after which, having been lured by his friends to unknown places,
he was henceforth led into the secret chambers of the rapists, who . . .
Is it possible that the corpse found in the lake was his?
The hands were bound, the court records say, but the witnesses dis-
 claim any recognition.

EL DESEO

Hoy tengo deseo de encontrarte en la calle,
y que nos sentemos en un café a hablar largamente
de las cosas pequeñas de la vida,
a recordar de cuando tú fuiste soldado,
o de cuando yo era joven y salíamos a recorrer juntos
la ciudad, y en las afueras, sobre la yerba, nos echábamos
a mirar cómo el atardecer nos iba rodeando.
Entonces escuchábamos nuestra sangre cautelosamente
y nos estábamos callados.
Luego emprendíamos el regreso y tú te despedías siempre
    en la misma esquina
hasta el día siguiente,
con esa despreocupación que uno quisiera tener toda la vida,
pero que solo se da en la juventud,
cuando se duerme tranquilo en cualquier parte sin un pan
    entre el bolsillo,
y se tienen creencias y confianzas
así en el mundo como en uno mismo.
Y quiero además aún hablarte,
pues tú tienes dieciocho años y podríamos divertirnos esta noche
    con cerveza y música,
y después yo seguir viviendo como si nada…
o asistir a la oficina y trabajar diez o doce horas,
mientras la Muerte me espera en el guardarropa para ponerme
    mi abrigo negro
a la salida,
yo buscando la puerto de emergencia,
la escalera de incendios que conduce al infierno,
todas las salidas custodiadas por desconocidos.
Pero hoy no podré encontrarte porque tú vives en otra ciudad.
Mientras la tarde transcurre
evocaré el muro en cuyo saliente nos sentábamos
a decir las últimas palabras cada noche,
o cuando fuimos a un espectáculo de lucha libre y al salir
    comprendí que te amaba,
y en fin, tantas otras cosas que suceden…

DESIRE

Today I'd like to run into you in the street,
and then we could sit down in a café and talk for a long time
about the small things of life,
remembering when you were a soldier
or when I was young and we used to roam the city
together, and in the outskirts, on the grass, we would lie
down and watch as the evening slowly surrounded us.
Then we listened cautiously to our blood
and kept silent.
And then we'd head back and you'd always say goodbye
        on the same corner,
goodbye until the next day,
with that carelessness we'd like to have kept throughout life
but can enjoy only during our youth,
when we can go to sleep peacefully anywhere,
        without a cent in our pockets,
when we still have beliefs and faith
in the world and in ourselves.
And I'd also like to talk to you
because you're eighteen and we could have
        a lot of fun tonight with beer and music,
and then I could go on living as if nothing had happened . . .
or I could go to the office and work ten or twelve hours
with Death waiting in the closet for me to put on my black overcoat
on the way out,
me looking for the emergency door,
the fire-escape that leads to hell,
with all the exits guarded by strangers.
But I won't run into you today because you live
        in another town.
While the afternoon slips by
I'll remember the wall on top of which we used to sit down
to say the final words each night,
or the time when we went to a wrestling match
        and as we came out
I understood that I loved you
or so many other things that happened . . .

Jaime Manrique Ardila

Como miel ahumada
la noche desciendo sobre el paisaje
y su oscuridad lo impregna todo.
La luna cuelga en el cielo,
redonda, plateada, un punto de referencia
sobre las distancias que el tren devora.
Nubes claras pasan enfrente de la luna.
Pensamientos cruzan mi memoria,
interponiéndose entre tú y yo
como la noche se interpone
entre la luna y el paisaje;
y la realización de este secreto
es la única sorpresa de este viaje.
La realidad se ha tornado monótona
como la geografía en la oscuridad.

Esta noche estamos viajando juntos.
Esta es la jornada de regreso.

El tren nos lleva de vuelta a nuestro hogar
a los sueños que soñáremos en nuestro lecho.

La noche nos lleva de regreso
a ese momento en el cual nuestros cuerpos al juntarse
se ajusten el uno al otro
como el clavo a la pared, el marco al cuadro.
Ahora, junto a tí, solo sé esto—
la misión de la noche es la de expandirse
a través del continente;
la del tren, conducir a los viajantes;
la de la luna, iluminar al espectáculo;
y la de la nube... pero no es acaso la nube
el pensamiento que se interpone entre nuestros cuerpos?
y no es el pensamiento, lo que separa el día—
con mis incertidumbres—
de la noche en la cual te amo demasiado?

Like smoked honey
night descends upon the landscape
and darkness pervades all things.
The moon hangs in the sky,
round, silvery, a point of reference
above the distances that the train devours.
Light clouds drift across the moon.
Thoughts cross my memory
imposing themselves between you and me
like night imposing itself
between the moon and the landscape;
and the recognition of this secret
is the only surprise this trip affords.
Reality has become as monotonous
as the shrouded landscape outside.

Tonight we are traveling together.
This is the journey back.

The train is taking us back home,
back to dreams we'll dream in our bed.

The night is taking us back
to that moment in which our bodies, joining,
fitted themselves to each other
like the nail to the wall, the frame to the picture.
Beside you now, I know only this—
night's mission is to spread
across the continent,
the train's is to carry travelers,
the moon's, to shed light upon the scene,
and the cloud's . . . Is the cloud not
the thought that imposes itself between our bodies?
And is it not the thought that separates the day—
with all my uncertainties—
from the night in which I love you too much?

New York, November 25, 1977

UNSUNG
HEROES *of*
ROCK 'n' ROLL